WHAT TOWN PLANNERS DO
Exploring Planning Practices and the Public Interest through Workplace Ethnographies

Abigail Schoneboom, Jason Slade,
Malcolm Tait and Geoff Vigar

First published in Great Britain in 2024 by

Policy Press, an imprint of
Bristol University Press
University of Bristol
1-9 Old Park Hill
Bristol
BS2 8BB
UK
t: +44 (0)117 374 6645
e: bup-info@bristol.ac.uk

Details of international sales and distribution partners are available at
policy.bristoluniversitypress.co.uk

© Bristol University Press 2024

British Library Cataloguing in Publication Data
A catalogue record for this book is available from the British Library

ISBN 978-1-4473-6597-6 hardcover
ISBN 978-1-4473-6598-3 paperback
ISBN 978-1-4473-6599-0 ePub
ISBN 978-1-4473-6600-3 ePdf

The right of Abigail Schoneboom, Jason Slade, Malcolm Tait and Geoff Vigar to be identified as authors of this work has been asserted by them in accordance with the Copyright, Designs and Patents Act 1988.

All rights reserved: no part of this publication may be reproduced, stored in a retrieval system, or transmitted in any form or by any means, electronic, mechanical, photocopying, recording, or otherwise without the prior permission of Bristol University Press.

Every reasonable effort has been made to obtain permission to reproduce copyrighted material. If, however, anyone knows of an oversight, please contact the publisher.

The statements and opinions contained within this publication are solely those of the authors and not of the University of Bristol or Bristol University Press. The University of Bristol and Bristol University Press disclaim responsibility for any injury to persons or property resulting from any material published in this publication.

Bristol University Press and Policy Press work to counter discrimination on
grounds of gender, race, disability, age and sexuality.

Cover design: Robin Hawes
Front cover image: Dave McClure/Velcrobelly

Contents

List of figures		iv
List of abbreviations		v
About the authors		vi
Acknowledgements		vii
Preface		viii
1	Introducing contemporary planning practice	1
2	Southwell: the privatised local authority	19
3	Simpsons: the values-driven global consultancy	61
4	Bakerdale: a 'traditional' local authority commercialising under austerity politics	105
5	OIP: the 'regular' planning consultancy	143
6	So, just what are planners doing?	182
Notes		199
References		204
Index		215

List of figures

1.1	The percentage of planners working in the public and private sectors in England, 1950–2018	7
2.1	Pedestrian access to a new retail development in Southwell	21
2.2	The planning team's tea tray	28
2.3	Kathy's hotdesk setup, showing the array of portable and fixed devices she needs to do her job	33
2.4	The edge of the green belt and the Everdale Fields development site	39
2.5	Upgrading a cycleway at a new housing development	53
3.1	The reception area at Simpsons	62
3.2	Tranton's fountains	69
3.3	A public sector planner speaks at the walkability event at Simpsons	79
3.4	Amanda's bake-off entry, 'Chocolate Surprise'	95
3.5	The Monday morning fresh-fruit delivery	98
4.1	The Bakerdale reception area	107
4.2	The Agile Wall	112
4.3	The kitchen at Bakerdale	124
4.4	The endless development-management decision-making process, with paper still in evidence despite digitisation	125
4.5	The Bakerdale planning office	128
5.1	The OIP meeting room	144
5.2	Stanley's desk	147
5.3	The recommended public inquiry layout	169

List of abbreviations

AONB	area of outstanding natural beauty
CIL	Community Infrastructure Levy
DM	development management
EDI	equality, diversity and inclusion
EHO	environmental health officer
ESRC	The Economic and Social Research Council
HIF	Housing Infrastructure Fund
HMO	homes in multiple occupation
KPI	key performance indicator
NIMBY	not in my back yard
NPPF	National Planning Policy Framework
PD	permitted development
PPA	planning performance agreement
QC	Queen's Counsel
RTPI	Royal Town Planning Institute
SA	strategic assessment
SPA	special protection area
TUPE	Transfer of Undertakings (Protection of Employment)
WITPI	Working in the Public Interest

About the authors

Abigail Schoneboom is Lecturer in Urban Planning at Newcastle University. Her research focuses on work with an emphasis on sustainability in urban environments. She has published numerous peer-reviewed articles and reports in this area.

Jason Slade is Lecturer in Planning at the University of Sheffield. He has broad research interests in planning theory and practice, with a focus on community involvement, and has published in journals such as *Urban Studies*, *Journal of Planning Education and Research* and *Land Use Policy*.

Malcolm Tait is Professor of Planning at the University of Sheffield. His research investigates the politics of planning and the professional work of planners, and has been written up and published widely in academic articles and reports.

Geoff Vigar is Professor of Urban Planning at Newcastle University. Geoff's research focuses on planning practice and urban infrastructure. He has published four previous books and over 50 refereed articles and book chapters in these areas.

Acknowledgements

The Working in the Public Interest (WITPI) study, from which this book emerges, was made possible by funding from the Economic and Social Research Council (ESRC, grant number ES/P011713/1). Ben Clifford (University College London), Zan Gunn (Newcastle University) and Andy Inch (University of Sheffield) made invaluable contributions to this book as part of the wider WITPI team. Administrative support was capably provided throughout the project by Imogen Johnson and Claire Horton. We also thank our advisory board and impact board for their insights and Matt Wargent for his early work on the project.

We owe a huge debt to the institutional gatekeepers, planning officers and technicians, planning consultants, elected members and other participants who graciously granted us access to their professional lives and accommodated us in their organisations as part of the fieldwork. In the interests of anonymity, we cannot mention their names.

We are grateful to Anna Richardson and Emily Watt at Policy Press for their support and advice in bringing this book to press, and to an anonymous reviewer for their helpful advice on an earlier draft. We also acknowledge the fantastic Dave McClure at Velcrobelly for his work on the illustrations.

Preface

This book has its origins in long-standing research concerns of its authors that culminated in an ESRC-funded project Working in the Public Interest (WITPI), which ran from December 2017 to July 2020. The project investigated ideas of professionalism and the public interest in planning, with a particular emphasis on redressing an imbalance in empirical work on private-sector firms. This book is one of two from the project, and we think it is unique in its in-depth accounts of what planners actually do.

In writing the book, we took inspiration from an ethnographic tradition that is focused on telling stories sympathetic to the point of view of our empirical subjects; in our case, a small number of planners in four organisations that we followed closely over a nine-month period. The result is a series of stories, punctuated with contributions to and from theory. A storytelling tradition exists in planning, but this book is unique for its extensive, long-term ethnographic engagement in four very different organisational settings and the resultant ways in which it tells its stories. It opens the black box regarding what the planner does all day and how decisions and policies are actually arrived at through the interplay of seemingly insignificant organisational issues, interwoven with power plays of money, political power and cultural capital. In doing so, we reject commonly adopted qualitative methodologies, such as case studies that rely solely on interviews, since what we think we do can be rather different to what we actually do. Interviews are always recollections and they render the past neater than it really was.

To narrate sympathetic accounts of planners' daily lives has meant that this book must create 'thick descriptions' of such lives. It is thus very different to most books in the planning field. As such, most of the text consists of four 'thick' case studies of planning practice. These are contextualised in an introductory chapter that follows this preface. The wider significance of our findings is highlighted along the way through the case studies, and is drawn together in a concluding chapter.

All four authors contributed equally to the book's production. Malcolm co-ordinated the project as principal investigator, Abby and Jason gathered the vast majority of the fieldwork, with some contributions and write-ups from Geoff and Malcolm. As such, Abby led on Chapters 2 and 3, with significant contributions from Geoff and Malcolm respectively. Jason led on Chapters 4 and 5, with contributions from Malcolm and Geoff respectively. Geoff led the production of Chapter 1; Malcolm led the production of Chapter 6. Geoff and Abby did the major editing tasks. In short, this is a team ethnography, based on sustained intellectual engagement, exchange and mutual support, that is much greater than the sum of its parts.

1
Introducing contemporary planning practice

This is not an ordinary book about town planning; rather, it is a collection of accounts from the coalface of planning workplaces in the public and private sectors. This chapter has two purposes in introducing the book. The first is to set out the themes that run through it and which are pivotal in debating the future for planning. The themes constitute the main elements discussed in our empirical stories, and in this chapter we review previous research to set the context for these stories. Second, we outline the methods underpinning our empirical work, which are grounded in the rich tradition of organisational ethnography that forms the basis of our analysis. The next section thus introduces the themes that underpin the book.

1.1 What matters in contemporary planning research: the book's structuring themes

The book has five main themes running through it, which are central to planning's future orientations: the nature and purpose of contemporary planning; the privatisation of planning; commercialisation and business practices in public- and private-sector planning; the nature of contemporary planning work and workplaces; and professionalism and the attendant ethics of planning work. Together they illuminate how contemporary planning is practised and to what effects. The themes have been determined through a literature review, but principally they have been arrived at 'bottom-up' through our empirical analysis detailed in the chapters that follow. Each chapter centres on one or more of these key themes.

Our first theme concerns the nature and purpose of contemporary planning. There is a rich literature here which is briefly explored in the next section. This discussion frames subsequent chapters which show how planning work is both much changed but also hugely resonant with past times. Perhaps the most significant element of contemporary planning literature attends to the much-changed political economy of planning, as neoliberal processes have come to dominate procedures of city-making and appear to bypass, or render ineffective, established planning processes and their attendant democratic safeguards (for example, Raco and Savini, 2019). Our contribution is to view issues such as these through the lens of the daily realities of planners, examining how they construct, interpret, resist or facilitate such challenges. Through this we see how the wider political economy is interpreted and made real in decisions about place futures. At a time when planning systems around the world are under great threat, not least in England, we highlight the complexities of doing even routine planning work, and thus we are able to speak to the possibilities and challenges of reshaping planning systems to meet contemporary social, cultural, environmental and economic challenges.

Our second theme focuses on privatisation processes and how these have shaped what gets done in planning, by whom and how. Key here is the shift from planning being a public-sector-dominated profession in the second half of the twentieth century to a situation where nearly half of UK planners work in the private sector. This is not a unique situation internationally (see Sehested, 2009; Linovski, 2019), but in much of the anglophone world it requires a reappraisal of how planning is conducted that decentres the state. Here we highlight what Wendy Steele (2009) describes as the 'hybridisation' of planners as public-sector work is outsourced to the private sector and planners work in settings which cannot neatly be described as either public or private. In such situations, projects are delivered through complex blends of public- and private-sector efforts. Chapter 2 of the book follows the daily experiences of a group of planners who are employed by the private sector but work for a local authority which has outsourced its planning function. Here the planners themselves are often contracted out to other local authorities to generate revenue for their private-sector employer, even while their primary identity might involve working for their council. Such complexity was unthinkable for much of the twentieth century and is important for understanding cultural shifts in individual workplaces and within the planning profession as a whole. Our case studies span public and private organisations, and as such highlight whether it matters if work is done by public servants or commercial employees, how public sector planners feel compelled to act in ways more traditionally associated with the private sector, and how future career trajectories are shaped by these shifting concerns and the organisational responses to them, viewed as far as possible through the moral and ethical lenses of the workers themselves.

Our closely related third theme explores the commercialisation pressures and business practices in planning that have reshaped planning work and the daily realities of being a planner. Chapter 4 centres on a local authority looking to commercialise many of its functions. While such efforts are part of long-standing attempts to show and account for the true costs of public-sector work, rapid changes, often forced by austerity politics, have seen local government charge for things that would have been unimaginable a couple of decades ago. How are these processes being managed and seen by planners and others? How are these new ways of working affecting how planners view themselves as professionals? Similarly, Chapters 3 and 5 provide accounts of the day-to-day realities of private-sector planners facing the sometimes harsh realities of the commercial world. Here we see how ethical compromises are made, how networking helps keep organisations alive and also how they can be vital providers of knowledge, resources and skills with which to achieve better planning outcomes.

Our fourth theme focuses on the sorts of work that planners are actually doing, what they think constitutes planning work, the pressures and opportunities that face them in their organisations, the workplaces in which they do their daily tasks and why this might matter. This is not simply an academic pursuit. If planning defies universal definition, and if the most we can say is that it is 'what planners do' (Vickers, 1968), then arguably we need to study what they actually do in greater detail than has historically been the case (Beauregard, 1998 (compare Healey, 1992); Forester, 1999; Abram, 2004; Majoor, 2018; Mack and Herzfeld, 2020). Planning ethnographies have also tended to focus on the exceptional: the life of a very senior planner (Healey, 1992), or a highly significant project[1] (Majoor, 2018). Our attention is rather on ordinary, everyday practices. Here we highlight the significance in such practices not just of what work is being done and how but of the emotional labour involved in contemporary planning work and, relatedly, bullying, micro-aggression, ideas of public service, compassion and kindness (Hoggett, 2006; Baum, 2015; Lyles et al, 2018; Forester, 2021). In doing so we bring into planning ideas from nearby disciplines which are similarly underrepresented, such as work-life balance, the role of class and gender in the workplace, the value of office talk – both professional interactions and also the everyday 'banter' that helps glue communities of planners together – and how organisational and planning cultures interact and are co-constituted.

Planning culture has become an important field of study in recent times (Sanyal, 2005; Inch, 2010; Othengraf and Reimar, 2013), and our research highlights its significance for understanding what is going on in planning organisations. It is curious that the cultural turn in planning has not generated much ethnographic data, and this book seeks to address this gap. Each chapter demonstrates the uniqueness of the four organisations' work cultures, but there are also uniting features that highlight that planners exist in groupings similar to 'epistemic communities' (Haas, 1992) or 'communities of practice' (Wenger, 1998) that serve to shape their responses and also their interactions with other professionals whose behaviours are, in turn, shaped by their own practice communities as much as by their employers and clients.

Such a discussion relates strongly to our final theme, which explores the idea of planners acting in the name of a profession and a public interest. The authority of professions have been under challenge for many decades, but professionalism has been seen as a potential bulwark against wider political economic forces of neoliberalism, although this is strongly contested (Suddaby et al, 2009). The question of how a professional mode of working aligns with societal challenges, particularly when undertaken in a commercial setting, is a key strand running through this book. In our empirical work we analyse what professional work looks like nowadays and the power that being a professional conveys through an analysis of the fine grain of everyday work environments. Through close observation of what planners actually do all day, in the following chapters we use the observed details of working life to offer our own take on planning practice as a potential buffer against neoliberal forces, reflecting on what forms of knowledge and skill might underpin an idea of planning as professional activity, and considering how planners learn, network and develop in the course of their careers.

The following sections explore these five themes in detail through an examination of selected literature. In each section we do not attempt an exhaustive review; rather, we highlight several writings which we feel get to the heart of the debates we are interested in. We return to each of them in Chapter 6.

1.2 The nature and purpose of contemporary planning

Our understanding of the nature of contemporary planning practice has been much informed by bottom-up qualitative accounts of practitioners going about their day-to-day work (for example Healey, 1992; Forester, 1999; Abram, 2004; Tait, 2011; Majoor, 2018; Mack and Herzfeld, 2020). These works, and associated research into planning practices, show how planning work is both much changed and also strongly resonant with previous decades.

What has certainly changed is the wider political economy of planning. Post-war planning in many parts of the world was driven by confident and comparatively well-funded local states. However, the simplification of complex societal problems by state planners in order to mobilise large-scale modernist projects also sowed the seeds of its demise as planning came to be seen as remote, bureaucratic, highly patrician and comparatively unaccountable. A wider negative perception of the public sector also then opened the door for the private sector to fill the void when planning itself came back in vogue in the UK in the early 2000s.

Certainly planning's association with the public sector meant that it was vulnerable to the same ideological critique as other parts of the, particularly local, state in the 1980s. The secretary of State for Planning, Nicholas Ridley, famously accused local government planners of 'locking up jobs in filing cabinets' and sought to undermine their power and make them more accountable. By the 1990s, UK planning had survived more or less intact, but managerialist regimes had crept in as they had throughout local government (Clarke and Newman, 1997). Notably, a regime of performance indicators now focused planners' attention on the efficiency of their operations. This focus had some useful consequences, preventing local authorities from sitting on planning applications indefinitely for example, but it also began to reshape the culture of planning work (Inch, 2010).

The period of Labour governments from 1997 to 2010 did re-empower planning to some degree but also loaded more and more responsibilities into it (a trend that has continued) and strangled it in procedural complexity (Gunn and Hillier, 2014). These complications served to further embed managerialist and neoliberal tendencies towards 'delivery' of development (Slade et al, 2021). Such complexity has become coupled with increasing legalisation, boosted by the profits available, and the absence of controls over gains made from land speculation as envisaged in the 1947 Planning Act (see Perez, 2020, for similar conclusions in a different national context). As we saw in Southwell, our case documented in Chapter 2, judicial review is threatened routinely by developers and their agents and often dropped on planners outside of working hours the day before a committee, for example.[2]

In addition, planning has suffered from the impacts of austerity, with a 53 per cent cut in funding for development management in the period 2010/11 to 2016/17 for example (Town and Country Planning Association, 2018, p 36). However bloated one might have felt planning to be, it is likely that such cuts have had a dramatic impact on planning practice, on what planners do and on what gets done; the following section explores this further. Local-government power in England has for many decades been undermined by central governments who have little confidence in the capacity, or indeed the necessity, of strong local authorities, in contrast to northern European governance systems (Hall, 2013). The contexts of continued centralisation and diminished local-government resources run through all the cases in our book.

Contemporary explorations of planning practice also emphasise how the objects of planning's attention have shifted across the decades. This mercurial tendency forms a major plank of one critique of planning (Reade, 1987; Evans, 1993), although others see it as an inevitable response to a changing world (Parker and Street, 2021). Planners are still primarily concerned with what happens to land and serving a public interest, even if that concept proves fluid and hard to define (Tait, 2016). In theory they are empowered to tackle a range of social and environmental issues through legislation such as the Climate Change Act 2008. In reality, their lives are governed in England by policy and ministerial decree which can and do change often. While their work takes heed of the wider statutory context, it is apt to reflect the political priorities of the day, locally and nationally, and thus planners are vulnerable to short-term change and have an adaptability to such change running through their practices and cultures (Gunn and Hillier, 2014). Such adaptability fuels critiques of planning from the likes of Reade (1987) and it is evident throughout the cases in this book, but we also note globally how planners push back against such trends, promoting, within the constraints of a particular planning system, ideas of what good planning entails and should achieve (Jackson, 2020).

This inherent flexibility in the English planning system has been used since the 1990s to prioritise allocating land for housing. The housing 'numbers game' (Vigar et al, 2000) as a discourse has largely crowded out discussions of good placemaking and of promoting environmental and social justice. The need for local authorities to demonstrate 'realistic' five-year housing-land supplies at all times means the 'acting space' (Grange, 2013) for planners to deliver communities' aspirations where these are in opposition to developers' has become very limited (see also McClymont, 2014). The idea of 'positive' and 'proactive' planning surfaces now and then but is evident largely in the planning of new, larger developments in the south-east of England, where market conditions are strong and public-sector planners appear rather more empowered. There is little planning attention focused on the management of previously developed areas beyond occasional interest in the future of high streets; community development and urban regeneration as foci for planners are much less in evidence compared with previous eras.

A further key change with regard to planning work concerns where it is executed. As the planning system became loaded with more complex assessment processes in the early 2000s, the number of planners working in the UK increased. The private sector moved to occupy these new specialist market niches. We now turn to discuss this element, as part of a wider privatisation of planning, in more depth.

1.3 Privatising planning

Before the Town and Country Planning Act 1947, planners were as likely to work in the private sector as in government.[3] The system created in 1947 required a cadre of public-sector workers, and 'planners changed from prophets to bureaucrats as they became the new servants of the state machine' (Cherry, 1974, p 139). So by the 1960s (see Figure 1.1), around 80 per cent of planners worked in local government, a situation which persisted until the late 1990s. Privatisation and commercialisation processes grew enormously in the 1980s, prompted by central government, but while some local authorities did start to look more closely at the costs of providing certain services, only one local authority, Berkshire County Council, was privatised, and planning escaped the wholesale changes forced on other professions such as probation and parts of health and social care.

The shift back to a situation in which almost half of planners work in the private sector began in earnest in the late 1990s and peaked and stabilised in the early 2000s. Again, this was less about contracting out planning services wholesale than about the growth of new areas of work within the system which the private sector moved to occupy. Typically, consultants were hired as

Figure 1.1: The percentage of planners working in the public and private sectors in England, 1950–2018

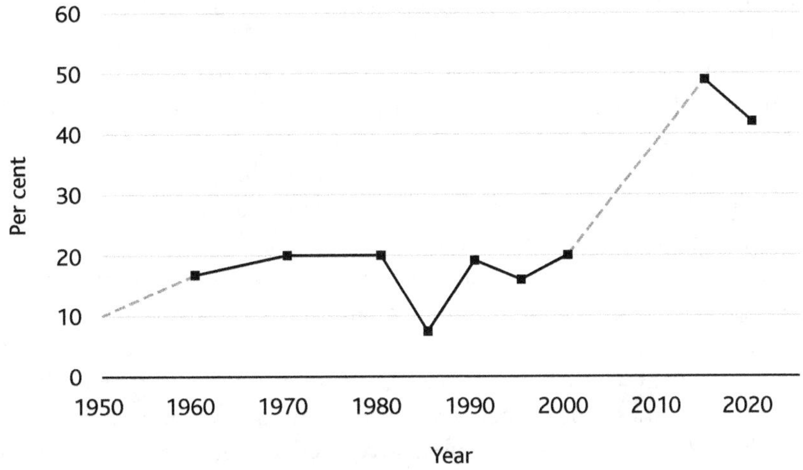

Source: WITPI, based on data from the Royal Town Planning Institute

experts to provide specialist knowledge, often regarding how to operate a new procedure such as a housing-land availability study, which their consultancy may have been central in devising in the first place! (Gunn and Hillier, 2014). In previous eras this learning of new procedures would likely have been done within the public sector. However, in many cases any spare public-sector capacity was being absorbed through professional planners learning how to navigate and operate increasingly complex legal and regulatory systems. Additionally, as more local authorities shed specialist functions such as urban conservation, the private sector took on such workload. As had been the case for many decades, the private sector also played an important role in working for the public sector to manage peaks in workload. One effect of this was to create divisions of consultancies that worked wholly for the public sector. The hybridisation of planners was thus mooted when, for example, private-sector workers might find themselves wholly or in part working for local government for much of the time (Steele, 2009). The complexities of these new arrangements are a feature of the cases that follow, and each highlight differences in the planning cultures that exist within them.

Despite the work of Steele and some notable others (for example, Loh and Arroyo, 2017; Linovski, 2019) private-sector planning – and planners – are under-researched. The complexities of the private-sector planning landscape should be noted: multi-national consultancies sit alongside smaller and sole-practitioner concerns. Sometimes companies focus on specialist niches and orientate themselves in very particular ways – with a strong social or environmental justice focus, for example, or indeed conversely, they may conduct work that others might reject for ethical reasons. Some favour working for the public sector to lessen the ethical compromises that might come from working for both developers and the state. But comparatively little attention has been paid to the differences and similarities in the work done within each sector, how the cultures overlap and differ and whether a shared professional identity remains (Campbell and Marshall, 2002; McClymont, 2006).

Full outsourcing of planning services from the public sector remains a very minor phenomenon, with eight local authorities having taken this route at the time of a survey we conducted in 2018 (Clifford, 2018). What are more common are a series of hybrid arrangements, with councils sharing specialist resources such as conservation officers among themselves and sometimes creating a more general pool of labour to share with each other and to offer to other local authorities on a for-profit basis (Clifford, 2018). Such actions by local authorities reflect a feeling that outsourcing to the private sector is expensive and not as effective as often advertised, despite central-government prompting (Slade et al, 2019). Thus, something of a process of learning has occurred in relation to the outsourcing of planning services, and some authorities have now chosen to 'insource' their planning functions again.

Much of this learning was predictable for several reasons. First, the complexity of professional service work and the fine judgements it entails suggest that importing the outcomes of outsourced work back into another organisation can be difficult. Second, planning often involves the ongoing implementation of research and policy that requires detailed knowledge of why the conclusions of the research and policymaking projects were arrived at (Barrett and Fudge, 1981). Here 'discontinuous outsourcing' can be particularly damaging (Perez, 2020). The translating of these outputs from outsourced processes back into the public-sector setting is unlikely to be smooth, not least as, third, they enter the messy, unavoidable world of local politics. Finally, outsourcing work to the private sector can imply a universalising dynamic that diminishes the depth of the local context. The embedded, local knowledge of place conditions, values and institutional relations that is so vital to planning work (Healey, 2010) can easily be sidelined in such practices. Despite all of this, private-sector planners working largely for the public sector are more common now than historically, and their work is much less ad hoc and more routinised than ever.[4] And in some cases these pitfalls of outsourcing are acknowledged in the construction of very different client relations, as we will see in Chapter 3 (and see Fincham et al, 2008).

1.4 The commercialisation of planning

The neoliberal turn has not only introduced market logics into planning via outsourcing but, increasingly, through attempts to make local authorities more financially independent and 'business-minded'. This turn is often captured under the phrase 'new public management' (Ferlie et al, 1996) and alludes to many different strands of change, from the reconfigured financial management of public services, performance measurement and improvement to the introduction logics of customer service to public services. All of these have shaped planning reforms, but it is perhaps performance measurement and logics of customer service that have shaped day-to-day planning work most profoundly. Measuring the performance of planning is not new – targets for the timely processing of planning applications have been in existence since the 1980s (and have a longer history; see Booth, 2003), but it is the linkage of these with ideas about serving customers that has been especially pertinent.

The idea of the 'customer' in planning emerged in the 1990s (Harris and Thomas, 2011; Clifford, 2012), and contrasted with prior perceptions of planners as engaging with 'citizens' or 'the public' (Thomas, 2013). In planning, the customer was most frequently seen as the applicant for planning permission, with various simple desires, such as for a speedy decision and clear provision of information as evidenced in the government-commissioned Killian-Pretty Review's key aim 'to identify and eliminate needless bureaucracy, root out unnecessary complexity, and make the system more responsive and customer focused' (Killian and Pretty, 2008, p 3). Subsequently, initiatives such as planning performance agreements were introduced to guarantee standards and timescales for local authorities (and applicants) in the processing of planning applications, with the threat of financial penalties if they were broken. Similarly, pre-application advice, which had previously been given for free and on an ad hoc basis by most local authorities, started to be formalised, with charges levied. These 'customer-focused' practices became far more prevalent as cuts to local-government funding were introduced after 2010. As noted in Section 1.2, significant cuts were made to local-government planning services, and managers were tasked with identifying new means of raising money (see Raco, 2018). Between 2010 and 2018, the proportion of income generated by planning fees related to planning applications rose from around one-quarter to about one-half, and services such as pre-application advice raised more than £50 million by 2018 (Kenny, 2019). The idea of the self-financing planning service started to seem achievable to many managers and was mandated for some by local authority chief executives.

Despite this shift, there has been little written on the commercialisation of local authority planning (see Slade et al, 2021), but as Chapter 4 in particular shows, there are significant implications for the work of planners. The Go To project that was introduced in Bakerdale explicitly sought to overhaul the delivery of planning services and introduce a clear commercial agenda to planning work. As Chapter 4 shows, this affected how planners interacted with applicants, accounted for their time and structured their advice. This commercially driven form of public-sector planning also has significant implications for professionalism and professional identity. Placing a greater focus on the client paying for a service has implications for how public-sector planners engage with other stakeholders. Thus, professional knowledge is in danger of being reduced to knowledge of how to navigate the planning system rather than implying a commitment to a wider set of values or distinct outcomes that might be generated by planning. As we will see, this creates a series of tensions for public-sector planners working in increasingly commercialised environments, and it is echoed in wider studies of local government (Pratchett and Wingfield, 1996; Needham, 2006).

Nonetheless, we need to be mindful both of idealising the public-sector ethos of local government planners and of creating a mythical time in which such an ethos was fully formed and under no pressure, as commercial and corporate impulses in local government have been in existence for many years (see Brindley et al, 1996). But the rapidity with which a commercial logic was introduced as being essential to the survival of local-government services is new and is happening at a time of unprecedented wider change to local authority finances (Amin-Smith et al, 2016). Such a situation presents unique tensions for planners as professionals, and through this book we seek to understand how they are dealing with this rapidly changing context.

Private-sector planners have of course been 'market actors' for many decades. Indeed, our two cases of private-sector consultancies also raise issues about how far commercial imperatives should drive planning work and how these might generate tensions with other professional commitments. Whether to take on a client or a project and how to frame advice are significant elements of private-sector consultancy work. Chapters 3 and 5 provide accounts of the broader contexts for such decision-making and present stories of business networking and other commercial practices. Here we sometimes see a 'macho' world of bragging and bravado alongside more-subtle forms of relationship-building with (potential) clients in a bid to capture commercial work. In highlighting the everyday activities of such planners we shine a light on a neglected area of planning literature.

1.5 What *do* planners do all day?

A guiding aim of our research was to answer the question 'What do planners do all day?' Or, to paraphrase Yarrow (2019, p 17), 'What is it like to be a planner?' In doing so we are alive to the diversity of planning work and wish to avoid a totalising idea of both planning practices and planners (Abram, 2004). Thus, there was never going to be a singular answer to this question. In our empirical work we have looked inside a range of organisations and tried to locate the skills and knowledge that planners deploy. Our research builds on rich accounts of planners at work which contributed to ideas of planning as a largely communicative practice with large amounts of time spent in meetings, on telephones and in general negotiating and liaising with others (see Healey, 1992; Majoor, 2018). The social relations underpinning planning work are thus as vital as they are in other related disciplines (see, for example, Yarrow, 2019, on architects).

In analysing planners at work in Foucauldian terms, Healey (1992) noted the deployment of moral-practical knowledge – *how to act* – as the most significant feature of planning work. Later Healey (2010) summarised that the knowledge required to plan consisted of: the capacity to know a place; the imaginative capacity to see opportunities (partly the ability to understand organisations, networks and power relations); synthetic thinking; and a capacity for judgement. Davoudi and Strange (2009) report that a variety of knowledge forms are deployed by planners mixing technocratic, positivist concepts and practices alongside more discursive ways of organising. They too emphasise action as a form of knowledge rather than as the application of knowledge; that is, knowledge of how and when to act. In terms of the actual knowledge in evidence, Rydin (2007) and, more recently, Parker and Street (2021) continue to highlight the synthetic/synoptic nature of much planning work, echoing Healey.

The similarities here show that while much planning research and scholarship focuses on changes to planning systems, what planners do is often little changed. In many ways this should not be surprising; what planning is trying to achieve has a degree of fixity, 'making places better', in Healey's (2010) terms, even if change is endemic. In focusing too on planners, in part as the agents of planning systems, we should note that as they belong to 'epistemic communities' or 'communities of practice', with shared experiences and sometimes values, change is likely to be slow due to such communities' inherent conservatism (Haas, 1992; Bickenbach and Hendler, 1994; Wenger, 1998). Here we note the significance of, 'shared assumptions; values and cognitive frames that are taken for granted by members of the planning profession' (Othengrafen and Reimar, 2013, p 1275). And for the individual planner, it is the interaction of the unique set of these factors in their environment that is crucial for us to understand. For example, some workplace organisations assert more overt cultural control than others (see Chapters 3, 4 and 5; Kunda, 1992). We see ethnographic research as being vital for uncovering these varying forms of control, and report on their significance throughout the chapters that follow.

Thus, within communities of practice certain forms of behaviour establish themselves and become stabilised. One significant aspect of public-sector planning over the years concerns the existence of a 'public-sector ethos' among planners working for local councils. Given the hybridisation agenda referred to in Section 1.3, Chapters 2 and 4 report on whether such a thing can be said to exist. In a similar vein, recent planning scholarship has pointed to the significance of kindness, care and compassion, as well as their opposites, displayed among planners, to colleagues, citizens and others, which are likely to be vital in getting things done, or not, in efficient and humane ways (Hoggett, 2006; Baum, 2015; Lyles et al, 2018; Forester, 2021). Here we also look for differences in coping and the emotional toil associated with planning work, in which intensification is a noted phenomenon. And we also note the value of solidarities and friendships present in all our workplaces. We are alive also to the added complexities of executing public work when planners must balance work intensification with the unresolved values inherent therein (Hoggett, 2006).

In highlighting what planners do, we are also conscious of the artefacts that they use, deploy and encounter (Beauregard 2015). Plans, maps and models have always underpinned planning work, although the development of digital technology may have reduced their significance, as have the space pressures in planning departments noted in our local authority cases. Nevertheless, planning involves complex assemblages of things digital and physical – people, cultures and behavioural norms among others, which our ethnographic research allows us to see.

1.6 Professions and planning's futures

As the discussion in Section 1.2 highlighted, planning's claim to professional status has been much debated over the past few decades. Planners themselves have often questioned the need to belong to a professional body and what they get from it (Thomas, 2002; Gunn, 2019). Those who assert planning's professional status note the skilled blending of tacit and codified knowledge alongside a range of other factors (Vigar, 2012). Others see a loss of key skills, such as design literacy, strategic thinking and policymaking, which were central to the planning project (Blackman, 2021). The particularly formalised nature of the planning profession in the UK compared with elsewhere in the world should be noted.

A key debate revolves around how far planning involves the deployment of universal principles that are learned both through education and on the job, through processes of codified and tacit learning (Durning et al, 2010). Such principles are blended with other forms of knowledge which encompass the unique nature of individual places under scrutiny, including their institutions and institutional histories, and thus the need for highly nuanced approaches to particular problems that can deal with the infinite depth of context that each place provides (Forester, 1999). Others conceptualise planners as having distinct roles to play in bringing people and knowledge together, a form of 'network professionalism' (Furbey et al, 2001; McClymont, 2014). Such arguments emphasise the judgement of the planner in navigating networks and the knowledge they contribute to them. As Sandercock suggests, planners blend their codified knowledge with other ways of knowing, such as 'experiential, intuitive and somatic knowledges; local knowledges; knowledges based on the practices of talking and listening, seeing, contemplating and sharing; and knowledges expressed in visual, symbolic, ritual and other artistic ways' (Sandercock, 2010, p 25).

Furthermore, being a professional is not merely about possessing a (codified) knowledge set but is also inherently related to identity, pointing to the deployment of this knowledge in settings and communities. Bickenbach and Hendler (1994) note the significance of a community of 'like-learned individuals', and Vigar (2012) suggests the importance of what happens in planning by understanding planners as a community of practice. The common educational background of planners and their interaction with a similar national policy context do indeed imply the existence of a national culture which sits alongside other cultural frames. However, the diversity of settings in which planners work, and particularly of who they work for, can inhibit unity. As we will show through the cases, divisions between public- and private-sector planners are frequently mentioned in conversation (see also Nelson and Neil, 2021), though these often tend towards stereotypical framings. In examining the actuality of work in a variety of organisational settings we get beyond stereotypes to explore how planners identify with other planners, citizens and other professionals, and in doing so we account for the relative significance of organisational and professional boundaries and allegiances.

More fundamentally though, planners' claims to professional status do not solely rest on knowledge or a community of like-learned individuals. They also relate to the ultimate purpose of their work and its societal value. Notions of planning's serving the public interest have been seen as foundational to its professional identity (Campbell and Marshall, 2002), and yet the image of the expert planner deploying technical knowledge in the service of the public has been critiqued for many decades (see Goodman, 1972). On the other side are market-oriented and public-choice critiques that see planners as self-interested bureaucrats inhibiting a smooth-running market (Pennington, 2000). These criticisms mesh with wider questioning of professional projects as self-interested means of protecting an occupational status under the guise that it is socially useful (Johnson, 1972; Friedson, 2001).

Certainly, the determination of the scope and content of planning in England by national government policy has undermined the profession's ability to determine its work independently (it might be viewed in Etzioni's (1969) terms as a 'semi-profession'). Nonetheless, planners still view the public interest as a lodestone that orientates their work, and it was something that many of those we engaged with wanted to talk about. Despite this, the definitions and scope of the public interest they were serving were less clearly delineated. This may indicate the different positions that planners take, particularly in relation to the market. As Gunn notes, 'a tension ... [exists] between the best interests of the public that councils are bound to serve, wider societal concerns including the environment and social wellbeing, and the interests of a business client who has paid, possibly at a premium, for an efficient, effective service' (Gunn, 2019, p 133). In turn, this indicates a fluid definition of the public interest that enables a wide range of positions and actions to be justified as following its logic (Lennon, 2017). This points to potential tensions in the professional project of planning, with some justifying their public-interest purpose through recourse to a technocratic allying of knowledge to a 'correct process', while others legitimate their work in terms of broader, but perhaps vaguely defined, values.

In thinking of planning work in these terms, does professionalism offer a bulwark to the pressures of neoliberalism and turbocharged capitalist development? Do planners think in the broader terms outlined by Sandercock, as mentioned earlier in this section? Do they have the acting space to act in these ways? And if not, how far does this undermine planning's claims to professional status given how planning is enacted currently in England? We return to these debates in Chapter 6, using our empirical data to shed unique light on them.

1.7 A planning ethnography

The ethnographic work at the heart of this book is unusual in the discipline and, as such, draws on a research tradition that may be less than familiar to some readers. Rooted in anthropology, ethnography is an approach to social research that generally involves an extended period of immersion and participation in the daily lives of those who are being studied. Distinct from natural-science-based or positivist research, ethnographers embrace the reflexivity of social research, the inseparability of the researcher's subjectivity from the social world they are exploring (Hammersley and Atkinson, 2007). As such, ethnographers create subjective, contingent interpretations that 'offend' some of the principles of natural-science methods; for example, that the researcher should not become a variable (Brewer, 2004, p 318). Contemporary ethnography acknowledges post-modern concerns about whether an objective and knowable 'real' world exists, while rejecting the idea that truth has to be abandoned altogether; here, ethnographers propose alternative criteria for measuring validity, justifying cautious claims to generalisability. As Brewer argues, 'This is the best ethnography can claim but it is more than enough' (Brewer, 2004, p 320).

Organisational ethnography is a specific research practice that is particularly concerned with understanding organisations as 'symbolic social institutions entirely rooted in people's practices for reproducing them' (Brewer, 2004, p 314). The organisation, for us, was a starting point to explore the working world of individual planners. As such, our ethnographic followings ranged outside the primary organisation for each chapter, and we conducted follow-up interviews with a range of others inside and outside the organisations primarily under scrutiny.

Among certain professions, there is a strong ethnographic tradition; for example, there is a wealth of ethnographies of police work, from Manning and Van Maanen's 1978 classic, *Policing: A View from the Street*, to Pearson and Rowe's (2020) recent treatment of police powers. However, ethnographic accounts of town-planning work are rare. While Healey's seminal work (Healey and Underwood, 1978; Healey, 1992) sparked interest in studying in situ planning practice, ethnographic studies, such as Majoor's (2018) account of how planners handle ambiguity, are few and far between (see also Abram, 2004; Mack and Herzfeld, 2020). Planning research is heavily dominated by interview- or survey-based methodologies and, as ethnographers have long argued, there is often a large gap between what people report they do and the complex reality of their lived experience.

Growing interest in ethnographic methods as a way of moving beyond organisational narratives and vocabulary (Sartorio et al, 2018) makes this book particularly timely. In planning research, there have been calls to pay closer attention to the day-to-day activities of 'foot soldiers' (Prince, 2012), to explore the significance of micro-practices and discursive regimes (Gardner, 2017) and to study emotional labour (Baum, 2015) and cognitively demanding ethics (Loh and Arroyo, 2017). We respond directly to these calls, deploying sustained participant observation of everyday planning life. Through this work, we shed light on how wider structural forces constrain and delimit yet are in turn influenced by the 'mundane' decisions and actions of planners.

Recognising with Geertz (2000, p 10) the 'knotted' and 'superimposed' nature of conceptual structures as encountered in the field, and the interpretative rather than objective nature of ethnographic practice, our goal is to understand planning work through a densely textured account that is aware of being one interpretation among many. As Van Maanen (1988) argues, the aim is to find more, not fewer versions of a story. As such, the value of our case studies might be measured by the extent to which they seem true to life, in terms of conveying the fragmented, often contradictory and irreducible nature of lived experience (Van Maanen, 1988, p 116). Such accounts are necessarily rendered in fine, close-up detail, forming a knotted 'thick description' of a lived reality rather than isolating variables that can be coldly measured from a distance. Indeed, as Geertz notes of ethnography, 'What generality it contrives to achieve grows out of the delicacy of its distinctions, not the sweep of its abstractions' (Geertz, 2000, p 25). We have thus aimed to preserve the raw subjectivity of our field notes, including some of our own distinct personal reactions, from which we reflexively consider the import and theoretical significance of our observations. Our work is thus impressionistic and confessional (Van Maanen, 1988); it turns 'up the background, enlarging the unremarked upon and mak[es] it remarkable' (Back, 2014, p 769, quoted in Yarrow, 2019, p 3). This approach has potential limitations; for example, subjects may 'perform' for the researcher, and we may amplify this. We have identified instances in our cases where we felt this was happening. But overall, despite inevitable limitations, ethnographies of planning practice have much to offer.

Our ethnographic research formed part of the three-year, ESRC-funded WITPI project, which foregrounded the growth of private-sector planning in the UK in examining the challenges of contemporary planning practice in England. The ethnographic component of the WITPI study comprised nine months of participant observation in five planning offices (three planning consultancies and two local authorities, one of which was outsourced). One of the consultancy case studies was abandoned due to unresolved issues around access. At the other four, we spent up to forty days in each location, generating around six hundred pages of field notes and dozens of interview transcripts. We shadowed planners at their desks, observed nuanced exchanges during meetings and immersed ourselves in the charged atmospheres of planning committees and a public inquiry.

We also engaged in 'participant listening' (Forsey, 2010) through conversations with planners, elected officers and clients or collaborators. These helped us triangulate some of our findings and interpret our observations in the field. Many important insights also occurred through informal conversations – while en route to a site visit or while waiting for meetings to start – and here we were able to get instant reactions to an event or confirm or deny our impressions of one. Sometimes, such encounters, such as with planning committees in local government, were heavily structured by established protocols, but mostly what we were observing were habits and rituals (see Rhodes, 2011); for example, the dynamics of 'banter' and collective tea-making (Schoneboom and Slade, 2020). We also reviewed a lot of documentation, such as planning-committee reports and draft plans, which allowed us to understand what was going on in meetings and other forums and primed us for what to ask our research subjects. Attempts to interrogate and analyse planners' diaries were initially helpful, but we did not follow this through systematically (see Rhodes, 2011 for a successful deployment of this method).

Our team comprised three planning academics – Geoff, Malcolm and Jason – and Abby, who is an organisational ethnographer. In creating the accounts featured in this volume, we were strongly aware of our own positionality: our whiteness, our different genders, our largely working-class backgrounds and our very different career stages and levels of exposure to planning work all played into the narratives we created together. What stood out for us during our fieldwork, what provoked or sat well with us, is deeply intertwined with our own subjectivities and critical intellectual orientations.

As a geographically distributed group of four, we were engaged in producing a 'team ethnography'. For each case study, we worked in teams of two, with Jason or Abby spending long periods in the field, while Malcolm and Geoff conducted fieldwork at key points and directed meetings and sensitive discussions with gatekeepers. Throughout the fieldwork period, we all engaged in reading and commenting on each other's field notes. Upon leaving the field, initial write-ups were generated by Abby (concerning Southwell and Simpsons) and Jason (concerning Bakerdale and OIP), and subsequent drafts were co-developed with Geoff and Malcolm, who led the analytical and theoretical synthesis across the cases.

Ethnography that draws on the insights and experiences of more than one researcher brings its own challenges and benefits (Erickson, 1998). While gaining from the peer support and mentoring that team members offered one another during the fieldwork, we grappled in particular with questions of voice and subjectivity. Here, we faced the writing challenge of synthesising first-person field notes generated by two different team members for a given case study. Leaning into these challenges, we sought to create a narrative aligned with the tradition of ethnographic fiction-science, in which the story becomes 'in part a fiction' (Watson, 2000, p 489) yet retains characteristics that make it social scientific. The field notes themselves, read and commented on by an audience comprising the other team members, had a performative, finished quality and a dialogical component that improved the integrity of the final write-up. The 'voice' in Chapters 2–5 is therefore that of the lead author, either Abby or Jason, sometimes incorporating field notes from, or acknowledging the presence of, another researcher; that is, Geoff or Malcolm. This results in a move between 'I' and 'we' within chapters on occasion.

Access to each site had been negotiated as part of the original WITPI funding bid, but early stages of the fieldwork required delicate negotiation regarding the level of access and type of research activity that was deemed acceptable. This process reflected, and provided meta-level insight into, the distinct organisational cultures we were studying. For example, one of the private-sector firms we studied was particularly open to respondent-led, quasi-academic engagement and engaged enthusiastically in an auto-photography exercise (Pink, 2021); at another site with a more conservative culture, reliance on researcher field notes was felt to be more appropriate. In a similar vein, one organisation desired the co-development of a detailed code of conduct, while others were content with a less formal understanding of roles and responsibilities. Across all cases, however, anonymity was achieved through the use of pseudonyms, and the fictional devices described earlier in this section also helped us to protect confidentiality. All organisations were offered opportunities to review the findings at different stages, and one of the case studies (Simpsons) involved a full respondent-validation process (Duneier, 2001) whereby we collaborated with key informants in reviewing and revising the write-up.

Just as each of the case studies had its own dynamics around access and validation, each also has its own shape and manner of unfolding; rather than constraining each chapter to a particular format, we therefore endeavoured to maintain the narrative voice that emerged from each case study while providing analytical threads that tie each chapter to the whole.

1.8. Conclusion

The themes presented here provide a brief context for the chapters that follow. These themes show the enduring nature of many debates within planning, such as whether planning is a profession, and if it works in the public interest, and they highlight how commercialisation and privatisation concerns in particular have fundamentally shifted what planners do and to what ends. We have also highlighted some weaknesses in the literature, both methodologically, in planning's focus on certain methodologies, and empirically, in its relative ignorance of private-sector practices. The stories that follow address these gaps simultaneously by building an account of planning from the ground up. In doing so, we focus on the practices that are being performed, on the situations that are being encountered and on the myriad relationships that planning work entails. In the final chapter we look across these accounts and return to the themes that frame them in arriving at our conclusions regarding the future of planning practice.

2

Southwell: the privatised local authority

Southwell is a local authority in Northern England. It is largely suburban, part of a wider conurbation, but with older town centres that have suffered a degree of post-industrial decline.

The chapter speaks to our themes of privatisation and commercialisation as large parts of the council have been outsourced, including the planning service to Theta. We spent several months following the core team of planners, most of whom were now employed by Theta. It was this arrangement, a public-private hybrid, that attracted us to the case. It threw up a range of interesting aspects of privatisation – such as the creation of organisational 'islands' and a tendency towards instrumental decision-making – but it also proved something of a red herring: the day-to-day planner's life was not so different from what we would expect in another local authority, such as Bakerdale in Chapter 4. As such, the chapter also provides a rich account of the everyday life in a public-sector planning office.

2.1 Arrival

This section provides a 'thick description' of Southwell Council's offices and the council planners. It grounds the reader in the realities of white-collar working life for many employees in urban edge-lands and for our planners in this case. It also serves as a brief introduction to planning pressures in the English urban fringe.

Riding the tram to the office park early on a summer morning, I travel in the opposite direction from most people, who are headed to the city centre. The windows of the houses get smaller, giving way to expanses of new build. It's about a one-mile walk from the tram to the council offices; there are no signposts for pedestrians, but I latch onto a scant trail of knowledge workers, with their manbags and reusable coffee mugs, who are making their way through the edge-lands to their offices, navigating the five-legged roundabout and walking along the pavement by the dual carriageway. As I get nearer, I cut off the highway onto one of the ancient rights of way that, somewhat incongruously, criss-cross the manicured landscape of the office park. Here, the yellow loosestrife is in bloom and allotment smells reach me over a tall fence. Back on the main artery of the office park, a team of landscape gardeners is maintaining the intentional curves of the corporate hedging and spraying weedkiller on the soil between the shrubs. I am one of about five pedestrians; the road is backed up with a mighty queue of near-stationary cars, filing slowly into work, punctuated by the occasional double-decker bus.

We are on the city-edges, in post-suburbia (Phelps, 2011); the buildings – a private hospital, an empty former government call centre, a pharmaceutical company headquarters, an improbable hotel that serves people for whom a business park is a destination – have a boxy sameness that you can't hold on to. The old town hall, a distinctive grade-II listed building on a busy high street a few miles from here, has been repurposed as a commercial business centre offering office and meeting space. The 'new' council offices brought its employees together – in the old arrangement, some departments were dispersed across several sites – but the location is anonymous and placeless. The official address is denoted by the unmemorable identifiers 'Sector 5' and 'Enterprise Way'.

Each building here has a vast expanse of car park round the back. So dominant is the car as a way of arriving at the council that the reception desk is oriented to face the back of the building, where the car park is, rather than the front door. There are four well-used code-activated bicycle sheds for employees, but members of the public who arrive at the front of the building by bike are left to their own ingenuity. Indeed, biking around here, as in much of the UK, requires insider knowledge of snickets in housing estates and a tolerance for bone-shaking surfaces. Now and then, though, somewhere along the route there is a short expanse of wonderfully smooth, rideable asphalt paid for by Section 106 (s106)[1] money that the council has extracted from a housing developer – an offering to the unhappy cycling-infrastructure gods.

Aside from the district's impressive pylons, there is not much in the way of visual or social stimulation to inspire a stroll to the shops in the newer residential areas hereabouts. Yet the landscape is constantly changing and growing – near the tram, across another enormous roundabout, a low-cost German-owned supermarket and drive-through coffee chain have recently appeared, with large signs to be seen from a distance. There are four lanes to cross, with a refuge in the middle. You wouldn't make it if you were mobility impaired; the nearest light-controlled opportunity is a substantial detour away (see Figure 2.1).

Nearby, new housing developments are springing up on greenfield land. At the Oakwood Park development, five hundred new homes are being built following a dramatic intervention by the secretary of state that overturned a rare refusal by the council planning committee. The planning committee had been bold in listening to the wishes of local residents and going against a central-government push to build houses regardless of the quality of the

Figure 2.1: Pedestrian access to a new retail development in Southwell

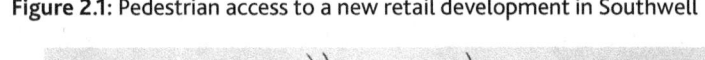

proposal. A large wooden sign bearing the logo of Vermilion, one of the UK's major housebuilders, at the site perimeter promises four-bedroom detached houses called 'the Prestwood' and 'the Berkeley' for around £200,000.

In spite of these signs of development, Southwell is far from being affluent. The council, like most in England, has been hit by cuts driven by an austerity agenda from central government which has fallen disproportionately heavily on local government.[2] This assault reflects a mistrust of councils that runs deep in English central-government culture (Leach et al, 2017). Southwell has persistently high levels of unemployment but is better off than some nearby areas, in part due to office parks like this. Here, well-paid white-collar work can be found, but the office park also houses call centres where the jobs are low-paid and insecure. A quarter of workers in the area who work a full-time job earn less than £20,000 a year; a quarter of Southwell's children live in poverty. There has been an upturn in 'survival crime' – people who can't make ends meet stealing from supermarkets; joints of meat in parts of Southwell come with security tags.

Labour hold most of the council seats but there are a few Conservatives and Liberal Democrats in more-affluent areas. During the last decade, most of the public services that the council delivers – including the planning service – have been outsourced to commercial entities. The ten-year 'partnership' contract to deliver planning services was rushed through a few years ago by a chief executive who came and departed quickly. Staff who were on council contracts have been 'TUPEd'[3] over to work for the new 'partnership' organisations, and the council logo is accompanied everywhere by the logos of private companies.

Cuts in financial support from central government have meant that over half the district's revenue comes from council tax, creating an incentive to build more houses. Indeed, central government requires Southwell to make eighteen thousand new houses appear here by 2032. Yet, many locals – including elected members and the planners themselves – worry that housing supply has become the be-all and end-all of Southwell's planning function. Will housing appear on every scrap of greenfield between here and the coast and into the green belt to the north?

Inside the council offices

The space inside the council building is bland and corporate, but with some relief provided by artworks and place-bound memorabilia transplanted from the old town hall. There are plaques commemorating industrial achievements, as well as a permanent display of contemporary council-owned artworks that are redolent of a less lean time in the public sector. In the lobby, an impressive, gilded portrait of one of the region's naval heroes hangs above leaflets about being ready for Universal Credit. Visitors are processed through the reception area; its black vinyl couches intermittently fill up with waiting people – a group of women thrown together by a common school-gate concern, a pair of suited professionals, an older man here to pick up a housing form. The planning committee meets just beyond the reception area in a large room with a sports-hall feel, and there are other glass-sided meeting rooms, but the main ground-floor feature is the canteen – which is cash-only, cheap and serves food of incredible freshness and quality. Visitors come from elsewhere in the office park just for lunch: salads with couscous, kale and halloumi; baked sweet potatoes; scones that taste like they are made in small batches, almost like homemade.

The planning office

The planners, a team of twenty-nine (a decade ago the number was sixty), inhabit two rows of ten desks in a large open-plan office on the first floor beyond card-controlled doors. Along a central aisle, columns bear the Theta partnership's motivational watchwords: 'Achieve', 'Aspire', 'Empower'. Large, unopenable windows offer views of the office park landscaping on one side and the spine road on the other. The office decor is generic, repetitive – brown desks, white ceiling tiles, metal filing cabinets on a grid layout – the air is a little stuffy.

Office space is under pressure – as a cost-saving measure, the council and its private partners have been shoehorning more and more people into the building and the space is becoming more difficult to work in.[4] The planning team used to occupy the entire east side of this floor but most of the space is now occupied by other teams that have different work cultures, some of whom are outsourced to different corporate entities. The smell of Domino's pizza sometimes drifts over to planning from the Revenues and Benefits team, whose motivational work culture, imported by their own outsourced entity, gives rise to lots of fun-at-work activities, their desks strewn with World Cup bunting or celebration balloons.

Due to space constraints, all of the planners work from home one day a week. If you arrive early, you can get a desk by the window; those who do the school drop-off get the aisle seats. Keeping hold of a chair is a challenge – many bear a sticker with the owner's name, but people often come in to find theirs has wandered elsewhere. Mugs and other personal items are kept in similarly labelled, movable filing cabinets under desks. Aside from laptops and computer wires, there is no clutter or visible disorder; paper is rare. You are not allowed to pin anything to the walls (there aren't many anyway), but one of the planners has surreptitiously stuck up the local plan map in an alcove and pinned the Community Infrastructure Levy (CIL) map to a grey metal cabinet. It's important to be able to see these in their entirety – something a screen can't give you.[5]

When seated among the planners, there is a white noise of talking mixed with heads-down work; fragments of chit-chat pass across the desks and there is movement as officers come over to consult with one another. Questions are asked to neighbours or along the rows: "Where's Stevie?" "He's on holiday, cycling." A huddle of younger planners puzzle over an application: "I think we might be able to argue this one", says one of them, sounding pleased. Across from them, a planning-enforcement officer is having a difficult phone conversation with a resident: "With all due respect, Mr Tyler", he says at intervals, in the steady voice of the public servant. Between colleagues, the banter is peppered with local dialect; many of the officers grew up round here.

The core team

Our sojourn in the planning team was mostly spent with a small number of officers: Kathy, the planning manager who oversees the team, and four experienced officers – Cameron, Amanda, David and Yvonne – who cover a mix of policy and development-management functions.

Originally a development-management (DM) planner and now in her third decade at Southwell, Kathy has risen steadily in seniority, and with the creation of the outsourcing arrangement in 2012, when a number of more experienced staff left, she became leader of the planning team. The commercial nature of the partnership has added a business side to her role that involves monitoring performance for the inevitable key performance indicators (KPIs) that govern what gets done and increasing the consulting work that the team does as part of the outsourcing arrangement.

Cameron, a principal planning officer, works largely in development management, processing planning applications. Known in the office for his eight-hole Doc Martens, he grew up in Southwell, in a New Town which boasted a brutalist housing experiment: "That's where they would wait so they could mug you", he told me, showing me a photo of the shopping precinct near his childhood home. He reads and thinks a lot about the state of the planning profession. When students come in for work experience, he gives them an article by UCL professor Yolanda Barnes, to drive home the idea that planning is not just about house extensions. The article has a great phrase in it – 'Think globally, act locally, panic internally.'

Amanda, who graduated in planning from the nearby university and grew up in Southwell, is also a principal planner with a preference for DM. From the start of her two decades here she has felt valued, like what she says matters. She loves the outdoors and, except when she has to go on a site visit, she often walks or bikes into work and tries to get out for a walk at lunchtime to clear her head.

Yvonne, another local, is a senior DM planner who has been here since her year-out placement from university. She is known in the office for being incredibly organised and systematic, approaching her work in a clear and ordered way that is well suited to the quick timescales of DM work. She enjoys the hands-on, front-line nature of her job, and without enjoying confrontation, has become inured to it.

David started his career around the same time as Yvonne. He is the principal planning officer who oversees the policy side of things. Originally from elsewhere, he came to university here and has stuck around. He is softly spoken, with a wealth of technical planning knowledge, and enjoys the challenge of wording a policy in a way that will stand the test of the real world.

Accustomed to Freedom of Information Requests and the notion of public-sector transparency, the team allowed us to study them over a nine-month period. There was a feeling that they wanted someone to know their working life, someone who might then tell the world about it while helping them make sense of it (see Rhodes, 2011, for a similar observation concerning civil servants). Focusing on particular episodes such as Everdale Fields, one of the district's strategic housing sites, we spent time in the office, shadowed individual officers, attended planning committees, went on site visits and attended meetings. We conducted interviews and a focus-group session where we fed back our findings to this core of officers and we carried out interviews with some elected members and others at Southwell who cropped up in our ethnographic followings.

The following sections relay our findings. We found a strong team, with much collegiality and knowledge exchange in evidence, operating in a high-intensity work environment where micro-aggressions from developers and members of the public were an accepted part of daily life. We observed planners in a lean team juggling a heavy, often unpredictable workload, sometimes splitting their organisational identities across two local authorities as part of the outsourcing contract, using technology that didn't always co-operate. We found a public-sector ethos that was alive and well, buoyed up by strong local ties and the everyday intellectualism and gallows humour that sustains the public sector the world over. The planners take pride in their work and get a sense of achievement in the day-to-day service they provide.

We found that the outsourcing arrangement was viewed with scepticism and a sort of black-humoured resignation. With or without the private sector, the planners largely accepted the need for a more commercial, pro-development outlook. While they expertly handle developers, the power asymmetry created by current central-government policy was such that the planners were often powerless against developers' will. Rather, planners focused on mitigating the worst excesses of development and winning back something for Southwell in terms of developer contributions for parks, bins and bike paths. When it comes to sustainability, there was little sign of visionary leadership in the council – unsurprising in a climate where resources are stretched so thin and a central-government mandate is lacking. In a context where master plans are vulnerable to compromise over viability claims, and where low-density, car-dependent development has become the norm, the councillors are sometimes, perhaps surprisingly, the most visible defenders of issues such as sustainable transport and biodiversity. The planners, some of them deeply attached to the profession's mandate to serve the public interest, share some of these concerns, but they sometimes lose sight of the bigger picture and, frustrated by the process, can regard this voice of the elected members as time-consuming interference.

2.2 Office culture

This section explores office life for Southwell's planners. It provides detail on how the team interacts and its underlying dynamics. We demonstrate how funding cuts and a proliferation of bureaucratic procedure are stifling creativity, and how team spirit and ideas of public service provide a glue that keeps the team functioning despite these wider trends.

Yvonne, who comes in early to avoid the traffic, has been in since 7:45 am. It's now mid-morning and she is reviewing comments that have come in on a major application; she reads and redacts them, then copies them to a large spreadsheet. Amanda is going over the paperwork for a contentious application that is about to go to planning committee – it's from Greggs Bakery, who are hoping to serve up their warmish steak bakes from a site that was previously refused a Kentucky Fried Chicken. She signs off on some work from a junior colleague and scans through her emails: it's October, but office Christmas plans are being announced already; there's a couple of 'delegated' applications due for sign-off and a reminder for an upcoming 'heat-network' meeting (see Section 2.7), the kind of meeting nobody wants to go to as it seems a non-starter.

She opens a pushy email from a planning consultant about an application that will turn a former nursing home in a conservation area into housing. The consultant is unhappy about how long things are taking. After conferring with Kathy across the tops of the monitors, Amanda writes back, politely but firmly, telling him that things are on schedule and his client will need to wait the customary amount of time. Moving swiftly through her to-do list to another application, Amanda opens up a scanned document, a hand-drawn tree protection order (TPO) from 1977, for a sycamore that is now encroaching on a vicarage in nearby Oldwell. Amanda checks what the applicant is saying they will do, signing it off to go upstairs to the legal team. At this point she realises she has lots of windows open on her screen, a result of the morning's multi-tasking, and she spends a few moments closing them down.

The planning team doesn't dedicate staff to particular roles, and officers are accustomed to triaging their time across a range of projects and functions. This multi-skilled approach is popular among graduate recruits, who feel they are getting exposure to a range of planning activities. At the same time, the balancing act can be challenging, and applicants, awaiting the outcome of their submissions, don't always understand the amount of multi-tasking and firefighting that the planners are doing.

With the team operating on a lean basis, pitching in to deal with staff absence is routine. The following day, the team are down an officer who had a caseload of thirty applications. Yvonne has not yet done anything she planned to do today. Her time has been diverted to training up Katie, a fresh graduate, so that she can take over some of the absent officer's workload. "I'll give you a crash course in viability", Yvonne says, inviting Katie to scooch up beside her so they can work together. They spend an hour like this, sometimes leaning in to ask things of Cameron along the row. It's a friendly, collegial atmosphere and Yvonne is patient, taking her time making sure that Katie is comfortable with the tasks in front of her, but there is also a thinly veiled sense of frustration that the team is so stretched. "We're now all overloaded", commiserates Cameron, "there's not much else we can do".

Workload has become more intense in recent years and, as in many contemporary public sector workplaces, burnout and its near relations stress and depression are not uncommon. Increased development in Southwell, coupled with a team that is half what it was in 2010, has meant larger caseloads for planners. More paperwork is needed than previously – this month's planning-committee agenda, which will review twelve applications, comprises 440 pages. New policies, such as Southwell's housing-space standards, add to layer upon layer of checks and balances. The many electronic systems that the planners use – for everything from timesheets to filing objections – eat up time, while the public's use of Facebook can easily generate a thousand objections to a single application. Meetings proliferate, in line seemingly with knowledge work generally (Sandler, 2017) and in planning particularly (see also Perez, 2020). Within this intensified work process, planners carve out ways to preserve the quality of their work. Mina, a planner along the row who is nearing retirement, tells me she makes a point of reading documents carefully and thoroughly; she insists on the importance of 'thinking time' to make well-considered planning decisions. Many of the officers use their mandatory work-from-home day to do work that requires deep concentration.

Team spirit and a public-service ethos

The planners are a close-knit bunch. Every couple of hours someone gets up and fills the tea tray with mugs; everyone is offered a 'cuppa' (see Figure 2.2). There are two married couples on the team, and the banter is rich with local wit, political savvy and shared cultural references. There's a strong sense that the people who work up here behind the glass doors are from the same soil as the public they serve. Yet, as a coping strategy, there is a degree of role-distancing from those the planning team serves. The planners, at times, seem to regard the outside world as a farcical realm that fuels their store of office humour. However, they are also caring people, committed to supporting one another and providing high-quality public service.

Figure 2.2: The planning team's tea tray

Jonny, one of the enforcement officers, is a master of office banter. He has a friendly local face, nourished by a diet of wry humour, and everyone seems to tune in when he arrives in the office. "What was that ding-dong you were having yesterday?" an officer along the row asks as Jonny sets up his workstation. "I was having the worst day ever", he replies, describing how a very angry citizen had been shouting and screaming at the other end of the phone. "He said I was more useless than an ashtray on a motorcycle", he recalls, smiling but conveying that part of his afternoon was ruined. He says that something he tried to explain about council tax accidentally set the man off: "After that he just called me a knob", he recalls. "Did he say he'll be going to the newspapers?" the guy next to me jokes. "He kept saying 'I have the power of the internet'", Jonny recalls to chuckles along the row.

The planners themselves are often the brunt of office banter. Yvonne is known for having a soft spot for animals and is obliged to join in the joking around whether the donkey she has sponsored at a sanctuary really exists. "Do you visit your donkey?" asks one of the officers. When she replies that she has never visited, Jonny says, "A donkey is not just for Christmas you know, Yvonne". There is further discussion about whether the donkey might be dead and the donkey sanctuary might be ripping her off – they should send a photo every day with the donkey doing something in front of today's newspaper, says Amanda. The joking dies down and we look at the photo of the nice donkey, "It's a good cause, Yvonne", says one of the officers. "It's a cause", corrects another.

There are running jokes in the office that help counter the stress of the job. Late one morning I look up and see a large yellow bear. It's Pudsey Bear,[6] accompanied by a councillor carrying a white bucket. People reach under the hotdesks for their wallets and there is talk about who is coming in wearing their pyjamas tomorrow for Children in Need, but the main discussion is about who is under the bear suit. Apparently, last year a planner called Joseph went out for an urgent meeting and a few minutes later Pudsey walked in; then, when Pudsey left, Joseph promptly returned. This has sparked a campaign that Joseph has to endure involving Cameron sending him a photo every time he runs into a giant costumed mouse or other suited creature at a shopping mall or leisure event: "I saw you this weekend, Joseph", he fires off with the photo.

In spite of these antics, a public-service ethos is much in evidence. Even 'Mr Angry', who had called in to complain about some rubbish that was being left by contractors working on a new housing development, gets to the person he wanted to reach. While nobody's in a hurry to call Mr Angry back and receive more verbal abuse, one of the enforcement officers calls the site project manager informing him that he is up to his neck in complaints, extracting a promise that the site will be tidied up pronto.[7]

Later that afternoon, Jonny takes a call from an upset resident. He talks to her patiently – "Do you need me to come out there?" he asks. The resident wants some excessively noisy building work next to her house stopped and Jonny explains that this is beyond his remit as the builders are permitted to do it: "In my enforcement work, I can't stop things for that reason", he explains, but he adds he can come and have a look. "I won't let you down. I promise I'll be there", he repeats a couple of times before hanging up. After the call there is a debrief along the row – the lady has been ringing up every day. A female planner along the row laughs: "If she gets me, she asks to speak to 'the man' ... and I say, 'Oh yes, I'll pass you right along to Jonny'". He shares a few more details about the caller, making light and irreverent fun of the call but adding, more solemnly as he prepares to go out on the visit, "She makes me promise because she says she has been let down by so many people".

'Greedy' developers provide a rich source of gallows humour in the office. In parallel to the Mr Angry conversation about the untidy contractors, a conversation sparks up about the Vermilion chief executive's bonus of £75 million pounds, which is in the headlines. One of the planners along the row says something about the director's smug facial expression and the unacceptable number of snags in those new homes, while another brings up a satirical Facebook page showing a photo of a lopsided pub with the caption 'Vermilion is now entering the pub business'. This disdain for the greed of the big developers sits alongside the fact that the council needs to meet its housing targets and must do business with these heavyweight, profit-orientated players in order to get the houses built. The black-humour part compensates for their participation in a planning system where they lack real power and can only focus their attention on helping the public get screwed that little bit less (McClymont, 2014).

In this vein, the intellectual bent of office banter is compelling and points to a deep conviction in the planning team that the big ideas that traditionally guided the profession must be kept alive. Cameron feels particularly strongly about the state of the profession and tries to stay abreast of unfolding developments, holding dear some of the principles he recalls from his university planning education. One afternoon we Google some of his old lecturers. His absolute favourite one was the charismatic, veteran planner Billy Goodman. Cameron vividly remembers Goodman's first lecture to the new undergraduates – he addressed the lecture hall, a roomful of silent new students: "What can planning do?" he asked. Silence. He walked up and down waiting patiently for an answer. "I'm going to need an answer", he warned. Time passed and eventually Goodman slammed his hand down on the table "No!", he exclaimed. "What can planning do? Planning can say no!" For Cameron this was Goodman's way of informing those who had chosen planning thinking they could spend time designing lovely places in artistic solitude that planners must sometimes make unpopular decisions.

Intellectual banter on topics such as the pros and cons of brutalism or a critique of Heather Campbell's take on the profession is not unusual. In addition, Cameron is the resident expert on parliamentary matters. As the Brexit debates became heated, Cameron's predictions about what would happen next provided a frequent current of office discussion: "There's a constitutional crisis and I'm supposed to plan towns", he exclaimed after one such bout, pulling himself back on task. During our fieldwork, he attended a lecture on the state of planning by Hugh Ellis from the Town and Country Planning Association, assiduously carrying out Ellis's homework assignment and working his way through the *Raynsford Review* in his own time. Some of the other planners, while not quite as vocal, share a critical engagement with the profession. One of the younger recruits recalls that he thought he had gone a bit off the deep end about planning ethics during his interview but was pleased that showing a taste for this sort of debate was in fact valued by the team and helped him get the position.

The planners function in a context where their practice is increasingly commercialised, something that is a general trend as well as a result of the Theta partnership. As we will see in Section 2.7, the council's plans – such as the master plan for its strategic housing sites – cautiously aspire to aspects of sustainable, equitable placemaking. However, the planners have few levers to pull that would bridge the huge gap between even these limited goals and the everyday realities of development. As a result, day-to-day work can seem removed from the big ideas about what constitutes good planning. At a recent Southwell visioning event, Cameron recalls, the goals being laid out were very instrumental: things like 'process three hundred applications per time period'. He urged the group to add what he calls "noble goals", stuff like making safe, affordable places. He was not opposed by those at the meeting but feels he was pushing against the current of how success, in the current system, is measured.

The human touch amid worrying trends

In spite of growing instrumentality, a resilient public-service ethos at the council is often palpable, something that is epitomised by Rosie downstairs at reception, who is the front line, dealing with all visitors to the council. Incredibly skilled at disarming visitors with her kindly face, she is fascinating to watch as she juggles all that happens at the front desk. This includes having to disappoint citizens – I first watched her help a man who had brought in a benefits form and wanted to see if someone could check it so he didn't miss the deadline. "They are a very small team and it is really hard to get one of them to come down", she said amiably but firmly. He explained that one of the reasons he had brought the form in person was because he didn't have the money for a stamp – he responded to her politeness and she helped him to hold onto his dignity.

Rosie's job is often to pacify people, make sure they see a friendly face in this big institutional building. This is something she takes very seriously. She thinks of those who enter as becoming part of her world and her investment in getting to know people pays off in them being nice to her back, even when things are not going smoothly. In a very natural way, she develops relationships with visitors, which does wonders when something goes wrong, like when someone isn't there for a meeting.

She is pleased at how she can connect people with a planning query to an actual human – there are set hours each week when citizens can see a planning officer face to face, and the rest of the week she directs people to the phone lines or the computers round the side of her desk. Overall, she is the human ingredient that might make some of the more faceless stuff palatable, workable. If you've met Rosie, somehow you don't feel bad about being directed to the website. Upstairs from Rosie's welcoming presence, the planning team also hold the operation together through kindness and genuine human warmth.[8] They show a good-humoured ability to cope with lean staffing and are capable of impressive juggling acts. Yet the planners' resilience also points to concerning trends in the wider system: a tendency towards instrumentality and leanness in how planning work and decision-making are carried out; an othering of the public as rather farcical and tiresome; an attachment to the 'big ideas' and a capacity for critical thought that, while well honed, languishes in the interstices of the system.

2.3 The Theta partnership: privatisation in action

Here we highlight how planners navigate the relationship with Theta through a mixture of resignation, role-distancing and quiet assertiveness. Theta's power emerges from the neoliberal context that shapes and limits the planning profession. Seeming on the one hand to be disengaged from everyday planning, it is concerned only with value extraction and exerts little direct influence on policy and decisions within the authority. Yet at the same time it insidiously fragments and operationalises aspects of the planning process, getting in the way of innovation and integrated long-term thinking.

Theta's influence on workflow

Theta has 'identified capacity' (that she doesn't really have) in Amanda's workload and have assigned her to work two days a week for Downstaple Council, a distant, rural local authority. Given the way development management works, it doesn't help to compartmentalise two separate workdays for Downstaple, so she does work for Southwell and Downstaple in parallel.

On a Tuesday morning I am shadowing Amanda as she works through her morning's tasks. Having wrapped up some Southwell tasks and closed down her extraneous windows, she switches her attention to Downstaple. She digs a separate phone out of her bag, a mobile, and plugs it in, showing it to me – "This is the Downstaple Phone". She navigates her two identities in a way that is impressive but also looks demanding. As well as having two phones, she has two different Outlook profiles, and there are also two databases for managing planning applications – Downstaple uses a clunky-looking system called Ocella, that she has had to master.

Amanda is handling thirteen Downstaple applications at the moment – she has never been there, but Google Maps is pretty useful and officers there do site visits. She spends some minutes on a query that has come in from a member of the public who seems upset that his comment has been deleted from the system. His message, which voices concern about the upset and distress caused to his elderly mother, has a genteel lilt; his postal address, which is something like Peony Cottage, Abbotsea, seems very far away from steak bakes in the post-industrial edge-lands. Amanda writes back politely, explaining that there was a technical glitch that is now fixed. Her email signature for Downstaple has only her name, the council name, and her mobile number. Downstaple's local paper has been asking why Theta staff hundreds of miles away are deciding the area's planning applications, but engaging in this debate is beyond Amanda's remit.

Theta's tendency to find room in people's workload for other assignments has the effect of making the Southwell team smaller and, sometimes, of removing expertise at key moments. Aside from Amanda, two other members

Figure 2.3: Kathy's hotdesk setup, showing the array of portable and fixed devices she needs to do her job

of the team are currently assigned to be at other sites five days a week, so they might not be around when reasoned decisions must be made on work they've done for the council. Poor integration of technical systems – you can't book a meeting room through the Theta laptops – leads to a clutter of devices on the officers' desks and frustration about slow or unreliable software, an issue that is compounded when trying to do work for multiple local authorities (see Figure 2.3).

Theta's drive for automation

The following week, as I settle into one of the desks and open my laptop, I notice that the usual background noise of office banter seems muted. A new-looking colleague wearing a top with enormous dog-tooth checks breezes past. "Anyone need any Timetracker help?" she asks, coming around to me and having a cursory look at what is on my screen. Amanda and Cameron quickly waft her away and I mumble something about being an outside visitor. "They've been here since last Wednesday", Amanda shares, "it's to do with Timetracker".

In spite of its malfunctioning tech, Theta is keen to position itself at the forefront of automation,[9] and has engaged the planning team in a time-and-motion-type study using a measurement system called Timetracker.

Timetracker is being used to gauge how long tasks take so that Theta can ultimately charge local authorities for these jobs in batches to be completed largely by robots.

"That's what they are doing in that little room over there", says Cameron, nodding over at a small glass meeting room in the corner that is entirely screened by venetian blinds. It is hard not to imagine a *Brazil*-type[10] setup in there: high-tech listening and watching devices, clipboards. Yvonne, who is on phone duty, is logging the length of each call on the Timetracker software and also keeping a tally on paper. The Timetracker colleague returns with a technical query for Cameron and Amanda about how a planning application from an adjoining authority would be handled. They respond helpfully, but there's something forced about the interaction.

In a way, Cameron explains later, the Timetracker idea isn't bad. His job entails some tedious processes such as checking through applications to see which have expired, a task which he feels could do with some automation. Studying what's needed to automate that task makes sense, and the data collected is bound to be informative in some way about how the team works. Plus, one temporary benefit of the Timetracker measurement exercise is that the planners are encouraged to focus on one task at a time, rather than their usual frenetic multi-tasking. He shows me something he has been reading – Cal Newport's *Deep Work: Rules for Focused Success in a Distracted World*. He explains that a lot of work tasks are shortly going to be automated, a bit like Fordism but for knowledge work. The way to stay employed and to find meaningful work, he explains, is to focus on the kinds of tasks that only humans can do. For him, in planning, this means doing the complex balancing act that he is skilled at: projects that require multifaceted judgements.

While there are some potential advantages, it's unclear who will capture the benefit of any gains made through the application of Timetracker at Southwell. It is clear to the officers that automation is going to be very profitable for somebody – the word in the office is that the guy who invented the Timetracker software has made a pile and is now off on a yacht somewhere. Meanwhile, some officers, while going along with it, are concerned that the measurement exercise is taking a bite out of their already intensified workday. They wonder whether efficiency gains would be used to stretch the team thinner and outsource them to other authorities at a profit, leaving less room for things such as professional development.

Another prevailing attitude is one of resigned good humour about the exercise. Given the staff's experience with outmoded, glitchy Theta laptops and software interfaces, Theta's effort to position itself as an IT innovator has generated some laughs. Also, since Timetracker is a system primarily designed for call centres, it seems unlikely to generate useful knowledge about complex planning work, in which professional judgement features at various parts of a typical process. Some of the planners find solace in the clumsy nature of the data-collection strategy, which seems unlikely to generate reliable data. In spite of outward compliance, there is a veiled hope that Theta's latest effort to extract value from the local authority will fall flat.

Having seen the large Unison displays outside of the canteen, I ask if the union has had anything to say about the time-and-motion study. Cameron explains that, although things were different in the past and many of the officers are card-carrying members, Unison no longer has any clout. Newer recruits are on Theta contracts and don't have the same union-won working conditions of the veteran officers who were TUPEd over from the local authority. These newer team members often don't see the point of losing £20 a month in union dues from their pay cheques. When it comes to things like flexitime, the TUPEd officers can move hours around within a four-week cycle, whereas those on a Theta contract have only slight flexibility within a given week. As a result, there is not much of a sense of union-based solidarity in the planning team and, if anything, the partnership has introduced a sense of haves and have-nots in terms of working conditions and salaries.

Encounters with Theta

It's a busy, buzzy afternoon in the office, and as usual, the quiet hum of focused work is punctuated by snippets of banter. Some musings among the planning technicians about going for a meal at Frankie and Benny's are suddenly muted by some deep, posh voices by the central aisle. I look up to see several loud-talking, tall men flanked by smartly dressed women; two of the men are hungry looking with smooth craniums and dark banker's suits; the third, who has the baby-pink face and tufty, sandy hair of a public schoolboy, is comically out of place in this northern, public-sector setting. He wears widely spaced pinstripes matched with a tieless, fuchsia, wide-cuffed shirt and a matching pocket handkerchief.

This group is here, it becomes apparent, to ask the planning team about how they are finding Timetracker. I cringe as I hear one of them move from desk to desk along my row; the difference in pay scale and social class between him and his interlocutor makes condescension inevitable: "Hello, nice to meet you, Betty, isn't it?" he asks in received pronunciation. "I'm Dominic, nice to meet you. ... So, you know why we are here, to get a really simple feel of what Timetracker is doing for you, how you are using it." Occasionally, as part of the niceties, he erupts with a moneyed "ha ha ha ha", straight from the diaphragm, that jars against the self-deprecating, local way of laughing. Most of the team play along, smiling and answering the "How is Timetracker for you" question fairly positively, but at one point I hear one of the technicians speak her mind in a timid but steady voice: "It's the worst thing ever invented, as far as I am concerned. Not being negative but, technically, what you want me to do is to stop service requests so that …" she trails off.

Hands-off but stifling innovation

David, the senior policy planner, isn't particularly enamoured of Timetracker, but in general he likes the fact that Theta doesn't meddle in his planning work and, like some of the others, has enjoyed some of the experience his consulting roles have given him outside of Southwell. It's a business, he notes, so it wants to earn money, but that ultimately means a hands-off approach day-to-day. Basically, he explains, Theta wants the team to get work in from beyond the district to meet its business-plan target: "There's pressure in terms of getting in external work and earning cash but Theta takes, at least in my role, no interest in the decision-making side of it."

When the partnership started, Theta's presence was more noticeable – they installed their own project managers who would monitor what was going on. Over time these have been drawn away to other ventures. David acknowledges that Theta, as a multi-disciplinary firm with a construction and engineering arm, does have an *interest* in the development that comes out of planning decisions: "By definition the local plan is an opportunity for Theta because the sites require infrastructure works", he notes, "but it's hard to say if they influence it in terms of the decision-making".[11]

However removed Theta may be from the detail of planning decisions, the council's relationship with them creates an instrumental tendency that potentially stifles innovation, limits responsiveness and rewards measurable activity and new aspects of professional planning work such as winning contracts and writing bids (Raco, 2018). What gets done is framed by what is and what isn't in the letter of the contract; an action plan is agreed annually and workloads have to be anticipated in the annual review; success means meeting KPIs. Work that falls outside of the core activity defined in the contract is charged to the council as an extra fee and, in a cash-strapped environment, is therefore less likely to be pursued, even if it is part of an emerging crisis.[12]

Creating islands

John Leavesley, Southwell's sustainability officer, is an archetypal public-sector veteran – a thoughtful-looking man with a wry manner, he has weathered rounds of austerity cuts and the shift to a public-private partnership without sacrificing his critical intelligence. Leavesley has organised the heat-network meeting (which we will discuss in Section 2.7), the meeting nobody wants to go to because they know the developers will refuse to engage in anything that might cost them money.

Over a cup of tea, Leavesley told me about Southwell's sustainability strategy. Southwell has two officers with a sustainability remit: as well as Leavesley, there is Simon Edwards, the district's active travel officer. Their roles overlap little, given that Edwards is focused on transport and Leavesley does a lot of energy work, but there is another key separator – Leavesley is employed directly by the council, whereas Edwards is employed by Theta. "I'm not up for grabs", explains Leavesley, highlighting that his role is viewed as statutory and can therefore not be outsourced, whereas Edwards works for the 'other side'. Leavesley adds that, as an outsider to Theta, he has become cut off to some extent. It can be a bit of an island, he explains, adding that, ideally, aspects of sustainability should be looked at in an integrated way but, because of the Theta/non-Theta split, this doesn't tend to happen.

I had a similar sit-down with Edwards, who is a soft-spoken sustainable-travel enthusiast. He has an outdoorsy, woodsman quality that seems out of place where he sits among the highways officers, some of whom are known for their passion for driving. He is focused on designing the built environment so that it is more convenient to walk or cycle, to make driving more of a pain – "filtered permeability" is his watchword. Fascinated by new ideas about rewriting the underlying 'source code' of a street for bikeability, he focuses his available resource on creating "one hundred metres of gorgeous [bike path]" rather than building a mediocre and dysfunctional longer stretch.

Although switched onto global urbanist developments, Edwards does not seem engaged with the political process at the council. Absorbed at the 'source code' level, taking on infrastructure one hundred metres of gorgeous at a time, he has never attended a planning-committee meeting and speaks little during our encounter of the wider council context. Unlike Leavesley, he seems fairly insulated from the dynamics of politics and power. Thus the Theta partnership has created a fractured line of command with islands of activity that disrupt the flow of communications and reduce integration. As one of the planners put it, "There is a level of separation now that didn't exist before the partnership."

2.4 Nailing jelly and the goalkeepers' union

In their daily work, planners navigate conflicting pressures while maintaining good relations with councillors, other professionals and their own managers. This section examines the micro-level organisational dynamics surrounding a legal ecological requirement from another government body. Here, the planners must balance conflicting governmental pressures relating to housing need and biodiversity, while maintaining the social capital in their networks essential to delivering this and other projects. Manoeuvring in this narrow space in and between organisations, unconscious alliances can be observed. Formal organisational boundaries are not necessarily the key delineations: *professionals with shared credentials form 'goalkeepers' unions' that emerge as shared concerns within a given project.*[13]

Nailing jelly

Large parts of the region's coastline are designated a special protection area (SPA), principally to protect coastal-dwelling bird species. Natural England has recently interpreted the legislation such that planning authorities need to compensate for additional 'recreational disturbance' resulting from people occupying new houses and tourist infrastructure and then, for example, walking their dogs at the beach. The council now needs to produce a 'Habitats Strategy' that demonstrates how seabird numbers can be maintained and increased. Numbers need to be monitored and measures, such as moving car parks further from nesting sites, will likely be needed to mitigate the impact of extra activity arising from new development. This all costs money and is to be paid through levying a charge on new development that happens within reach of the coast.

It has been proposed that Southwell partner with Overcombe, a neighbouring authority, to hire wardens to monitor bird numbers and patrol the coast at key times of year while jointly funding capital projects. How this works in practice is yet to be determined. Local authorities across the region have come up with different charges on development, and partnering with another authority brings benefits but also a series of things to be worked out – who employs the wardens and what happens if development doesn't come forward at all or as quickly in one or both authorities being chief among them.

Kathy has requested a meeting with Natural England to iron out some of the details. Around the table are several of the planners plus the Southwell ecologist Margie Symonds and Bea Tunstall, who represents Natural England. Kathy stresses at the start of the meeting that this is urgent due to a planning application for one of the strategic housing sites, Southwell's Everdale Fields (see Figure 2.4 and Section 2.6), where the planners will need to know exactly what to demand from the applicant. Deciding the fee to charge for the habitats strategy is also now the only impediment to the release of a £17 million pot of government infrastructure money that has been secured for Everdale and another strategic housing site.

A particular frustration for the planners is that Natural England signed off on the local plan three years before and the Community Infrastructure Levy just last year but have now unexpectedly added in this new demand. Kathy explains that developers are getting impatient and frustrated: "Sorry to pass that on", she says, "but the goalposts have moved since the local plan and developers are quite concerned". One developer has done their own calculations based on the option of providing alternative mitigation and things have gotten contentious as they say they will pay only £200 per new house.

Figure 2.4: The edge of the green belt and the Everdale Fields development site

There are also outstanding questions about how far inland development needs to be for charges to apply: 6 km is a cut-off used in other places, and Southwell visitor surveys indicate there is a bit of a drop-off in visits to the coast at this point, but it is somewhat arbitrary and will illogically split in half one of its two strategic housing sites. Some authorities have two zones where different charges apply, reflecting that if residents are further away from the coast they are likely to visit less often. Kathy raises the difficulty of selling the rationale for the charge to developers and residents. "People outside 6 km will say, 'Why me?'" she adds. She explains that tensions will emerge with viability (including carefully negotiated contributions for other aspects of sustainability such as play areas or cycle paths) if costs are high. This is particularly problematic for more-marginal brownfield development in Southwell, which the council wants as it usually outperforms greenfield development on wider sustainability grounds. The shifting goalposts and the 'rock and a hard place' nature of the situation are making viability negotiations with the developers difficult: "At the moment it's like nailing jelly", says Kathy, driving home the difficulty of acting as a go-between without clear direction from Natural England.

She also points out the pressure on the planning service from other central government diktats, in this case to deliver a five-year housing land supply. "So we need clarity from you", she says to Bea. For the strategic housing sites, she proposes a meeting between Natural England, Southwell and the developer consortium to nail down the details (or the jelly), but she is aware that, in a commercialised public sector, government bodies may charge the council to meet with them in this way. "Do you want to charge to meet us?" she asks Natural England in a raised-eyebrow fashion. "Not if it's part of a planning application and we are a statutory consultee", Bea replies. Reassured, Kathy points out the reason for her wariness – there were hiccups over a high-profile community project because the charity leading it had to pay several hundred pounds to meet each of the public bodies and could not afford it. They agree to set up the meeting and Kathy concludes things in a conciliatory tone, aware that she has needed to be firm about the planners' unmet needs: "I'm sorry we outnumbered you", she says to Bea.

The goalkeepers' union

Overcombe has offered to manage the wardens that might be employed across the two authorities. In May, the two local authorities meet to thrash out some of the finer details, each bringing along an ecologist and two planners. From Southwell, David, the senior policy planner, and Priya, another planning officer who has been heavily involved in planning for the SPA, are here, along with Margie, the council ecologist. Roger, Overcombe's ecologist, is slightly old school – small, wiry, bearded, thick glasses, thinning but wildish dark hair, and shy but with a confidence that comes from a solid upper-middle-class upbringing. This seems to give him a bit of authority over others in the room.

David is concerned about the delivery of houses in Overcombe: whether they will actually get built and what happens if they don't. He also questions whether Southwell really needs two wardens given the much shorter length of its coastline compared to Overcombe's.

Roger is firm in saying yes, the number of wardens will be determined by the number of people coming to the SPA and the pressure from extra houses. Here the talk gets technical around visitor numbers, origins and destinations. Roger says, in justification for the 6 km and 10 km cutoffs, "What's interesting about our dog walker survey is its very similar to others, with a drop-off in numbers around 6 km". This type of evidence is good enough for Margie, but the planners want more, anticipating having to account for policy based on such evidence in quasi-legal forums such as planning inquiries. The ecologists drift together, their professional orientation, their goalkeepers' union, stronger than organisational allegiances.

Following some discussion of Overcombe's relatively robust finances, Roger, in an assuredly upper-middle-class way, implies that his authority is ready to crack on. He has more discretion to act in his local authority than David. The ecologists are more certain of their agenda, and he and Margie are aligned in their thinking – you can count seabirds and dog walkers – whereas David's game is nailing jelly, the endless round of negotiations within and beyond Southwell. Talk turns to costing possible projects, signage, moving a car park, dog walking areas, land purchase and shifting Community Infrastructure Levy regulations. More layers of jelly-nailing complexity loom against a backdrop of ever shifting central government requirements.

Finally, David asks how Overcombe came up with their £500 per house figure. "We have developer acceptance around £500", David says simply. Priya is astounded: "We can't do that, we need evidence up front", she says. While allegiances form on professional lines, local authority and place-specific planning, cultures vary, and tacit knowledge of local politics, developer positions and organisational know-how are needed to assess what is and what is not possible in particular places, even in adjacent local authority areas.

Manoeuvring within the council

Back at Southwell, the seabird saga continues with an internal meeting to make sure further work isn't wasted due to being vetoed by the higher-ups. The planners, Kathy and David, along with Margie the ecologist, are meeting Tony Hall, a head of service. Priya, who has done most of the work on the habitats strategy, can't attend as she has been seconded by Theta to another authority.

Tony oversees planning, ecology, environment and about a quarter of the council staff. He takes charge, outlining what he thinks this whole thing is about, and looks for clarification of the current position. He revels in the identity of a straight-talking fixer; direct but also self-aware, he often pushes an issue and then realises he may be being too direct and rows back. He quizzes Margie hard about the legal demands of the scheme, looking for what they absolutely have to do. He outlines members' desire to bend the money from the seabird strategy to satisfy other objectives such as extending the upgrades to the Sandy Bay promenade.

Margie patiently points out that this example doesn't work as it is likely to bring more visitors to the coast, specifically the rocky foreshore in this location, and thus disrupt the nesting birds. She adds that about £160,000 per year will be needed for monitoring, as without this data you can't tell whether you are meeting the demands of the legislation.

Tony, slightly alarmed, says that the deputy mayor, Ned Kirk, won't spend that sort of money on surveys. "I am purposely being challenging", he adds, noting that Kirk isn't very fond of birds and that this is a sticking point. One of the officers quips that Kirk doesn't like dogs either and so maybe he will like this proposal as its anti-dog? Tony suggests he isn't very fond of much, "such as spending on sustainable transport, people" he notes wryly. Frustrated, Margie reiterates the legal necessity of the survey work, and Tony retreats a little, noting that the argument he needs to take to the members is "We don't have a choice".[14]

Pressure on already stretched staff

The discussion unexpectedly turns to the idea that Southwell might do its own thing rather than buy into a warden service run by its neighbour. This has major implications for Margie's workload. Tony raises the idea, saying that Kirk will want more direct control over the money, but Margie speaks up, insisting she doesn't have time to manage two wardens.

The meeting gets tetchy and uncomfortable. Kathy, as head of the planning team, is willing to consider the idea of Southwell going it alone, while Margie, the ecologist, is not. She objects to the workload implications but also sees the social capital she has developed with her fellow ecologist-goalkeeper disappearing over the horizon.

As the discussion develops, Margie becomes more isolated. Tony explains that he is keen on employing staff directly to "build resilience and capacity". Demonstrating an impressive grasp of what Margie does, he tries to assuage her concerns by suggesting that one of the wardens could be her assistant so she can do the more interesting community work she used to before austerity cut it all. However, Margie is unconvinced, and the goalkeeper's union re-emerges: "I've spent a lot of time with Roger in Overcombe [working on this]", she says, reiterating that having people to manage will take more of her time. Tony tentatively suggests she could go back to working five days a week from her current three. "I should hand my notice in", she replies. And in that moment, she is, after fifteen years' service at Southwell, more than half-serious. I walk out with her. "I am seething", she says, unnecessarily. She is particularly upset that Priya, on an assignment for Theta, was not able to be there to back her up, as she could have provided more of the reasoning behind the proposal to share the wardens across authorities.

In many ways, juggling opposing interests is a planner's bread and butter. It demonstrates the judgement gained tacitly in the workplace and the synthetic knowledge work central to planning (see Chapter 1). However, as the unfolding of the habitats strategy illustrates, these tensions and contradictions can take on a pathological bent, wrought with ugly surprises that sour working relationships, contradictory pressures from government that make the planner's task impossible or stubborn disinterest in even statutory aspects of sustainability at higher levels of the council. This situation is exacerbated by the secondment of staff by Theta to other authorities, part of the privatisation deal that brings in income but causes organisational disruptions where institutional memory and tacit knowledge is lost at key decision-making moments.

This difficult process represents a lot that is hard to account for in government work: the probing, the discussing, the abandoned options. How might the Theta Timetracker account for this when the simple outcome is all at odds with the amount of resources that go in? How will the accounting work when the council is in effect doing the bidding of another government agency who aren't paying for the organisational time and effort? The outcome is yet another meeting to thrash it out, to nail more jelly to the wall.

2.5 Planners, politicians and the planning committee

This chapter has explored the work rhythms of the planning office, showing that planners often find themselves between a rock and a hard place in trying to accommodate the various powerful actors that they are compelled to serve. We now turn our attention to the councillors, the elected local politicians who deliberate alongside the planning officers, and the highly significant but under-researched arena of the statutory planning committee. The planning team's relations with councillors are good, but reveal tensions rooted in a sense of disappointment about the scale and type of development that is going on in Southwell as well as their relative powerlessness to affect it. The members were very much involved in the local plan preparation, and demonstrate ownership of it, a process reflective of strong engagement between officers and members during its production. At the same time, this ownership leads to strain wherever it appears compromised, particularly around environmental sustainability issues.

"Murdered hedgehogs"

Southwell Planning Committee is in session in the gymnasium-like room beyond reception. Amanda had been expecting the first application, which is for a small retail development and gym, an add-on to an existing city-edge retail park, to be passed by today's planning committee. Going in, she had a sense of how some of the councillors would vote, but there is always something of a wildcard factor, which today unravelled over a particular member's concern about "murdered hedgehogs". This concern unleashed a deeper current among the members of disappointment at broken developer promises, as well as their grief at seeing the district's green spaces disappear.

After Amanda's presentation and her officer recommendation to approve the retail development, Councillor Baker, who has the air of a kindly, watchful local grandmother, speaks up, worried about the loss of woodland that the development will entail. We have just looked on the big screen at a Google Maps photo of a swathe of woodland in the corner of the site. Many of the trees in the photo are apparently already gone, but the applicant, the all-powerful Earl of Overcombe, who owns much of the land around here, wants to remove more trees so that the new retail development can be seen from the road. Councillor Lovett, who has a no-nonsense aura, asks what percentage of the trees will be lost. The committee chair, Councillor Reed, a consummate committeeman who aspires to a statesmanlike bearing and has little taste for a public set-to, plucks a supportively small number of trees out of the air: "It looks like about 10 per cent", he says.

Baker, not appeased, wonders aloud whether the retail unit (a typical tin shed that boxes off one side of a large car park) will be a vibrant place. Councillor Archer, thick-set, slow and deliberate, takes up the baton, wondering whether concerns raised by the biodiversity officer and landscape architect have been pushed to one side in the officer recommendations.[15]

He adds that he is unconvinced the proposed replanting will be properly managed by the developer to protect wildlife – "We take the measures to encourage wildlife and then go and cut the grass", he argues. "A family of hedgehogs was recently murdered in this way", he informs the room, adding that it is something he read about in the papers.

Vague as the murdered hedgehogs are, this strikes a chord of discontent among the members; they are tired of approving things only to find the ameliorative measures that developers are supposed to take never quite materialise. Baker chimes in: "I'm disappointed that we leave so many things open", she says. "Promises have been made that haven't happened."

Archer's thought process has an infuriatingly blundering quality. He speaks slowly, often hitting dead ends, relaxing his mind around an issue, allowing himself to follow a train of thought, lacking the inhibition that would cause an ordinary person to give up the chase or the filter needed not to bring things up in the first place. It is a bit like watching a toddler put shapes into a Fisher Price Shape Sorter. However, he often gets one of his shapes in with a satisfying effect – in this discussion he hits on the sense of ownership that the members have in the local plan. He directs us to point 4.7 of today's documentation and quotes from the biodiversity officer's comments, "This is unacceptable and contrary to the local plan", concluding that he will be opposing on these grounds.

The conciliatory chair is keen to regain some perspective on Archer's comments. "We have to balance it in our own minds", he notes, reminding the committee that they are not bound to subscribe to the opinions of the biodiversity officer. We are reminded that the development is not in a wildlife corridor, that some shrubbery has been proposed. "The applicant wants visibility, so it's a difficult one", he muses. However, the mood has shifted in favour of the hedgehogs. "I'll vote against unless we can keep the trees", says Councillor Baker. It goes to a vote and the application is narrowly defeated.

Back upstairs in the office there is some analysis. "Murdered hedgehogs!" says Kathy, looking faintly exasperated at the tendency of the committee to throw up surprises. "You can't underestimate how much the members are bothered by biodiversity issues", one of the officers muses. "There is a cumulative effect on the members of seeing their greenspace disappear", another comments. Amanda looks back at the Google photo that seems to have fanned the flames of the discussion – it turns out to have been an old photo as much of the woodland has indeed already been cut down by the developer – the council had a complaint about it, one of the officers remembers. "They have taken an awful lot out", Amanda says a bit sadly, "There's almost nothing there now."

A couple of months later the committee reconvenes to discuss the resubmitted application. "This is the one you might remember fondly from October", says the chair. The earl has compromised and abandoned the plan to cut down the remaining trees. "This committee has spoken and the trees have miraculously reappeared", announces the chair with his customary wit and perhaps a note of pride that the earl's power has some limits. He quickly moves to a vote and the members all vote in favour of more car-oriented, city-edge development, albeit with a few more trees.

How far is the post office?

Southwell has worked hard in recent years to reach high standards in council-owned-and-operated care homes, and they aren't going to let developers put something shoddy in their patch. At the next planning committee, the first item on the agenda is a proposed care facility next to a busy road in Pitthead, in the north of the district.

Councillor Baker is the first to question again and raises the issue of amenity: "We need care facilities, but *within communities*", she stresses: "How far are they from a post office or a pub?" Cameron quotes Policy DM5.7 of the local plan, which asks for such integration; it's adjacent to existing housing, so in that sense it's integrated, he notes, perhaps rather broadly interpreting the policy. Councillor Baker isn't giving up: "How far is it from the pub, and the post office and the church?" she asks. "There's the Lidl", says one of the members with a note of humour. The Lidl is on the murdered hedgehogs' site, through a lot of 'wiggly-worm' new housing development, a good way to the south.

The tenor here among the more vocal members is that this is the 'fag end' of a 'big wodge' of land allocated for housing on which the Earl of Overcombe as landowner has made a tidy sum, and it is being fobbed off to the voiceless. The feeling is that if you have mild dementia when you go into the home, it's going to accelerate pretty quickly with just the weekly minibus to get you away from the drone of the dual carriageway. Councillor Baker says the demand for the facility exists, but the distance from community facilities means she won't support the application.

Baker does not carry the day. The vote goes 6–2 in favour and we move to the next application. It's for ten four-bedroom houses on the site of a former pub that is situated in the bottom of a wooded valley with no other housing in the vicinity. Councillor Stobbart, who keeps a weather eye on sustainability issues, asks about public transport to the proposed development.

The highways officer notes it's over eight hundred metres to the tram but about four hundred metres to bus stops north-east and north-west. Stobbart asks where the nearest primary school is, given that these are four-bedroom family homes, and there is a bit of scurrying from the officers to provide an answer. Councillor Lovett asks about play space, and Amanda, on the back foot, zooms in on the application to show there is a bit of fenced grassy area which could be an informal play area.

Councillor Gallagher, drawing on his local knowledge, returns to the bus stop issue, noting that the bus stops are both at the top of long, steep hills: "It's ridiculous", he says. Amanda uses Google Street View to point out that there is still a bus shelter nearby and it's in good condition. I check later and the only bus that goes past the shelter is a school bus once a day in each direction to a secondary school. We move towards the vote and one of the members notes that this is a useful contribution to housing land supply – the councillors are well aware of the constraints posed by the housing targets. Councillor Gallagher is the only vote against.

During planning-committee sessions, members' concerns that services need to be more walkable from new development or that biodiversity is threatened often jar against the pragmatic assessment of the officers. The officers are accustomed to the demands of a system that, in order to deliver housing, requires a certain resignation to developer power (McClymont, 2014); here, 'Is it bad enough to refuse?' wins out over 'Is it good enough to approve?' We explore this relationship more thoroughly in the following section.

2.6 Public planners, developers and their agents

Key to delivering development in Southwell are developers and the planning consultants and other built-environment professionals who represent them. In this section we use a case study of a large greenfield housing development to illustrate the complexities of delivering such a scheme at a time when the public sector is limited in terms of the tools it has to shape the final product. Much of the negotiation that affects what gets built happens in meetings, and this and the following section lean heavily on meeting observations, providing a window on a terrain of huge importance that is not given enough attention in planning research.

Between the city and the seaside is Everdale Fields, an area of land earmarked for major housing development that will help Southwell deliver a healthy chunk of the eighteen thousand new houses they are required to build by 2032. The site, which has established residential neighbourhoods most of the way around its edges with a bit of green belt to the north, is a mosaic of farmers' fields with a village in the centre. Favoured by dog walkers who tramp its perimeter and criss-crossing footpaths and lanes, it's big enough to lose your gaze in and to feel a sense of openness and distance; the sky takes up a lot of what you see. Wood pigeons fly with surprising elegance long and low over the fields. At the edges are the plants and flowers of urban cracks – copious brambles and nettles; tall dandelions that, freed from gardens, have stretched themselves out. The ground varies a lot, from dry scrub to bulrush-fringed marsh. In one pocket, a copse provides shelter and dappled shade; the buffeting wind drops away and the air is alive with bird calls. The ground here, a small rug of clover, is marked by rabbit droppings, and there are human signs: the remains of a fire in a hollow; a faded packet of tomato-ketchup-flavour crisps.

"It's a lovely place to walk", says a man in his sixties walking his dog along the edge. "There was a fox just over there the other day", he recalls, pointing to the field's edge. For the trained eye, the site is rich in wildlife. The local natural history society recently published on its website an overview of the birds that take advantage of the site's habitats: skylarks, reed buntings, yellowhammers and, usually not far off, the kestrel. Depending on the season, we are told, the visitor might be charmed by the cheerful calls of dancing meadow pipits or arrested by the plaintive cries of lapwings and golden plovers. Redwings and fieldfares, arriving from across the sea, make their first pit stop here to feast on hawthorn berries.[16] At ground level, we are told, we may be lucky enough to spot a weasel stalking its prey, or the hoof prints of roe deer.

In the middle of the expanse is a cluster of houses – Everdale Village. Outwardly promising from the whinnying horses of its stables and the antique plough at the entrance, it has a suburban hodgepodge feel. Its centrepiece is a large, unsightly pub called the Prince of Wales, complete with faux-Tudor panelling and faux-leaded uPVC windows. The interior is furnished with a wall-to-wall black-and-white tartan carpet that runs around the small bar. It's a popular weekday lunch spot for older folk who drive in and use the big car park at the side. The food menu features daily specials such as 'Thai Thursday' and two mains for £7.95; Viennetta and Arctic roll are on the dessert menu for £1.

At the entrance to the village is a planning notice for the first application that has come in, for 424 houses in the south-east corner of the surrounding fields; there will be four thousand in total, spread across the area. The barman at the Prince of Wales is not convinced that the houses will ever materialise. "They've been trying to do that for forty years but it'll never happen", he laughs. A customer along the bar disagrees, "Don't listen to him, he's an idiot."

The Everdale master plan

"I think it's hard for people", observes Yvonne, "I think they feel like it's a bit of a dictatorship sometimes. We're dictating what's happening in the area that they live in." We are in the planning office talking about the master plan for Everdale Fields. "Development needs to happen to support this country", she notes, adding that the master plan has been designed to provide a mix of housing types that matches the council's own assessment of future housing need in Southwell. Yvonne observes optimistically that housebuilders nowadays have to take some responsibility for the impact of their developments: "Historically, going back to the '70s and '80s, you probably got very little contribution from a developer", she notes. "I think the roles have changed ... the developers now contribute to make their development acceptable."

The master plan for the site, aimed at meeting government-prescribed housing numbers while working within local political constraints and the need to protect birds and other wildlife, was carefully developed over several years. There was organised opposition in the community. As Kathy recalls, local campaigners had come up with the view that houses were being built hedge to hedge, that the whole of Everdale would be covered in houses; there was particular concern about protecting the character of the village.[17] The council needed to attach the development to established settlements so that incomers would have access to the services and facilities that existed within those communities, but had to achieve this without igniting the ire of existing residents.

Working within these constraints, the council employed consultants who developed a 'concept plan'. More consultants were then appointed to move things forward and fill out the details. The resulting design is a series of connected beads, or blobs, of housing that adjoin the suburbs hereabouts rather than the village. A link road connects the blobs, and a 'wildlife corridor' buffers the development from the village. The master plan says that the site will 'encompass a park ... a natural, verdant environment serving local communities and wildlife'.

Resident comments, collected at public engagement events in 2017, bear witness to community opposition to the plan. One resident poignantly expressed the value that the space, in its wholeness, offers: "I often walk there for peaceful reflection and, standing in the centre of the fields, seeing St Luke's church off in the distance and listening to the sounds of nature, I feel as though I'm immersed in the countryside, not in a town." Others, worried about loss of biodiversity, asked why the council is building on greenfields when there are numerous other options; there is a specific objection to the narrowness of the proposed wildlife corridor in the south-east corner of the site. There are concerns about whether the houses are really needed and whether local people will be able to buy them: "Who round here can afford £170,000?" asks one concerned resident who has looked at how much the 'affordable'[18] houses will cost. Amid concerns over sprawl and over-development, there are worries about pressure on schools and there is great distrust of the 'arrogant' highway network manager's modelling for the additional traffic. Consultees, cited in the engagement document, voice similar concerns. Sustrans points out that the current proposal does not follow the council's own design guidance. The Overcombe and Southwell Nature Conservancy raises a concern that the planned roads and meagre or poorly implemented buffers will dislocate and fragment the site, rupturing its wildlife permeability.

There is an occasional positive comment: "It seems a lot of careful thought and listening has gone into the layout in general", but there are also claims that the planning officers are out of touch with the impact of current development on local communities, particularly in terms of impacts on traffic and air quality, and there is suspicion that the council is creating extra housing in order to boost council-tax revenue.

The council's responses to each resident comment repeat throughout the engagement document like a mantra: 'Southwell is growing. To accommodate this growth we need to build 18,000 new homes by 2032.' 'The Council seeks 25% of new homes to be affordable.' '52 of the 65 housing allocation sites in the Local Plan are brownfield sites.' 'Existing tree groups, copses and field boundaries will be retained where possible.' 'Planning applications will be required to show that there are no negative effects on the highway infrastructure.' As a result of the engagement, several changes to the master plan are recorded – the wildlife corridor, at a pinch point in the south-east corner, has been widened, and a pedestrian route has been moved to appease neighbours worried about anti-social behaviour.

The development consortium

Each change in the plans for Everdale Fields requires delicate and often uneasy negotiations with a consortium of housebuilders. The master plan quite ambitiously brings together several – each of whom owns a different set of farmers' fields – to deliver the four thousand houses. The site is of a scale that Kathy refers to as all or nothing: "You need that critical mass of development", she explains, "to get the right quality of place and the right infrastructure to support it".

A couple of the developers are major national operators, household names: Overcombe Holdings, the earl's property development arm, also owns a slice, and there are other players; Southwell itself owns a slither of the land. To finance the necessary infrastructure, such as the link road, tram stop and primary school that are needed for the site as a whole, the developers need to work with each other. The process, which has taken several years, has involved Southwell planners in a highly resource-intensive process.

After the approval of the master plan, the officers expected that the consortium would continue to move in concert. Instead, while there is still some collaboration among the developers in applying for pots of government infrastructure funding, the alliance is fragile. Also, the earl has gotten in early and submitted his application for 424 houses (with 1,184 parking spaces) as a stand-alone application, creating anger in the consortium around Overcombe Holdings' commitment to the wider project. "I think their aspiration was always to try and come in and be able to get that bit of the site away without having to be involved for the longer time", observes Kathy. "It's only about 10 per cent of the site, and it's an easy win, because you can get access into it from the existing highway network ... and they can be in and out [of the wider scheme]." As time passed, the officers became more concerned about the lack of developer collaboration: "It's a very difficult thing for rival housebuilders to have to work on", notes Kathy, "but this development can't happen if the infrastructure isn't provided".

Meetings with developers

In ongoing discussions about delivering the master plan, the planning officers skilfully manage developer tantrums and exhibit strong negotiation skills. However, the power asymmetry between them and developers means their control over the outcome of discussions is heavily circumscribed. Attempts to work collaboratively to create and deliver a cohesive placemaking vision are undermined by the unwillingness of competing firms to work together. At the same time, both sides take refuge in hoped-for panaceas, such as the driverless car, that will relieve them from the burden of planning for a sustainable future.

"We are all aware of costs"

Harvey White, who heads up the earl's development arm, is sitting around a table with some of the officers. The meeting is focused on discussing progress at Everdale Fields and on Overcombe Holdings' plans for their bits of the site. Kathy and Yvonne are here along with Daniel and Will from the transport and highways side of the council. White has a practised restraint about him and a disarmingly quiet, mild way of talking. I expected him to be posher and more stand-offish, but he is affable; I have to remind myself of the Latin inscription that is carved into a treetop tourist attraction at the earl's nearby stately home: *Parvus pendetur fur, magnus abire videtur*.[19]

The meeting gets going and we home in on some details about cycling provision. Will notes that Harvey has proposed putting a cycle route on only one side of the road. Harvey answers smoothly that the "original aspiration was to put a cycle route on both sides but our application won't go that far ... simply because we are all aware of costs". He continues, "Let's put forward a reasonable ..." but Will interjects that Southwell has a requirement for an early-adopted cycleway that will be on both sides, reminding Harvey that this requirement was based on earlier discussions with the developer consortium.

"So, this is an internal agreement", says Harvey, intimating that he didn't know about it and hinting that it may be tricky for the council to enforce. To get him off the defensive, Daniel adds that it is possible to sacrifice some of the planned road space to accommodate cycle lanes on each side. "So you're telling me it would be just as cheap?" asks Harvey, perking up. He tests the waters again: "You want both sides?" he asks, adding, "We think a cycle path on one side and a footpath on the other ... how much of that discussion might be at the Section-106 stage?" Will replies firmly, "We think at the planning stage." "OK, fine", replies Harvey, not pushing further.

Harvey has adopted a strategy of acting surprised regarding details that he knows about already. He approaches money-related aspects that are already decided as though they might still have some wiggle room in them. When cornered by a cost that seems unavoidable, he finds ways to display his power to go back on arrangements to build houses if the market takes a downturn, reminding the officers that the earl's passion for solving the alleged housing crisis will ultimately be determined by market demand.

We move on to housing numbers. Yvonne asks about the increase in units in the application that has come in from Overcombe Holdings at the Everdale site. The council was expecting 333 units for this piece of land, but the application is for 424. Again Harvey begins his quiet work, noting that 333 was not the physical capacity of the site but that it was simply the number that triggered the need for a bus gate.

Yvonne, concerned, explains that with 424 units there will be knock-on effects for the overall housing number in the master plan; the numbers have been carefully worked out for each member of the consortium. Harvey suggests somewhat offhandedly that Yvonne could shave off some units from elsewhere on the site to allow him to build his extra 91. He continues his pursuit, "We don't think this upsets the master plan by moving to 400 ... I don't think it is at physical capacity." Yvonne is unmoved and says, "We'll need to assess this and come back to you", suggesting a separate meeting, or possibly several, to discuss this part.

Harvey wants to know how long the determination of his application will take and asks if it will be twelve weeks, Yvonne deflects this latest attempt to negotiate a detail that he already knows is fixed: "It will take sixteen weeks", she says calmly.

"The boys versus the girls"

It's the next meeting and in come Yvonne and Amanda with four men who are here to discuss the Overcombe Holdings application. "It's the boys versus the girls, I see", says Harvey as they take their seats.[20] Harvey and his colleague Damien have brought with them two others, Gregg and Jules from Aphid, a small firm that Overcombe Holdings use for their design work. Gregg, Aphid's founder, is a large rugby-built man in his forties, an architect who exudes tightly balled-up hatred of planning officers almost from the moment he enters. Jules, his waifish, angular colleague, is dressed in uninterrupted blackness from head to toe.

During the meeting, Jules disarmingly engages with everything in a designery, problem-solving way. Gregg, by contrast, says everything loudly and, like Harvey, seems rather uncomfortable with women. He repeatedly uses Yvonne's name when he talks.

An objection to the earl's 424 houses has come in from Vermilion, one of the other consortium members. Clearly angry that their competitor has jumped the gun, they are objecting to the increased number of houses in the Overcombe Holdings application. Damien notes that Overcombe Holdings are in the process of setting out their position on this. Yvonne reminds us of the need for the consortium to continue to work together, explaining that because the Overcombe Holdings proposal has come in as a stand-alone application, consultees are looking at something that has no mitigation. She gives examples: there is no allotment provision or primary school; there is insufficient open space for play. One particular problem, Yvonne explains, is that the primary school in the master plan is going to be on land that is owned by another developer, and they haven't submitted their application yet, so we will need to put our heads together to come up with a solution.

Harvey finds this tiresome. He wants to be given a cash number so that they can make their financial contribution and get on with building some houses, without taking responsibility for delivery. "We can't deliver a primary school that is in another part of the site", he urges. Amanda chimes in, "That's our issue too, it's a conundrum." There ensues some more conversation about the complications of extracting Section-106 contributions for something that will be built on third-party land. Again, Harvey is firm that Overcombe Holdings' input should begin and end with some kind of payment and the council can work out the tricky details. "We have to make sure that the master plan is delivered", is Amanda's rebuttal. The subtext here is that the Everdale Fields site was allocated on the basis that developers would work collaboratively to deliver the full vision laid out in the master plan, which includes not only the link road, the primary school and allotments but also a network of cycling provision joined up to a new tram station in the north of the site. Harvey is not convinced: "There is no way we can guarantee that your tram is delivered", he says grumpily.

Damien relieves the tension by moving us onto the cycleway design; there is a tricky pinch point in the layout: "Those cycleways don't get any narrower, do they?" Gregg, the Aphid director, interrupts; he is annoyed at Southwell's insistence on a 4.5 m width (see Figure 2.5). He mentions that he has already clashed with Kathy about the lack of wiggle room on the cycle paths given all the other constraints they have to work with. "We're

Figure 2.5: Upgrading a cycleway at a new housing development

hoping, Yvonne, you'll be able to appease her", he says with an unsettling mix of flirtation and threat.[21]

Gregg is looking for a bit more appreciation for the changes they've made to the design so far, and he brings us around to the thorny issue of visitor parking. While 4.5 m cycle paths will clearly encourage active travel, Southwell's parking standards are what the planning officers refer to as "generous". "We know your highways department is like the 1980s ... like the '70s,"[22] Gregg says disparagingly, arguing that there should be more flexibility in the system to allow for better design. "Are you meeting visitor parking standards?" asks Yvonne. "We're a little bit down", answers Gregg testily. "You guys were utterly inflexible. Where the hell does it go?"

"How many units would you have to lose to meet the visitor parking standard?" asks Yvonne, subtly reminding the developer that they have exceeded the number of units they were expected to propose on the site. Gregg asks the name of the highways officer he needs to talk about visitor parking with, and recalls that they've already met and have the same hair colour: "Ginger on ginger", he joke-threatens. "Boxing gloves on, I can take him."

The mood suddenly lightens as Harvey invokes the driverless car panacea. Jules and Gregg join in with the banter; in ten years' time, with self-drive technology, there'll be no private vehicles, so all this discussion is a waste of time, they laugh. Amanda chips in that this is something they've been just saying in the office as well, that in a decade or so nobody will own a car any more. Harvey adds that he saw a German system recently where people don't have a car and just ring one up when they need one. "Like a big taxi?" asks Amanda. "They're all Mini Coopers", he laughs.

A matter of density

Much of the discussion around Everdale Fields boils down to issues surrounding car-centric suburban development. While Southwell's planning officers are passionate about placemaking and are intellectually committed to sustainable development, the day-to-day practice of planning at Southwell demands accommodation of the realities of an unsustainable, developer-oriented planning process that tends towards sprawl and is exacerbated by the district's own parking and highway standards.

That said, the planners tend not to problematise low-density development. At the Everdale site, which has one compact section but will tend in the main towards lower density, the planners believe that building at higher density would jeopardise the quality of place that they can offer. Cameron's experience of growing up in a failed high-density housing experiment in nearby Middlecroft has perhaps had an influence on the team.

The council's insistence on 4.5 m cycle paths is encouraging, but the summoning of the electric and/or driverless car to ease tensions signals the powerlessness of the officers against developers. For planners who lack agency, it provides a soothing eco-modern way out, precluding deeper engagement with what is really needed for sustainable development. The following, final, section explores these ideas further, looking at how the prospect for visionary planning is constrained at Southwell, while also celebrating the planners' ability to maximise their limited acting space in ways that serve the public interest.

2.7 Constrained visions and limited acting space: what can planning achieve?

Southwell's planning service operates, like many others in England, largely at the mercy of developers. While policies such as that relating to cycle-path width are somewhat enforceable, the officers are wary of digging in their heels lest they upset the developers they depend upon for housing delivery. Central-government rules dictate the council must demonstrate they have five years of housing in the pipeline, and, if they have not met this requirement and refuse a proposed housing development, the threat of a planning appeal looms large. Knowing this, arguments surrounding viability are used by housebuilders to limit what the council asks for, and this makes it difficult to refuse a development over issues such as biodiversity or air quality. This section shows how such constraints, alongside a lack of public-sector funding, foreclose the implementation of a vision for sustainable development in Southwell. On a more hopeful note, we examine a counter-trend whereby Section-106 finance was beginning to benefit the poorest parts of the district. Yet, this example also underscores councils' dependence on private-sector development coming forward. In a context where planners' acting space is severely constrained and resources are limited, the purpose of planning is reduced to reining in neoliberalism's worst excesses rather than advancing a sustainable alternative.

The meeting nobody wants to go to

Amanda asks if I want to come with her to the heat-network meeting; it's the meeting that she'd previously told me nobody wants to go to. It's a great idea but everyone knows the developers will not go for it because they feel it is not marketable.

A heat network is a way to eliminate the need for gas boilers in every home, providing sustainable heat.[23] Heating makes up around a third of an individual household's carbon budget, so inefficient home heating is a major contributor to climate change (Climate Change Committee, 2016). However, responding to a powerful developer lobby, central-government backtracked on commitments to increase the statutory requirements on energy efficiency in new homes, preferring looser statements of guidance that often leave local authorities with little negotiating power with developers. Central government has a pot of money for feasibility studies, but heat networks rarely feature in mainstream commercial housing development.

We arrive at one of the upstairs conference rooms; it's cold, which is funny, given the topic of the meeting; the projector, drained of energy, emits a murky light. John Leavesley, the sustainable energy officer who has organised the meeting, says that we are expecting a few more people but indicates we'd better get going to stay on time. At the head of the table with his laptop projected on the screen is Duncan from PPG, a professional services firm that Southwell has hired to do a heat-network feasibility study for the two strategic housing sites, including Everdale Fields. Also present is one of the council's heavy-hitting senior managers, Malcolm Thomas, who interrupts Duncan's presentation at intervals, paying particular attention to who is going to pay for things. Another manager, Lee, sits low in his chair asking practical, salty questions delivered in broad local dialect, oozing scepticism but trying to find a way forward.

Duncan from PPG is an engineer. He wears a blue crew-neck jumper with a shirt underneath and his forehead gets blotchy at points when the meeting gets political and away from the technicalities of pipe diameter. He does not shy away though, and is firm about the role the council would need to take in requiring developers to come on board with a heat network. This is something that, as those present at the meeting increasingly articulate, they are powerless to do.

The meeting starts with a reminder that the developers have so far been unresponsive to invitations to discuss the heat-network idea. Duncan states plainly that if the developers at Everdale Fields and the other key strategic housing sites are not on board, a scheme has no chance. He says that to make this work the council will have to ban gas boilers, mandating participation in the scheme. He emphasises the opportunity that will be squandered if we do not install the heat network on these virgin sites along with the other pipework.

Duncan explains that although the upfront costs of the heat network look scary, the project can be financed by selling power and through avoided costs. Unfortunately, at £1,000 per metre, the low density of the proposed housing at Everdale and the other strategic site greatly inflates the heat network's cost. However, Duncan still sees some ways forward. He suggests that part of the costs can be met by making the houses a little more expensive. By adding £1,000–2,000 onto the price of each home and having homeowners pay upfront now, he explains, later costs related to the government's low-carbon transition can be avoided. Unfortunately, this is a cost that the authority, not the developer or homeowner, will shoulder: "Who will pay those transition costs in fifteen to twenty years?" Lee asks. "We will", says Leavesley. "The government should be telling us that on any strategic site you need to do this, then we could insist", he adds.

"Has it been done elsewhere?" Lee asks. Duncan tells us about the Exeter Cranbrook site where that council forcefully specified that the area had to be covered by a heat network. "No ifs, no buts", he says. He lays out some of the details, adding that councils can de-risk a heat-network project by committing their own buildings to it. Lee observes that, down south, some councils have the assets and clout such that local plans can be written in a way that says installing a heat network is what you *have* to do, something that is not economically possible in Southwell. Furthermore, he adds, Southwell no longer has much in the way of buildings to commit; many have been sold or are in private hands.

Emphasising the powerlessness of the council, Amanda interjects, "If the developer says no, what can we do?" Trying to be helpful, Lee offers to hook Duncan up with the developers, but reminds him, "We can have the discussion, but we can't insist." Mindful of housing numbers, Amanda adds, "If it comes to the crunch, we'll be refusing applications and we don't want to get down to that."

Towards the end there is a sense of doom about the prospect of engaging the developers. Malcolm becomes more vocal about how the developers are never going to sign up to this, how the numbers, in terms of up-front capital cost, will be totally off-putting to them. Looking for ways around the problem, Leavesley asks whether there could be a "soft-dig" approach whereby the channels are dug without the pipework. Here, Lee notes that it could be dangerous to build a network before the houses are built in case developers back out and the houses are never constructed. Trying to keep the idea alive in spite of his scepticism, Lee asks if it is possible to implement the network in embryonic form at a couple of council buildings and branch out in the future.

Trying to sound supportive yet also needing to point out the inevitable failure of the idea, he adds, "It's the cost and who's going to pay. They will just say no." He notes that timing is also a big problem as the process is too far along; there are some murmurs that this sort of thing should have really been started five years ago in the local plan.[24] "We don't have any power to insist", Lee concludes. Amanda remarks that the planners are in delicate viability discussions with the developers now. Lee adds that there are upcoming viability workshops and that the developers' opinion is that there is a large viability gap, so it is bad timing to add in a new demand.

Lee offers up a developer name – it's the evasive Harvey White from Overcombe Holdings – for Duncan to talk to: "But it would have to be separate from the business-case discussion." He is clearly nervous on this point and knows how Harvey will react: "If the bottom line is affected, if it's negative, they will be not interested." The group wonder whether any of the consortium members might have heard about the Cranbrook scheme, as this might help sell it. The meeting closes with some more pessimistic comments. Lee says, "When they see the price tag they'll tell you to get lost." He pauses, and adds, "In a nice way."

Herding cats

While extracting finance for the heat network is near impossible, the level of housing development in Southwell has generated a significant amount of money from s106 payments (see endnote 1 for this chapter) that developers pay to councils to mitigate the impact of their activity. Southwell has initiated an s106 sub-committee tasked with keeping track of the money raised and ensuring that it is equitably and intelligently distributed. The sub-committee is there to ensure the elected members have more input into agreements that were previously figured out between officers and housebuilders; it also aims to address political disagreements between members about how and where money is spent.

At a sub-committee meeting in the large fourth-floor meeting room, Kathy and I take a seat at a huge table, a scale appropriate to the big committeemen in the room. Chairing the meeting is Tony Hall, head of service, who sits opposite us; he wears an open-collared shirt, his tie folded on the table, signalling that he is en famille. To his right is Mack Watson, a seasoned cabinet member and councillor. He is fairly quiet except when it comes to jokes. Next to him is the Rabelaisian figure of Ned Kirk, deputy mayor and councillor for one of Southwell's most deprived wards, whose misanthropy was referred to in the seabird strategy reported in Section 2.4. He peppers his strongly opinionated speech with bantery jokes, sounding from these exertions as if he was once a heavy smoker.

The manly, working-class atmosphere is palpable, and after witnessing the condescension of the visitors from Theta, it is reassuring to see a display of local colour at the top levels of the council. At one point, while we are working our way through a list of applications for derelict pub sites, it becomes apparent that Mack is rather too familiar with all of them. "I used to drink there", he says of the Rye Lane Social Club. Kirk asks how come all the places Mack has had a drink in are falling down. "It's when he gets barred", quips Tony, joking about the financial impact of losing Mack's custom.

During the meeting, Tony emphasises that the point of this new sub-committee is for the council to have a more strategic approach to how s106 money is spent. He explains that, for each application, the council's job is to try to get as much as they can, adding for Mack's benefit that s106 is "the art of the possible, what we can get away with".

Kirk wants a clearer picture about how much money there is and where it is going. Tony explains that chasing where s106 money has gotten to across multiple complex agreements is not yet a straightforward process: "It's like herding cats, but we're getting there", he says, adding that the council have advertised for a new financial officer to implement a tracking system: "There'll soon be someone in post to herd the cats", he assures Kirk.

At the next meeting, we are joined by Neil Allison, the council's senior manager for investment, who seems to have started some of the cat-herding in advance of the new officer's arrival. His manner provides a break from the workingmen's club aesthetic, but he joins in successfully with the banter. Kirk's tone is initially a bit prickly – some members, he explains, are frustrated that, having borne the impact of development, their s106 money is being spent on upgrades to a distant park; there is also a concern that the poorer wards, where there is little development, are not receiving any improvements.

Neil has prepared a briefing note for Kirk, an attempt to lay out the big picture, that includes satisfyingly chunky numbers. He reads out a total of £10.7 million not yet spent, covering 142 agreements, pointing out that education, at £4.9m is the biggest item. He adds that there is £16.4m in the pipeline based on applications that have been received and approved but which are not yet started on site.

A happy 'ker-ching' sort of feeling spreads through the room, conjuring images of shopping sprees for nice new play equipment for the kids in scruffy areas; 100 m stretches of gorgeous cycleway seem to materialise before our eyes. This, it seems, is the full piggy bank that Southwell has created through its pro-development approach. Kirk checks that the strategic housing sites are not yet in these calculations and sounds pleased. If he had spectacles, he would be tapping them on the page and nodding. He wants to know if the spreadsheet can be used to tell us how manoeuvrable the money is – "Can we tell if there is money that can be used for the school build-out that's needed in Pitthead?" Neil confirms that the numbers show there is potential there to fund the school.

Kirk is letting it sink in, sensing that he has good news to take back to the members; there is a vague sense that he has won the lottery. "So this is lying in the bank? There is £10.7m lying in the bank?" he asks. Neil points out that there is also an additional £5.1m for offsite affordable housing that can be put anywhere in Southwell, even in the more neglected wards.

Towards the end, Tony announces that we now have a start date for the new hire, and there is some discussion about putting a briefing note together for the larger board meeting about how this s106 management process is being handled, about the spreadsheet tool they are developing – there is a feeling that the sub-committee have done some work that needs to be shared – "For them to learn from!" says Kathy.

2.8 Conclusion

What then is planning *for* in Southwell? The discretionary nature of English planning means that its purpose is always at the whim of central government. For them, planning is currently useful principally for delivering housing. Thus, housebuilding dominates planning decision-making at Southwell and, given other pressures, this has serious implications for sustainability. The unyielding burden of housing-delivery numbers leaves developers calling the shots. Volume housebuilders have little motivation to drive innovation in sustainability; their preference for greenfield sites, their fixed palette of offerings and their short-term need to boost the bottom line dictate what gets built and what doesn't. The master-planning episode discussed in Section 2.6 is most illustrative of this. In much of mainland Europe, the public sector leads on this type of urban extension (Hall, 2013). In England, typically no one has the power to lead, to assemble land and infrastructure in a wider public interest. The result is a pragmatic mess generating huge transaction costs. These costs are subsumed into both public- and private-sector organisations as they attempt to 'nail jelly to the wall' in endless rounds of shuttle diplomacy and developer brinkmanship.

The Southwell planners' task is to skilfully nudge developers towards slightly better outcomes and respond to externally imposed mandates such as the habitats strategy in a way that does least damage to their delicately negotiated plans. With visionary leadership foreclosed, they make the most of limited acting space (Grange, 2013), helping distribute s106 windfalls as equitably as they can, a Robin Hood approach that delivers resources where most needed yet, in relying on developer contributions, further cements the monetisation of planning and its need for more development.

Meanwhile, the partnership contract with Theta, with its narrow instrumental focus, stifles innovation. There have been upsides to this privatisation: staff get to experience work in other places, facilitating knowledge transfers for which there are fewer opportunities in the public sector as budgets for conferences and professional development have been cut. But the downsides are disruptions and loss of institutional memory in Southwell, coupled with lots of transaction costs in interfacing between Theta and the council (see Perez, 2020, for a similar conclusion regarding planning in a very different context).

The officers are alive to the noble ideas in planning. Yet, while developer power is sustained by weak and contradictory government policy, and the planners' work remains intensified and harnessed to the value-extracting logic of Theta, their prospects for stepping back and contributing to a visionary model for sustainable placemaking are worryingly slim. Higher purposes of planning – of social and environmental justice – surface in the cracks of the system but are largely foreclosed; rather, planning is intensely pragmatic, and planners become ever more skilful in the art and science of 'muddling through' (Lindblom, 1959).

3

Simpsons: the values-driven global consultancy

Simpsons is a multi-disciplinary, global organisation known in the UK for positive, collaborative relationships with clients. Our ethnography centred on a small planning team based in the firm's Dunthorpe office. Gaining direct access to Simpsons' clients was a sensitive challenge and we agreed to engage with client projects that had been recently completed, coupled with spending time in the office observing how the team learns and works together.

The case highlights the realities of contemporary planning practice in the private sector, and led us to a discussion of how such work can be executed in the public interest. It demonstrates the importance of relationships to Simpsons' business model and uniquely illuminates how strong collaborations help public-sector clients build capacity. Consultants displayed agility and flexibility in managing workflow and they skilfully navigated a shift towards large-scale projects featuring multi-headed clients that comprise more than one organisation. While Simpsons' high-performance work culture is rewarding for these driven individuals, their achievements come at a personal cost in terms of work-life balance, while their intensified work schedule is characterised by decreasing time for thought as well as by a loss of control over how their work is used.

3.1 Arrival

This section offers a 'thick description' of Simpsons' work environment, which is designed around cutting-edge 'officing' principles. We also introduce the planning team, grounding the reader in the types of planning work carried out by consultants in large, multi-national corporations, as well as explaining the processes of shadowing and collaboration that were used to create this account.

Simpsons occupies several floors of a Victorian former printworks that is situated on the outer edge of the city's creative district. A high white counter, topped by a hothouse plant, almost conceals the receptionist (see Figure 3.1). Once checked in, clients and visitors are greeted by the smell of good coffee and received in a smart, comfy couch area decorated by artsy photos of high-rises from around the world. Elevated halfway up the wall is

Figure 3.1: The reception area at Simpsons

a shelf with an illustrated book setting out the firm's philosophy. The toilets are the type you'd find in a nice hotel. Each stall has a hardwood door about eight feet high and the mirror is gently backlit.

Backstage, the planners occupy two rows of a long, bright office that also houses transport engineers, architects and other teams. The office, which smells faintly of candles, toast, coffee beans and pricey soaps, is a mix of hard and soft textures in muted colours – the exposed brick on both of the long walls is softened by a greyish-blue carpet. Thought has gone into acoustics, lighting and airiness: harsh sounds are softened by baffles suspended from the ceiling; slatted lighting encasements enhance the daylight coming in through the openable windows. The side where the planners sit has a pleasant view over a nearby park with a boating lake. The less-favoured, noisier side looks out onto undeveloped land, a dual carriageway complete with a tree that has a hurled shoe in it.

The desks, which are in short rows, are white and spacious. Each has a high-spec ergonomic chair and is adjustable to standing height, giving the office a creative-industries aesthetic. An always-busy kitchen area is seamlessly woven into the space, featuring a snug of comfy, booth-style couches, a long table with stools, a proper counter and cupboards full of clean mugs and bowls. A few times a day, a slightly careworn young woman from an outside cleaning company in jeans and a tabard comes and runs the dishwasher, keeping the kitchen area tidy, but there are also posters about putting things away and cleaning up after yourself.

The room is broken up by steel columns, painted in a warmed-up industrial grey, that once supported machinery but which are now used as purchase for strands of blue and grey paper stars and subtle Pride bunting. Intrigued by the building's features, I look up its history. Here, Victorian journeymen often worked in stuffy air without a break from breakfast until early evening; a fifteen-hour working day was routine.

No phones ring in the office as Skype calls and headsets are a recently introduced norm, but every day in the late morning an instrumental version of 'Food Glorious Food', that I initially mistook for somebody's mobile phone, rings out signalling the arrival of an outside sandwich vendor. Hearing this refrain in a factory conversion is an amusing commentary on changing work rhythms – like their Victorian counterparts, Simpsons' employees often work long hours, but they can do so while enjoying a tasty baguette at their ergonomic desks.

Meeting the team

It's a Tuesday morning and I sit down in one of Simpsons' comfy booths with Brett, the most senior member of the team. Brett, who came to Simpsons after some local authority work as well as a stint in a harder-edged consultancy, is known in the industry for her analytical ability and social skills. Dressed in an educator-meets-designer style, she appears relaxed and collegial but with a super-smart intensity, like she would quickly spot any nonsense on a project.

Brett has brought along a handy organisational chart and talks me through the team's make-up. The three most senior planners, Brett, Amanda and Lauren, each have over ten years of experience; they were all trained by Nate

Cartright, an "amazing brain" who, after a stint in a local authority, now heads up the entire Dunthorpe office. During her career, Brett has directed her skills towards finding the "killer piece of evidence" on several major planning applications and is currently employing her relationship-building skills to help deliver a massive infrastructure project; she is also involved in several collaborations that contribute to Simpsons' research profile. Amanda, who is a little younger than Brett, is known for her phenomenal work output and all-rounder planning capabilities, which were honed during a tough recession. Lauren, who came to Simpsons from a local authority, is an "engineering-friendly" development-management or DM planner with a lot of highly technical coalface experience; she's in high demand, especially on multi-disciplinary projects.

At a more junior level is Xander, an artistically talented young planner who originally studied architecture, coming in through the graduate programme after his planning master's. He has been with the firm for three years and is thriving; as part of a recent promotion, he's gradually taking on more responsibility. There are also some very new recruits – Jack, a mid-career planner who was recruited from a smaller consultancy and has some previous local authority experience, and Leah, who has come in through the graduate programme. Recruitment can be very competitive due to a sector-wide planner shortage and tends to rely on personal networks to bring good people on board. During the fieldwork there was some change in the make-up of the team – with two planners moving onto teams in other cities (this is one of the perks of Simpsons' fluid organisational structure). This gap was quickly filled by Jack and Kate, a senior planner with expertise in community engagement who had been in another of the firm's offices for a while.

At any given time, Brett explains, the team is engaged in a range of big and small projects, from a huge national infrastructure project that takes up large chunks of various team members' time to medium and small projects that spring from long-standing relationships with local authorities. These include green belt reviews and land viability assessments, as well as supporting aspects of master planning for brownfield sites. The team is also involved in planning applications and consent work for large public-housing concerns, infrastructure-related bodies and developers with a local-authority-friendly profile.

The team, in keeping with Simpsons' broader structure, does not have strict hierarchy or line management. Brett tries to focus on letting people follow their preferences, opening the door to projects but leaving them to follow their interests and inclinations. Yet this also involves shaping the team so it can flourish, trying to keep a balance between policy and development-management expertise. Simpsons' planners are individually responsible for ensuring that their time is filled with billable work. They tend to be committed to part-time roles on projects, aiming to base-load with a regular project that gives some stability and allows in-depth engagement. They fill their remaining time up with other projects. "Intellectual kicks", explains Brett, come from smaller projects, but, as we discuss in Section 3.6, these can also be more stressful, involving a complex but often highly rewarding juggling act.

A fieldwork journey

During the fieldwork, much of my interaction was with senior planners Brett and Amanda, but I also spent time observing the rest of the team during the regular business day as well as at professional development events and team meetings. We indulged in some playful, participant-led photography, whereby the team took pictures of their tea and coffee rituals as a 'can opener' to discussion about their working life (Schoneboom and Slade, 2020). This interaction was rounded out with individual interviews as well as a focus group held with more-senior members of the team towards the end of the project. I travelled to two different locations to interview Simpsons' clients – Carol Blyth in the post-industrial town of Tranton and Dirk Morritt in the city of Northby. I visited several of the firm's offices, attending a Simpsons business-development event on walkability; I observed a planning committee where elected members deliberated the Merton Wharfside application – a large housing development that Simpsons was involved in; and I spent a pleasant couple of hours with Tamsin May, an independent planning consultant who is one of Brett's long-time collaborators. I also interviewed, via Skype, Simpsons' equality, diversity and inclusion (EDI) director, Nadia Russell, about work-life balance in the firm, and chatted with Toby Graham, an engineer-turned-architect whose innovative health-related work intersects with that of the planners.

The fieldwork highlighted the importance of relationships to the team and allowed me to explore how the planners navigate the need to maintain their professional independence and pursue their passion for progressive planning outcomes while serving clients. We gained immense respect for the planners' ability to work with intensity, to push projects forward and prevent things from falling through the cracks. Exploring the planners' work-life balance, we also reflected on the line between exhilarating, meaningful work and potential burnout. Our subjective interpretation of life as a Simpsons planner is captured in the following sections.

3.2 Relationships

This section documents the importance of collaboration to Simpsons' work. It describes how clients benefit from Simpsons' capacity-building ethos; yet it also reveals how, in an austerity climate, local planning authorities are bringing in Simpsons to plug gaps left by devastating cuts to their core teams. This section also chronicles the vulnerability, in terms of dealing with client micro-aggressions, that reliance on strong relationships and networks can create for the consultants, exploring the ramifications of an emerging new world order involving multi-headed clients and large projects.

A safe pair of hands

Part way into the Simpsons fieldwork, I noticed that my notes were unusually well organised, that I was not doing my customary amount of procrastination over difficult aspects of data organisation and analysis. My field notes were named meaningfully; I had a staged plan for the next phase of inquiry, which I'd figured out with Amanda and Brett's help. I had even taken, albeit intermittently, to ironing my crumply academic outfits. I started to wonder if this is how Simpsons' clients feel, whether working with Brett and Amanda might give them the sort of boost in efficiency and lucidity that I was experiencing. How nice it would be if Simpsons would come in and run my whole life for me.

Lauren, one of the senior planners, feels that clients recognise the security that Simpsons offers: "We're a safe pair of hands to get that piece of work done well." On applications and reports, she adds, "we actually try *and need* to keep to timescales … you move hell and high water to get it in by that date". But it is not just the welcome timeliness. To be engaged with Simpsons, I started to feel, is to be connected to a capable set of people who, for the time you have paid for, are dedicated to bringing out your own abilities, increasing your influence and mobilising their own networks and skills to make things happen.

It is common for businesses to stress the value of relationships with clients, the need to listen, to understand and to tailor advice to their needs. Patsy Healey (1992, p 16), in her shadowing of a senior planner in their workplace, noted the significance of people knowledge – the 'ability to relate to participants at a personal level and to get behind their concerns and appreciate their realities'. Increasingly, relationships are between fellow professionals, heightening the move away from more traditional roles centred on technical competency towards 'network professionals' who draw together abstract and localised knowledge in multi-disciplinary settings (Furbey, 2001; Vigar, 2012). This section explores how relationships were conceived in Simpsons, a company that prides itself on a particular quality of interaction with clients.

Relationships as value

What Simpsons has is relationships, Amanda explains, adding that relationships are an extremely valuable part of the business that are nurtured with care and sacrificed only where absolutely necessary. The Simpsons planners pride themselves on a form of networked co-production rather than "parachuted-in" expertise or adversarial practice: "One of Simpsons' core values", says Kate, "is this ability to collaborate across teams internally or externally with clients and other organisations".

She observes that, by contrast, many of the local authorities she has been exposed to tend to be more siloed, with a lack of communication across departments that should work together. Brett likens Simpsons' contribution to a sort of adhesive that can transcend this compartmentalised approach, empowering local authority planners to raise their heads above the parapet and extend the influence of their work: "You're going to help them take it forward and do other things with it or open it out or link it … we are helping them see how their work is related to another colleague's piece of work. So, you're kind of that glue in between."

Forging relationships and activating networks is integral to Simpsons' inner workings and is a key part of the socialisation process for new recruits. In this vein, Brett observes potential recruits to see if they offer tea to their fellow candidates or just help themselves. Offering tea to colleagues is a "house rule" that translates directly to good internal networking as well as effective listening and sharing when out on secondment. As a multi-disciplinary firm, Simpsons is known for forging innovative links across specialties, often with an academic spin, which can in turn help clients make new connections or develop new understanding. For example, Toby Graham, an in-house Simpsonian visionary, whose work overlaps with the planning team, have brought together water engineering and architecture to create new ways of looking at social value in infrastructure projects. Graham's work is part of Simpsons' research arm that boasts partnerships with a significant number of universities worldwide. Linked into this network of resources and expertise, whether as a client or an employee, you feel more switched on, more like ironing your clothes.

The complete package

Brett emphasises the two-way nature of how relationships work for Simpsons, the buzz that she gets when her abilities align with those of her clients or co-consultants, and how this can create a "really complete package". She is quick to acknowledge the strength she draws from engaging with certain "frighteningly bright" clients, co-consultants and academics in her own network who challenge her intellectually as well as providing opportunities for critical reflection. During one of our meetings, she gets talking about Tamsin, the independent consultant whom she and Amanda have worked with for over a decade, building sustained relationships with some clients. Tamsin has always had gravitas, explains Brett; she is respected and gets respect for her challenging senior roles in local authorities. Brett and Amanda have had repeated successes by bidding together with Tamsin for local authority work: "She's our secret weapon", Brett smiles. This form of work hints at wider trends in expert labour, particularly in terms of collaborative working beyond and across the usual boundaries of profession and firm (Evetts, 2011).

I take the train out to Holton, where Tamsin is based, to talk to her about this special collaboration. I like her from the outset – she has a pleasant, wise, approachable and open manner. I tell her about the effect that Brett and Amanda's spirit of getting down to work has had on my own level of organisation. She concurs: "Their analytical skills are phenomenal, their work output's amazing." Tamsin confirms that she brings to Brett and Amanda's party her own deep, continuous embeddedness in local authority settings, a profound understanding of "what levers to pull, who to get to know" as well as empathy, drawn from her own career experience with local authority actors: "It really is combining everybody's strengths", she agrees.

Simpsons as an ally

Several years ago Brett, Amanda and Tamsin did some policy support work for Carol Blyth, planning-policy group leader at Tranton Council, which required a significant amount of technical planning work but also involved helping the planning officers navigate tension with senior management over the local plan. The connection forged during this original assignment has grown into a trusting relationship and subsequent collaborations. I travelled to Tranton to meet with Carol and talk about her experiences as a Simpsons client. Brett was keen for me to meet her, explaining that Carol has a diffident exterior but has great integrity in the council because she has stayed there through thick and thin.

Tranton has the mix of grimness and grandeur that you'd expect of a post-industrial Northern town. Next to the railway station, the brutalist, multi-storey car park and market is being demolished and large billboards advertise a new development that will provide 'A new Heart and Soul for Tranton', which has presumably had both ripped out during decades of austerity and recession. Passing through the arcade, where you can get pie, peas and gravy for £3, you are swept upwards toward the newish European-style fountains (see Figure 3.2) and a free museum that features a video re-enactment of Tranton's history: "Skilled men have come from far and wide", a hopeful nineteenth-century textile worker announces, shortly followed by a proud, striking ex-miner from the 1980s who looks straight at the camera: "Our fight with Thatcher weren't about greed for higher pay." A short walk downhill from the museum, the council offices are in a pleasant, modern building. Carol comes down and greets me in the well-lit

Figure 3.2: Tranton's fountains

lobby and takes me up to one of the meeting rooms upstairs where we chat about the origins of her ten-year relationship with Simpsons.

In an austerity climate where local authorities have been cut to the bone, Carol sees Brett and Amanda as firm allies, constants in an otherwise volatile planning system. In engaging them for the local plan preparation work, Carol knew that Simpsons was in good standing with local authorities and didn't do the kind of work with developers that would present a conflict of interest. Simpsons' technical skills and their wider experience of the examination process were invaluable in reviewing the evidence base her team needed in order to ready themselves for examination: "We were asked to look at quite a lot of green belt release … and we'd not done a lot of green belt review at that time, which from a planning officer point of view was very concerning", she explains. Carol's officers also faced a challenge from senior management, who wanted them to proceed without some of this evidence. At a time of low morale, she feels, Brett and Amanda were really supportive to her team and were well liked. "Had they been seen by the team as a kind of a threat", she explains, "then that would've been more difficult". Carol feels that they listened to her officers and talked to senior management in a way that supported the officers' interests, giving their concerns external validation.

Spending public money to bring in a third-party consultant is not a decision Carol takes lightly. In the case of the local plan preparation, she felt that a "fresh pair of eyes" was needed to see if they were on the right track. She notes that, given the challenge from management over whether particular aspects of the evidence base were needed, Simpsons played an important advocacy role: "They were very helpful in supporting myself and the team in explaining the planning system to non-planning managers that we'd got at that time." She sees value in the extra scrutiny that Simpsons can provide through its arm-length evaluation of the planners' decisions, but she weighs this carefully against the available budget and the desire to nurture her own team. "We certainly think we need to try and do more in-house to develop our own expertise and professional development and retain that knowledge internally", she notes, adding that this is ultimately better for her team: "It's better for team morale as well if we can increase people's knowledge and experience and give them a chunky piece of work that they've actually got time to learn and research how to do."

Capacity-building as a business model

Carol's aspiration to do more in-house, to *need* Simpsons less, is entirely consistent with the Simpsons planning team's business model, which is based on capacity-building. As Kate, one of the senior planners explains, local authorities see value in client-side learning: "We don't just take a piece of work away and work in isolation and then chuck it back at them, we bring them on the journey with us." Brett adds, "It was something we made a conscious decision on. If you're keeping everything back and they have to keep asking you every time … that's not really a good service, because you're not empowering them." The team therefore actively pursues a collaborative approach that simultaneously builds the client's knowledge. Simpsons' approach to co-produced knowledge, and enabling learning is in line with their wider philosophy, but it also brings wider benefits. Additionally, it represents an approach that moves away from traditional notions of technical expertise towards one that mixes this with a broader conception of consultancy as a collaborative process (Kirk and Vasconcelos, 2003; Fincham et al, 2008).

This model, based on sharing knowledge, leads to repeat business when the client faces a new type of challenge. As Amanda explains, "They'll come back to you next time because they've felt safe when doing that piece of work." Carol's relationship with Amanda, Brett and Tamsin has become a close professional relationship and her trust in their abilities and what they give back to her team has led to a sustained working relationship whereby Simpsons carried out Tranton's subsequent green belt review and sustainability appraisal work.

A commitment to capacity-building in the public sector helps Brett, Amanda and Tamsin to reconcile their private-sector affiliation with a strong public-sector ethos. "I was always motivated to work for local government", explains Brett, adding that she enjoys the ability to influence and work with local authorities while maintaining her ability to offer an independent view. Amanda, whose partner is a local authority planner, takes a similar view, noting that they tend to promote sites that are already allocated: "We don't really do council-bashing, we don't do that." Simpsons' capacity-building, non-confrontational approach gives her peace of mind: "I need to be able to sleep at night. ... I don't want to sell my soul, it's not really worth it."

Similarly, as an independent consultant, their collaborator Tamsin has dedicated her career to supporting the public sector: "I have always had a very, very strong public-sector ethos. And that was absolutely what I wanted to do", she says with conviction. She adds that her consultant identity has given her much-needed flexibility to manage her work-life balance while dedicating herself to supporting local authorities. Tamsin's decision to work as a solo practitioner while maintaining her public-service ethos reflects wider trends in the search for work-life balance among female professionals (Annink, 2012).

In an austerity climate where capacity in the public sector is being aggressively eroded and where plan-making is becoming increasingly technical, Amanda, Brett and Tamsin are highly unlikely to be short of work. The loss of technical expertise has been one trend: for example, UK local authorities lost 35 per cent of their conservation specialists between 2006 and 2018 (Historic England, 2018), but Tamsin also explains that over the last ten to fifteen years there has been a wider drain of experience in local government with the demise of good generalist planners. As the work becomes more instrumental and specialised, she feels, strategic and tactical thinking are major casualties.[1] In a stripped-down context, where public-sector teams are continually gutted and reshuffled, Simpsons' consultants, somewhat ironically, can provide a sense of stability and belonging, combining both technical expertise and strategic nous in a desirable package.

I talked about this with another Simpsons client, Dirk Moritt of Northby Council. His council has just brought in a new manager to cut back the planning team, and Dirk notes sadly that very few local authorities can afford to keep expertise in-house. The cuts at Northby will dismantle a team that has won many awards: "We've had a lot of in-house capability in the last twenty years", he observes, "I think we have been unusual. That's just finally been stripped out." Simpsons, he adds, has been doing an increasing amount of environmental modelling work for Northby, and there has been some joking among his colleagues that Simpsons is taking over the council. In a context of cuts and shrinking in-house capacity, where morale is at rock bottom, the Simpsons planners are recognised as harbingers of the coming hatchet, yet they are simultaneously valued for their technical skill and ability to integrate with what is left of a given team.

Vulnerability

Clients know how important relationships are to Simpsons, and this can place Simpsons in a vulnerable position, creating pressure when projects expand beyond their original scope or when its independent view is not what the client wants. Simpsons can be at the mercy of clients' capricious timelines, and disagreements among multi-headed clients can put budgets and individuals' personal time under pressure. Unpredictable time crunches happen most often with private-sector clients who have less-formalised procedures than local government. However, the planning team can also be subject to last-minute demands from council clients that can strain their resources and patience.

One morning, I come across Amanda, tucked away at one of the hotdesks in the back of the office, looking harried and like she has no interest in keeping up a Simpsonian veneer of wonderfulness. Her voice has a bit of a croak, and she looks like she's had it up to here. I ask how she is and she makes a sort of groan and says, "Oh, just people being unreasonable and expecting things done to unreasonable deadlines." She explains that Simpsons is doing some work for Polborough Council, helping them with the first stage of a large infrastructure bid, involving some work around flood risk and other factors that will allow them to secure various brownfield sites. Although there is a Simpsons secondee on site, for some reason the client waited until they were about a week away from their deadline to let Amanda know that a huge amount remains to be done. The main part of the report narrative has not come together and much more work is needed.

Amanda tells me that things came to a head last week when the client dumped a large volume of documents on her; many of the documents are complex and fifty or sixty pages long. The client expects Simpsons to extract the necessary data from them and produce a cohesive report that draws everything together. They want the work immediately, and although Amanda tried to push back on this last-minute request as she has other work scheduled, they insist the work needs to be done by the deadline, which is basically today. As we talk, Amanda reveals that part of the reason she is upset is because she has had to lean on the understanding of a client in Stopton by asking them to wait for work that she was supposed to be doing this morning so that she can meet the Polborough client's tight deadline. She has also had to sacrifice her day off, which she usually spends with her son, and has had to arrange last-minute nursery cover for him: "People assume that consultants have capacity", she says with a note of exasperation. The subtext is that since the work is being done at an hourly rate, by squeezing Amanda in this way, the client will get a report, which should have taken a month, done at low cost.

Simpsons is also involved in working on increasingly complex projects, something that is seen as an emerging trend in this line of consultancy. A decreasing amount of work is with one client on a simple scheme, with Simpsons' consultants now often managing other consultants on multi-year, multi-player infrastructure projects. In particular, multi-headed clients with poor governance can cause serial problems for the Simpsons planners, leading to heavy investment of non-billable time and resources in brokering relationships. Amanda is involved in another piece of work for Somfortby Council, where a range of clients – a housebuilder, a farmer and two local authorities (Somfortby and an adjacent landowning authority) – have collectively commissioned Simpsons to carry out a viability assessment, looking at land that is suitable for residential development. Simpsons is at risk because the various parties keep arguing with each other and will not sign off on the work: "No one can agree", says Amanda, "they just argue between themselves". She adds that while she needs to finish the commission and move on, the clients are not bothered about how long it takes: "They're fine just going to meetings, saying they don't like it, you know?"

The situation is complicated by the fact that the local authority client that owns some of the land is angry at Simpsons for not including all their land in their recommendations. The client wants Amanda to ditch the master-planning considerations that were part of the brief, which she has used as a professional basis for her decisions on which land to include, and make a representation on the land as might be done for a single private client. To make things worse, the farmer has gotten wind of this line of reasoning and is now demanding that all of his land also be included in the recommendations.

Amanda is worried because not only is Simpsons at risk of the project going way out of scope but also the client may just refuse to pay for the work that has been done. The consortium members are incapable of agreeing, and they are demanding a time-consuming level of nitty-gritty detail rather than a broad-brush cost assessment. If the project breaks down completely and the client refuses to pay or accept the work, Simpsons would have to accept the loss of a relationship. Simpsons could walk away and keep the moral high ground around the master-planning issue – the planning team have taken such financial hits before – but harder to deal with is the fact that walking away risks damaging valuable (and potentially work-generating) future relationships. They have previously done a lot of work with one of the local authorities involved and would not want to lose their relationships with this particular client.

With good relationships at stake, raising the topic of money is also a continual challenge for Simpsons' staff – Amanda is steeling herself to send an email communicating to the client that more money will be needed if they are unable to wrap things up. The desire to help clients is often in tension with the financial necessities of being in business, and the bond Simpsons' staff develop with clients may increase their reticence to discuss fees. More generally, the issue of fee-setting is particularly difficult for such professional work, with reluctance to be drawn into price competition, as well as the difficulty of standardising services and appraising value, noted in the literature (Auty, 1996).

Later on in the fieldwork, I had the opportunity to talk about Simpsons' need for relationships with Nadia Russell, the organisation's EDI lead, who is based in London. She agrees that relationships can be highly nourishing for Simpsons' staff and that they are a key source of value creation for the firm. But she also sees the vulnerability of Simpsons, particularly around their reluctance to jeopardise the potential for repeat business with a client. Simpsons' staff, she feels, must constantly navigate a sense of ambiguity around client relationships, asking, "What is the state of the relationship today?" She frames this as a continual process of making decisions in the face of "micro-aggressions" from clients. I am impressed that she has chosen such a strong word. Later, I talk to Brett about Nadia's framing and she particularly likes the phrase "micro-aggressions" – "I've dealt with a few of those already today", she says.

The new order

Brett is giving a talk at the office Knowledge Café, a well-attended lunchtime affair with sandwiches and snappy talks, mostly by architects. Brett's talk is titled 'The Future's Bright, the Future's with our Competitors'. She starts with an image of how she used to work with clients back in 2009; it depicts a simple flow from Simpsons to the client, sometimes with the addition of a flow to and from a sub-consultant. Her next slide shows how this has changed in 2019 – it depicts a bunch of logos from national multi-disciplinary consultancies. She observes that she now spends her days working directly with people from these organisations in a complex web.

Simpsons has always done a lot of infrastructure planning work using its multi-disciplinary capacity. Recently, Brett and her team find themselves operating in a new order, working with co-competitors on large multi-player infrastructure projects, part of a wider trend towards public- and private-sector fragmentation and the increasing organisation of expert labour into projects (Lundin and Söderholm, 1998). As Fincham et al (2008, p 188) note: 'Distinctive labour forms within professional services may be critical for knowledge-intensive work', and perhaps fertile ground for new forms of urban professionalism (Metzger and Zakhour, 2019). This way of working, alongside firms that have very different norms and cultures, demands highly developed social skills. Although they are nominally competitors, they need each other and must work with each other on these massive schemes. Having taken on a major role on one of these projects, Brett's day currently involves conversations with members of a dispersed, often non-Simpsons team, facilitating communication and navigating different viewpoints and needs of the people who are doing the work.

For Brett, this presents a next-level challenge – how to create a trusting relationship and get things delivered where she can't use traditional face-to-face influencing skills. At the Knowledge Café, she makes the case that Simpsons is ideally suited to meeting this challenge. She notes the importance, in this situation, of defining clear roles so that these competitors can get the best from one another, so they can also face client challenges by supporting one another and giving out the same message. While some competitors might see this kind of cross-organisational communication as a risk, she notes positively, it is the sort of thing that plays directly into the skill set of the Simpsons planners.

Later, when she and some colleagues are discussing the implications of the new order, Brett elaborates on the opportunity that this represents: "We are becoming more and more recognised for our ability to collaborate with others. And I think that's why you're seeing us get more involved with competitor co-consultants than maybe others." Within the mega-project that she is involved with, she is helping co-competitors to "leave everything outside", and she draws on her social skills to bring the dispersed team together through lots of emails and phone conversations: "I tend to be the person people phone when they're not sure what to do next, and that's sometimes around them just offloading and feeling comfortable." She is convinced that it's a niche that Simpsons is well suited to, but she is also conscious that the time she spends on the subtle art of relationships is not always fully acknowledged – when it's done well, nobody notices, she laughs.

Brett has always enjoyed working at the meeting point of different interests, different dimensions of a problem, and sees facilitation of multi-player projects as a natural extension of this: "All my career has been about convergence, the sweet spot where everything meets", she reflects. Although she is rising to the challenge of the new order and sees it as a business opportunity, she is still evaluating the kind of integrity, in terms of upholding Simpsons' values, that is possible when working with co-competitors at this scale. She also finds the work emotionally draining and has had to go on a conscious journey to embrace this role. Looking to the future, she feels that this kind of complex, multi-player project is likely to become more common and that simple consultant-client projects will become more of a luxury. It's a daunting future but also a possible opportunity. Indeed, as Linovski (2019) notes, the increasing complexity of projects fuelled by greater regulatory oversight, in Levi-Faur's (2009) terms, 'regulatory capitalism', might be seen as an opportunity for technical and co-productive expertise, the sort that Simpsons seeks to draw together. "Problems are getting harder", Brett says, "there's less money around, less funding, less public-sector money, more parties with interest, more laws to navigate and you need to have good, creative, holistic, engaged solutions. That's quite a challenge, isn't it?"

3.3 Independence

This section explores the consultant mandate to provide clients with independent advice rather than make decisions for them or bend to their will: it charts the planners' efforts to nudge clients towards 'good' planning regardless of a client's vested interests. We also explore here the learning that takes place at Simpsons and how this is disseminated within the team and widely across the organisation, the planning profession and beyond. Additionally, we document how larger projects with multi-headed clients are becoming more common, creating greater complexity in the management of relationships and, potentially, reduced influence in moving clients towards sustainable planning outcomes.

Only advise

While navigating client relationships, 'Only advise' is a mantra that private-sector consultants need to internalise and embody.[2] Although many consultancies sell their services as providing 'solutions',[3] in many cases what is being offered is expert advice rather than the actual making of final decisions. As Amanda explains, "We generally would advise a client but we wouldn't be able to make a decision for them. We would say, 'We recommend you do this', but we can't make them." Often, the client takes Simpsons' advice. Amanda offers, as an example, a piece of work the planning team did for West Harbyshire, who wanted to work out if they could allocate part of a big area of land as an employment site in their local plan. It was a very technical piece of work that looked at floods, highways and ecology. Simpsons looked at all the constraints and recommended a potential site boundary, providing the client with a master plan illustrating their recommendation.

For Amanda, this is "a really nice story where the council trusted our judgement". The land is now allocated in the local plan and Simpsons have won some subsequent work on the planning application for it. She contrasts this with the multi-headed client in Somfortby (see Section 3.2), where the decision-making process does not flow smoothly from Simpsons' recommendations. Brett adds that, although the Somfortby work is very technical, how it is actually used will hinge on governance and politics that are out of Simpsons' remit. In private-sector consultancy, she notes, you "keep your political opinions to yourself".

As a new team member, the graduate planner, Leah, has quickly internalised this way of doing business. She is currently working on a green belt review for Friargate County Council using a methodology that has been designed by Simpsons colleagues, evaluating boundary durability for various parcels of land. Simpsons' input is limited: "We have no say in what they should do", explains Leah, "we basically just assess it and they make all those judgements and decisions themselves". While Leah's socialisation as a Simpsonian is her first professional role, planners who join the team from the public sector sometimes have difficulty in adjusting to this different advisory capacity. As Amanda notes,

> 'If you've come from a client role and you're suddenly in a consultancy role, actually that's quite different. If you've been able to say, "Do it this way, I'm the boss", you come here and actually you can't say that, you can only advise … you can only ever advise or recommend. Actually, that's quite a big change.'

While limited to an advisory role, the Simpsons planners are also keenly aware of their ability to influence the client, albeit subtly. As Brett muses during the focus group we convened to talk about different types of client relationship, Simpsons planners are perhaps particularly known in the industry for this type of nudging towards sustainable planning outcomes: "I think it's something that we do that others may not."

Quite often, Lauren adds, a client will want to do things a particular way when this is not the way that the Simpsons planners would do it if they were making the decisions themselves. Here, a common strategy is to open the conversation by presenting the client with options: "It's about explaining the pros and cons of their approach to them. Ultimately, it's their decision as to the way that they want to do something, but I think it's about communicating quite often how you might take that approach and do something slightly different." This is a carefully navigated process in which the client must not feel put upon. She notes that one of the benefits of being in a multi-disciplinary firm is that planners can draw in technical knowledge from various disciplines to back up the options they are suggesting, slowly bringing more people into the conversation: "I think part of the value is that we can back our options up with actual technical expertise easily because everyone is under one roof."

The Simpsons intelligentsia

While this art of persuasion is handled subtly, it is pursued with a conviction that is rooted in the planners' professional values. Before considering the individual planners' values in detail (see Section 3.5), it is important first to note the high-profile nature of Simpsons' commitment to progressive planning and how this forms a key part of the client experience beyond the details of an individual commission. Public-interest-focused values are embodied in Simpsons' very visible work on issues such as green energy, which are championed by an organisational intelligentsia and disseminated via in-house publications and events. Advocacy around these issues forms a backdrop to the Simpsons-client relationship, acting as a vehicle for urging existing and potential public- and private-sector clients towards equitable planning outcomes. This may be more common than the stereotype of the private consultant as a value-free 'gun for hire' might indicate. The holding of values similar to those of public-sector clients was noted by Loh and Norton (2013) as a key finding of their survey of private planning consultants in the US, with commonalities often located around the importance of affordable housing and protection of open space.[4] Nonetheless, Simpsons package their approach in a distinctive fashion.

Attending a walkability event one evening at Simpsons' Kentpool offices, I sit down with forty or so public-, private- and third-sector attendees to hear a range of presentations from local authority clients and Simpsons visionaries. The presentations are given in an open space in the centre of the office; we sit at white tables adorned with fizzy water, wine, crackers and showy wedges of cheese (see Figure 3.3). Around my table are an academic, a representative of a local community trust and a planning officer from a nearby council. There are also a couple of local authority planners who have come in from a more far-flung local authority on the train – Simpsons is currently helping them with master planning for a major development; they have a day-out aura, and are keen to enjoy the hospitality and learn more from the speakers.

Roberta Weinsach, the first presenter, who is here from London and has co-authored the Simpsons publication on walkability, blows me away. She speaks energetically, commanding the room easily. She starts out by describing herself as a "passionate pedestrian" and tells us she is here to get us enthusiastic about walking. I am intrigued when she describes herself

Figure 3.3: A public sector planner speaks at the walkability event at Simpsons

not only as a transport planner but also as an anthropologist. She likes the alliteration of 'passionate pedestrian' but prefers the more mundane word 'walker'. What follows is a crisp, digestible tour of theory and practice around walkability, loaded with useful statistics and qualitative insight, as well as a nuanced condemnation of Uber and a warning against the insidious distraction offered by driverless and electric vehicles. As the presentation progresses, she presses the business case for walkability, offering numbers related to the "pedestrian pound" in urban shopping/eating districts. "People who arrive on foot spend more", she says with conviction.

By the time Weinsach is done talking, I am having one of the starry-eyed Simpsons moments that I experienced from time to time during the fieldwork. Her presence makes me reflect on other Simpsonians from this echelon that I have met during the fieldwork – Brett is one, as is the EDI director, Nadia. Their issue-driven intellectualism exists alongside Simpsons' business side in a carefully managed symbiotic relationship. They shine and influence at educational events like this, which simultaneously (as is explored in Section 3.5) direct their powers towards serving both the public good and business development.

Independence as integrity

Supported by the output of the firm's intelligentsia, Simpsons' integrity is derived not only from the planners' technical skill but also from their reputation for sticking to their independent advice while fostering enlightened and sustainable planning practice. In turn, this source of integrity is valued by local authority clients who are seeking to minimise risk or challenge at inspection. As Carol Blyth from Tranton notes about the sustainability appraisal work that Simpsons carried out for her, there are particular types of work that warrant public expenditure on a private consultant, "otherwise we'd be assessing our own policies and proposals". She adds that there can be a public perception that in-house appraisals lack sufficient scrutiny: "They'd think it'd been done with less rigour than if an external party had done it." Although Simpsons does work for some developers, this can be interpreted, according to another local authority client we spoke to, as valuable market savvy that adds credence to their advice, rather than as a conflict of interest.

Serving the client is, undeniably, a central aspect of Simpsons' core values. In the firm's philosophy, which forms the foundation of the organisation's commitment to humanist, equitable conduct, this matter is dealt with unambiguously. "We must earn our clients' trust", the firm's vision statement urges, "by prioritising their interest when we carry out work for them". Carol Blyth is keenly aware that engaging Simpsons to carry out an appraisal for the council can be interpreted as Tranton buying someone in to say what the council wants, and she notes that this criticism has been levelled at the council during the examination process. Giving strategic advice to the client is indeed central to the level of service that Simpsons' planners provide. For example, Brett describes a scenario in which, during some brownfield development work for Sleekmoor Homes, Simpsons advised a phased strategy of eight applications that allowed them to meet an affordable-housing requirement across thirteen sites without antagonising the local authority. Similarly, Brett's work for an electric car production facility expansion in northern England hinged on Simpsons' finding the key piece of evidence that enabled the application to be part of a more comprehensive scheme that could deliver sufficient infrastructure.

While committing to serve the client, the Simpsons planners pride themselves on sticking to their independent advice and not changing this based on what the client wants them to say. In doing this, Simpsons draw together both more 'traditional' notions of professionalism, based on established expertise and independence, and newer, more agile, client-focused work, particularly through sensitive shaping of expertise as advice.[5] This process is carefully managed. For example, some things are said in person but left out of the written version of the advice to give the client the wiggle room they need. The right to an independent view is also built into the organisational structure, including the right not to work on a particular project: "If you're not 100 per cent on board with something, you don't have to work on it", Brett explains. She notes that when Simpsons accepted work on a particular controversial project, the board ensured that clauses were written into the contract to allow employees not to participate in that work if they didn't agree with it.

Technical expertise and neutrality

When it comes to working on difficult projects, a certain refuge, in terms of professional integrity, lies in the very technical and 'objective' nature of much of the work that the planners do. As Brett notes, "We're motivated by doing something technically well." She explains that even when compiling or reviewing evidence on a thorny infrastructure project, Simpsons' job is to make sure that this assessment includes the negative impact as well as any positive outcomes that might result from the proposed scheme.[6]

She also sees one of Simpsons' key roles as providing a "linking point" that opens up the viewpoint of the client to broader perspectives on the issue. For example, on a recent controversial scheme, the Simpsons planners acted to "bring in the bigger picture to those people to say, 'These are the wider considerations you need to be aware of'". Producing an environmental statement or other "neutral" piece of evidence, for Brett, can justify Simpsons' involvement in difficult schemes: "For us, that's the right territory because it fits our values. We are a company that is independent … if there's going to be a bad impact, we will say that."

The need to compromise

As with all consultancy, clients can try to pressure Simpsons into doing their bidding. Furthermore, as already mentioned, difficult clients – especially those with weak governance – take projects out of scope; this generates internal pressure to compromise, which is potentially stressful for individual Simpsonians, who must juggle their own internal reputation, in terms of not making losses for the company, against their professional integrity as planners.

The fractious, multi-headed Somfortby project, where the local authority wants Simpsons to forget the master-planning aspect of their brief and recommend the East Farby land, ends up putting considerable pressure on Amanda. She knows that any compromise will threaten her professional integrity, but at the same time she needs to balance this against Simpsons' business interest, not only in keeping the relationship with the client but also in terms of her need to maintain her reputation within Simpsons as someone who can effectively manage projects. After some negotiation about the report, Simpsons agrees to show the previously omitted East Farby land on the diagram, but shaded differently from the land that has been recommended for allocation. The differently shaded part is distinguished as potentially developable but requiring further work.

Amanda is clearly troubled and professionally shaken by the turn that events have taken. Simpsons' recommendations were based on technical planning considerations such as whether a proposed area is linked to the original settlement. Amanda's professional position has been compromised by agreeing to include areas that are not consistent with this in the recommendations (albeit with qualifying phrases and different shading). She feels that Simpsons is being somewhat bullied into this by East Farby's misunderstanding of how independent advice works.

As this challenging project goes on, without new fees being added it could make a loss. At Simpsons, difficult projects become part of an internal list that is seen by colleagues and higher-ups, Amanda thus needs to use her personal time to prevent the project making a loss (and thereby potentially damaging Amanda's reputation at the firm). Loss-making projects become very visible through a sort of 'wall of shame' effect that deters Simpsonians from allowing their projects to run over time or budget. In terms of Simpsons' wider portfolio of projects, it is not a large project or a threat to the income stream, but Amanda is concerned that she would look like someone who dropped the ball.

Reflecting later on the project, she remains professionally unhappy with the report, but she is resigned to the compromise under the circumstances. Such a situation is not unusual in the field of planning, particularly in terms of advising public-sector clients, with their necessarily political character and wide-ranging and contested objectives.[7] However, as explored in Section 3.5, in this value-driven business model, Simpsonians find such compromises particularly hard. Amanda accepts the outcome but is not able to dismiss it: "I couldn't marry up what Somfortby needed, what the developers needed, what East Farby needed", she laments, "I couldn't marry it all up to make it work for everyone."

Influence and large, multi-agency projects

The Simpsonian evangelism around sustainability is authentic; while technical 'neutrality' helps the planners to highlight areas of concern to clients. However, in a complex planning arena where Simpsons is part of a jigsaw of organisations, this 'neutral' evidence can nevertheless become part of a narrative constructed by powerful interests, potentially acting against the public interest. As projects move through various iterations in which the planners' involvement and level of influence may wax and wane, choosing projects and clients that align with one's professional values can be challenging. This raises questions about navigating competing obligations to uphold standards of professional and technical knowledge,[8] to be part of a wider set of actors involved in planning and to promote values that are personally held. Research in this area has tended to concentrate on public-sector planners (Campbell and Marshall, 1998), though Loh and Arroyo (2017) highlight the self-awareness that planning consultants must employ in order to act ethically.

A month or so before the walkability event, I attended a gruelling six-hour planning committee related to the Merton Wharfside planning application. Merton Wharfside is a controversial urban development that the Simpsons planning team had originally been involved in. This site has great eco-potential, and the land is mostly in public hands, but it has been through a number of iterations and the public-sector client, who wanted a more commercial approach, replaced the Simpsons planners with a more aggressive consulting firm, Blake Dyson. Other Simpsons teams remained heavily engaged in providing evidence related to aspects such as traffic modelling, and were present at the planning committee giving evidence.

It's about 8 pm at the Merton Planning Committee and the packed room is getting stuffier. The public in the room are largely over forty; there are occasional, daring violet streaks in the hair of the women, and a library-reading-room look to the men, fulfilling the characterisation that one speaker gives of Merton as a "city of intelligent, thoughtful people". A ruddy-faced businessman from central casting addresses the room – he is Roger Barclay, the chair of the region's Local Enterprise Partnership: "Any place needs to grow if it wants to prosper in our modern economy", he starts out, dismissing a question about how the city will avoid congestion issues with a nod to the two rows of suited consultants – many from Simpsons – who occupy the front of the room next to him: "Expertise has been thrown in there on the transportation side to make sure we avoid gridlock", he assures the elected members who are about to vote on the application.

In this context, Simpsons' 'neutral' technical assessment appears as part of a 'wall of suits' comprising players from various powerful firms and entities committed to driving through the application in spite of eloquent objections from high-profile local activists and community members, who castigate the application as a missed opportunity for a car-free development in the city centre, right next to a huge railway interchange in a city with high levels already of active travel. At one point, Anthony Noble from the Merton Cycle Campaign urges, "Wouldn't you prefer to walk in a clean, low-carbon Merton Wharfside and know that your decision helped make it happen?" At another key moment, an emeritus professor of transport planning (who, I found out later, was criticising the work of his own former students who now work for Simpsons) challenges the Simpsons evidence, calling their traffic modelling confused and inconsistent. Speaker after speaker from the local community condemns the public engagement as a farcical ceremony.

The power imbalance in the room is palpable. It's something about the immaculate business attire in the front rows. The twenty-eight other speakers are topped off by a professional oration from Damon Cruikshank, the heavy-hitting, non-Simpsons planning consultant who has been brought in to drive the application through. He speaks weightily: "The case for granting planning permission is compelling … this is a genuinely ambitious vision for the site." One of the members, Councillor Staith, confronts Cruikshank and his grave intensifiers: "You are ignoring what the people of the city are telling you", he thunders. Cruikshank's answer is a solemn assertion of power and technical certainty: "The facts are that a huge amount of engagement has taken place."

As already stated, the Simpsons planners were no longer involved at this stage of the game. Nevertheless, the process made me reflect on the milieu in which their work unfolds. As Loh and Arroyo (2017) note, the abilities of planning consultants to 'nudge' clients towards 'planning values' can be compromised in a competitive market, and certainly might be more challenged when they are working on multi-headed projects. Simpsonians, already limited to an advisory mode, can become entwined in projects where their technical expertise legitimises agendas that perhaps seem open to influence but which might move completely out of their control. As multi-player projects become the norm, lines of influence and relationship-building between Simpsons' planners and clients are increasingly disrupted; using one's powers for good becomes ever more challenging.

3.4 Time

This section looks at planners' skills, notably how consultants navigate project beginnings and ends, especially when projects run over or develop 'long tails'. We document how hourly billing gives time a purposive and focused quality; yet we also note how this can clash with less instrumental evaluations of how work might be carried out. Observing the planners' skill in adapting to workflow, and their knack for accommodating work that lands unexpectedly, we reflect on implications for wellbeing as well as work quality.

Beginnings and ends

It's the Monday morning team meeting, where the planners each summarise what they are going to be up to this week. Amanda gives an overview of how a new commission is going and explains that she will also be wrapping up a couple of what she calls "minor projects", one of which has been dragging on for a while. "So you're in the projects-that-never-die phase", jokes Brett. "You need to get rid of that one", she says, slightly more seriously, as the chuckles die down.

Simpsons is good at beginnings and ends, and this creates clarity and purposeful energy during a project. Time at Simpsons has an intentional quality that I was aware of throughout the fieldwork, from my bounded six-week fieldwork chunks to the emails that would fire out from Amanda's desk right after every research-related meeting. Getting an employee badge at Simpsons took one day, whereas at my local authority research site it took over a month. A pleasant result is that, in spite of this time-consciousness, things don't feel rushed; during the period of time allocated to a particular task, you feel you have the Simpsonians' full attention.

My first one-to-one meeting with Brett, which lasted a full two hours, felt surprisingly relaxed. In a consulting world where time is money, I had assumed that she would be more obviously counting the minutes, but instead I had the sense – as was evident during our subsequent meetings – that this time had been purposefully allocated in her diary. Time is very important in the world of Simpsons' planners, yet, despite this, literature on planning frequently privileges the spatial over the temporal, missing a significant element of what it means to 'do planning' (Mbiba, 2003; Laurian and Inch, 2019). In many ways, the management of time was 'part of the organisational actors' ongoing active production and reproduction of their social context' (Nandhakumar and Jones, 2001, p 194).

Simpsons' planners aim to plan their work around a three-month cycle; they complete weekly timesheets in which every hour of a 37.5-hour week must be accounted for. Most of their time is expected to be attached to billable activity, but activities such as business development and training might also take up a portion of their hours in any given week. Within this structure, projects such as Somfortby (see Section 3.2) that develop "evil tails" are troublesome. As Simpsons' EDI lead Nadia notes, the need to ensure that a discrete project does not become a "forever relationship" exists in tension with the hope for a continued relationship and future commissions. Simpsons' consultants therefore need to be skilled at ensuring that projects end when they are supposed to. When closure becomes challenging, Amanda sometimes brings in Carl Forbis, a senior Simpsons business leader who is very skilled at managing such negotiations without harming the relationship, to help finalise the project with an élan that she feels she is still acquiring.

During team meetings, the planners collegially press each other on the issue of wrapping things up, cultivating a normative dislike of things that drag on. At another team meeting, Amanda asks for an update on the South Glenny project. Jack indicates that progress has been held up because of a drought. "It would be nice to get rid of it", she offers, "it's been going on for ages". Jack, understanding the premium placed on closure, reassures her that Lauren, who is overseeing the work, is "keen to draw a line under what they've done". Pushing things forward that are in danger of stalling is a key Simpsons skill, and the team meeting provides a forum where the planners urge each other to nudge officers who have gone to ground or chase contacts who are endangering a deadline.

Time as money

Simpsonians are keenly aware that the client is paying for their time.[9] Leah, the graduate planner, notes that she has to be mindful of the fee when apportioning her time so that the work recorded in her timesheet is consistent with the budget for a particular project. In Amanda's view, timesheets create less faffing about: "Every hour you charge to that timesheet knocks off your project [budget]. It kind of makes you feel, 'God, I need to get on!'" This need to get stuff done and sorted is felt particularly acutely when the Simpsons' planners are doing work for developers, who are very conscious that time is money and need to see a return in a relatively quick timeframe, often demanding a clear cost justification for every additional element that Simpsons proposes to include.

Local authority clients generally appreciate Simpsons' focus on efficiency, but there can be interesting temporal clashes. Amanda notes that the Simpsons planners created a method for one local authority's green belt review based on minimising site visits to those that were deemed necessary to the work. While Simpsons was focused on giving the client a robust method that was quite quick to carry out, feedback from the client indicated that they, in Amanda's terms, "had no issue with it taking them ages" given that they had people based in the district who might enjoy and value the site visits as part of their professional work. Amanda notes that this preference was tied to different work rhythms in the public sector, where "there's not necessarily the same pressure in terms of actually hours on paper or hours on a computer because it's not monitored in the same way".[10]

As noted in Section 3.2, cases like Somfortby in which projects are extended by local authorities who are not concerned by Simpsons' need to cost time out by the hour can be a source of frustration for the Simpsonians. Frustration also emerges during procurement when agreements have to go through four or five layers of sign-off in a local authority before work can go ahead. However, during the fieldwork, the Simpsons planners also acknowledged the value of this alternate local authority temporality, whether in terms of the building in of needed checks and balances, allowing holistic and well-considered approaches to messy planning problems, or in terms of connecting planning officers to place in a professionally enriching way that has value to the community they serve.

Ready to jump

Consultants not only need to keep projects to time but must also be ready to jump when work suddenly lands. The Simpsons planners display impressive flexibility in responding to sudden demands.

At the team meeting, Amanda thanks a couple of team members for helping to get the latest round of housing work – making the case for allocating or continuing to allocate eighteen different sites – done in a very tight timeline of ten working days. The work was sent off on time, she updates the rest of us, and now it's "down tools" to wait for the next step. Later, she fills me in on this feat, explaining that the work on this major initiative had landed quite unexpectedly and the clock started ticking right away: "We basically had two weeks to deliver it." The first day was devoted to evidence gathering, furiously downloading data from the client and chasing information from particular project managers, "so really good for relationship-building", she notes as an aside. Based on the evidence, the Simpsons team, which also involved fellow planners at Seathorpe, produced three-pagers for each of the sites, circulated drafts, incorporated comments and edited them for consistency, working together to hit the deadline.

Simpsonians become skilled at triaging existing work to accommodate these "just-dropped" commissions. As Amanda explains, she is accustomed to sudden switches: "The ability to go, 'Right, I was doing *this* work, but now I'm not, I'm doing this'." Working with developer clients can involve very productive relationships and a sense that everyone is pitching in, but as mentioned earlier, developers are also known for making last-minute demands, which can sometimes become quite aggressive and adversarial. In this vein, Amanda recounts her dealings with Rita, a representative of a developer client on a different project: "[She] used to ring me about stuff that her own team hadn't delivered and then go, 'Right, you need to sort this out. Now'." This kind of sudden demand is one of the types of client micro-aggression that Simpsonians accommodate for the sake of relationship-building. Amanda notes that, although the demand had landed with no advance warning, she would invariably respond, "Of course I can, Rita", as this meant Rita would grant more work to the Simpsons team.

The team maintains a spreadsheet that details work that is under development (often involving time-consuming bidding processes) as well as commissions that are already under way. During the team meeting, we review and update the section titled 'New work', in which there are about forty lines of data – National Rail off-route work; Sanditon infrastructure study; PRP recycling facility; Gospen High School (Sleekmoor Homes); A64 bridge; Brookhaven IDP; Woodshott green belt and so forth. There is quite a mix of projects, from huge multi-player initiatives to discrete facilities, some for private-sector clients, many for local authorities. Individual planners on the team can find themselves juggling multiple projects, and this, coupled with the tendency for work to land suddenly, can lend the work a 'bitty' or fragmented feel, with potential implications for quality, a situation that is, again, often dealt with by staff members doing work in their own time. Simpsons' need for agility can also be a source of pressure on staff, particularly for those who are on less than a full-time contract, something that we take up again in Section 3.6.

Where clients demand work be carried out on ungenerous timescales, Simpsonians are able to perform skilful juggling feats, and the fast pace can be exhilarating, yet as they respond to these demands and move rapidly between one project and another – in a wider cash-squeezed context where clients are sometimes not allowing sufficient time for a project – there is the possibility that expediency trumps thoroughness. The potential for conflict between rapid work within tight deadlines and high quality, time-consuming examination of planning cases has been widely recognised in the literature, yet this almost exclusively focuses on the work of public-sector planners and particularly those involved in development management (Glasson and Booth, 1992; Carmona and Sieh, 2004). This situation might, however, be understood to exist more widely in planning.

3.5 Hunger

This section explores how Simpsons' company culture promotes curiosity, resourcefulness and self-reliance. We observe the sometimes frustrated efforts of senior team members to inculcate these qualities in younger recruits. Simpsonians successfully develop their passions for social and environmental justice through networks of influence in ways that create value for the firm. At the same time, the need to meet the bottom line and serve clients' needs circumscribes this commitment, particularly during economic downturns.

Valuing curiosity

We are gathered round a small table in one of the glass meeting rooms for 'Focus Hour', the planning team's answer to professional development. The whole team is here, including Lauren, who is back from her week of resilience training in Boston. Brett asks Xander to introduce Focus Hour to those of us who are new. With some input from the others, Xander emphasises the idea of professionals coming together and, rather than just listening to an outside authority, instead learning to regard *themselves* as experts. "We came up with the term 'team-based professional development'", he explains, adding that the planners are encouraged to come up with their own specialist topic to speak on, learning directly from each other's experience.

Today, Brett is speaking about infrastructure-led development – she starts by explaining that one of the things about Simpsons is that you are able to "follow a couple of wormholes", pursuing lines of interest that may not relate directly to current projects but that you may later bring into your work. The meat of Brett's talk is Toby Graham's health-centre work. As mentioned earlier, Toby, an engineer-turned-architect, one of Simpsons' 'amazing brains', is engaged in an interdisciplinary, cross-sector framing of healthcare provision that uses existing community assets to improve health outcomes. This kind of thinking, Brett explains, allows a more open-ended and holistic process than usual, one focused on solving social and environmental ills together.

During Brett's talk, Amanda is the first to ask a question, signalling to the others that it is fine to interrupt at any time. Lauren chimes in, linking Toby's ideas to the resilience stuff she learned on her course in Boston last week; Kate identifies some connections to the work she is doing on the Felby Water Park. Brett concurs that clients might find this infrastructure-led approach helpful; Northbolt Water, one of their clients, has been able to think more holistically about their land asset, with potential social and environmental benefits, she adds. The conversation branches out beyond specific client concerns to wider social and methodological issues, from political short-termism to the place of quantitative analysis within this kind of work. One of the other planners meditates on the dominance of benefit-cost ratios in local authority decision-making, and at some point in this open-ended exchange, we find ourselves musing about Tony Blair's decision to go to war in Iraq.

Focus Hour represents an attempt by the team to move beyond traditional forms of knowledge creation. Such efforts at promoting group identity, which are often seen in firms whose main business is the provision of specialised consultancy, leverage individual creativity and expertise as an organisational resource (Robertson et al, 2003). While the discussion is freewheeling, Brett skilfully brings it back to how she is hoping to use this knowledge in her own work. She feels it has possible relevance for major initiatives such as the Sanditon tidal barrier, particularly since the government knows there is a funding gap and that they will need to find a different way of having an economic conversation with community stakeholders. There will need to be new ways of talking with clients about what's in it for them, she explains. Her framing is a reminder that Focus Hour has a strategic as well as a merely intellectual purpose; it celebrates the alignment of personal passions and professional goals.

Hunger among younger recruits

The lively and stimulating hour is almost up. Brett asks if the people who haven't said much want to add anything. This means Jack and Leah, the younger members of the team, who have been listening in attentively but pretty much silently. Neither of them wants to add anything. "We're just tuning in", says Jack agreeably, and Leah nods that she's the same but soon chimes in with a smart-sounding question that Jack then adds to, pitching his ideas into the discussion.

The Simpsons business model requires planners to be hungry for knowledge, curious and resourceful, skills that result in a useful bag of tricks that can be placed at the disposal of clients. One of the aims of Focus Hour is to inculcate in newer recruits the performance and practice of being curious – Amanda notes that, in recent years, some of their younger planners have struggled with presenting themselves as hungry for knowledge, so Focus Hour is a way of nurturing and celebrating a learning culture across the team. While some studies of younger recruits in consultancies stress the need to appear 'client friendly', with a focus on dressing smartly and being seen to be 'professional' (Anderson-Gough et al, 2000), at Simpsons the expectation is for a deep, vocational engagement with one's professional role. Recruits who develop and display this level of internal drive tend to excel in the firm.

Amanda explains that her own 'hunger' was honed during the 2008 recession, when work dried up and she was under pressure to feed herself. "A lot of the [current] team just weren't here for that era and the fear it created in you", she reminisces, "I remember going for my lunch and basically you were just like, 'I might not be here [tomorrow]'." She recalls that the task of letting individual staff go had fallen to a manager who travelled around the firm's UK offices delivering the bad news in person. "We were literally watching, checking his diary to see where he was going", she recalls. Brett notes that, having endured this hardship at the start of her career, Amanda will "turn over many stones" to look for work, remaining constantly on the lookout for new work possibilities and new nuggets of know-how that might add a string to her bow.

Today's younger hires, thankfully, have not had to endure Amanda's recession-based precarity. Unfortunately, being less 'hungry' means junior colleagues can be less energetic, not only about intellectual pursuits but also about drumming up new leads. The spreadsheet used in the weekly team meeting to review business possibilities is aimed at encouraging what Amanda calls a "culture of thinking ahead" rather than sitting back and waiting for work to land: "We should all be trying to generate leads", she says, noting that everyone should understand that work doesn't just magically land.

The need for self-reliance

Amanda also observes a tendency for the newer generation of recruits to ask for help before trying to find the answers for themselves; she tries not to be overly helpful but finds it difficult to leave juniors to sink or swim. In a consultancy climate where individual planners are largely responsible for filling their own time, self-reliance and autonomy are indispensable. Junior team members are usually base-loaded with one or two major projects, and learn to fill up the remainder of their time with billable work, working out how to prioritise and triage projects. Instead of a strong hierarchy of project management, each team member is responsible for communicating their availability to the others. Senior members of the team see their role as being to open doors for more-junior colleagues but leave it up to them which opportunities they choose to pursue.

This can be confusing for new recruits, Amanda notes, but she feels that the lack of clear line management is actually liberating, giving planners room to develop. Once you accept that you are in charge of your own destiny, she adds, things become more straightforward: "You are in control of what you do. If you create some relationships and generate some work and keep yourself busy, just do it, no one's going to bother you". This sense of finding something that you are good at and getting on with it is particularly apparent among senior members of the team, who are rewarded with a high degree of autonomy.[11] It also represents a more entrepreneurial attitude towards work, something that has been underplayed yet is arguably important for planners who wish to influence society's direction of travel around key issues (Frank, 2007).

Broadly defined value and productivity

Kate, one of the senior planners, feels that Simpsons' business model is currently giving her the room she needs to pursue one of her intellectual kicks – a passion for tackling climate change. A geography graduate, she came to Simpsons through the graduate programme after pursuing an IT career in which she honed her project-management skills before returning to university to do a master's in planning. Her communication style in team meetings is precise and on point; she can be a little stern when it comes to ensuring that things are moving along. One afternoon we grabbed the chance to chat about her work in one of the cosier upstairs meeting rooms. In conversation, she comes across as much warmer and deeper, driven by a concern for social and environmental justice.

While at Simpsons she has specialised increasingly in stakeholder engagement for infrastructure projects. She has always been interested in the voice of the community, in how grassroots movements can work side by side with policy to create change. She has an abiding interest in environmental issues – her undergraduate dissertation was about Agenda 21 – and she is trying at the moment to raise the profile of climate change. "One of the things that I like with Simpsons", she says, "is that you can follow your interests. So, I've just started having a bit more of a detailed conversation about climate change and where we as planners can play more of an influential role".

She is hoping to use her Simpsons network to bring together key specialists who can help shape the conversation:

> 'What I want to be doing is getting them on board to help influence and upskill the planners, so that we can go out and then have those

meaningful conversations with our clients and adopt an advisory and influencing role with the people that we speak to day to day.' (Kate)

Kate feels that the climate change conversation needs to become standardised as part of every planning project, and she is committed to applying her tenacity and project-management skills towards achieving this goal: "Basically, since Easter I have just been every day talking about climate change", she says with conviction. In considering how best to influence practice, she is particularly interested in the potential of devolution to produce a shift in power away from Westminster to the regional level, where planners might focus their influence: "I think the fact that different combined authorities have been declaring climate emergencies before the government has officially declared it is really, really interesting", she explains.

Kate's commitment to stay ahead of the curve in understanding the climate change policy agenda harmonises with a business model that produces 'altruistic' outputs while monetising this work for Simpsons. Shortly afterwards, at a lunchtime Knowledge Café, the director in charge of environment and sustainability announces the imminent publication of Simpsons' new guidance for local authorities. It's called *Climate Emergency: From Declaration to Action in 7 Steps*. The guide offers substantive information organised around seven points to help local authorities structure their forward thinking. But it is, of course, also a way to drum up business. It ends with a contact list of named 'local authority climate emergency liaisons' from Simpsons offices around the country who stand ready to field enquiries, offering reassurance in capital letters: 'WE CARE DEEPLY ABOUT THIS, AND WE CAN GUIDE YOU.'

Reconciling profit and the public good

Simpsons' commitment to 'equitable wealth', as laid down in the firm's philosophy, helps the planners to feel they are reconciling profit and the public good. Simpsons' ownership structure and its solid investment in research around cutting-edge issues provides, in the view of many of the Simpsons planners, a mechanism for serving the public interest. Leah, the new graduate planner, points out that in a lean, target-driven context in which local authorities have less capacity to do visionary work, Simpsons' research activity around progressive planning serves the public interest.

In the firm's official narrative, profit is aligned unproblematically with altruism. For example, Simpsons' investment in equality and diversity is directed at 'sharing our stories about diversity and equality within our teams and with wider society', and it is also predicated on EDI as 'living the Simpsons values through a sound business case'. As another case in point, Toby Graham's interdisciplinary health-centre work promises an innovatively holistic approach to tackling social deprivation *and* is also being pursued as a tool that Simpsons can sell while continuing its cycle of research investment. Furthermore, Kate explains that becoming a leader in tackling pressing social and environmental issues such as climate change may be a key recession-proofing strategy for Simpsons:

> 'A lot of our business currently is within infrastructure schemes and they've only got a certain longevity, so we just need to look ahead and think what next. I think there is so much change happening that if we can grapple with that and help shape that, then I think that's going to place us in a really strong position.' (Kate)

As discussed in Section 3.3, Simpsons' value-driven culture and specialist knowledge must be reconciled with consultants' limited influence, including their 'only advise' mandate and their pragmatic need to serve client interests. Such a tension has been noted more widely in knowledge-intensive firms, with ambiguity of role between 'expert' and client-facing 'consultant' being central to managing this contradiction for workers. As Robertson and Swan note in relation to an engineering and biotech firm, a strong culture of reflection on values is a crucial component for maintaining such an ambiguous role (Robertson and Swan, 2003). At Simpsons, this culture is continually reinforced through documents, social activities and training that promote the alignment of altruistic and business goals.

Simpsons' work nonetheless takes place within a wider set of structures, both economic and social, that can run up against these authentic commitments to progressive, evidence-based influence on society. The planners are acutely aware that local government austerity has shaped the environment in which they work, opening up opportunities for consultancy work while also denuding local government teams of capacity. Their response – to frame engagement with local government as support and capacity-building – is deeply felt but occurs against a backdrop of wider political and ideological shifts diminishing the role of planning and wider trends towards outsourcing work, often at the expense of well-represented, stable, unionised public-sector jobs.[12] There is additionally a need to frame the more exciting, blue-sky work with an eye to adding value to Simpsons' portfolio of work and potentially developing a commercial position that may generate a profit in the coming years. If such projects cannot support the bottom line, then economic downturns mean that wider pressures come into play that make this work vulnerable. As Nate Cartright, the office leader, notes, work that is not is directly billable is more difficult for the organisation to sustain in an economic downturn.

For Leah the graduate planner, the key is where Simpsons sits in terms of how central an attitude of "Let's make as much money as we can" is to the firm's day-to-day operation. Having grown up in a socially deprived area of a nearby city where her father was a clergyman, she greatly values being part of a company that is oriented towards something more than profit. She recalls that while still a student she developed an interest in the firm, noting that all the students in her year held the company in high esteem: "I think for me they just came across that they weren't focused on money, they weren't focused on targets, they were focused on genuinely making a difference." So far, she feels that the work she is doing fits this expectation even while operating within the constraints of the client relationship: "We do work with our values", she says, reflecting on the projects she has worked on. "I'd like to think we're working in the public interest."

3.6 Icing

This final section examines how sector-wide dynamics of work intensification, coupled with Simpsonian work commitment to "put the icing on the cake" for every project, play out in terms of work output and work-life balance. Revisiting the demand for agile, flexible planning work alongside the need to cultivate client relationships, we see a rewarding yet concerning investment of consultants' personal time above and beyond the hours that they bill for. The team's efforts to protect their work-life balance unfold against a structural backdrop that, increasingly, requires overworking, not least on the larger multi-client projects that are more and more common.

The concept of work–life balance has become an ever more important issue in workplaces. An 'always-on' culture stimulated by digital technologies, as well as by higher expectations of service and fluid career paths, has added challenging pressures (Green, 2004), and planning and built-environment professions are not immune to this. For client-facing planners who are nominally in charge of managing their own workloads, such a balance has become increasingly elusive (Tait et al, 2020). For consultancies such as Simpsons, the ability to navigate the pressures of a rapidly changing external environment, in which projects are complex, with multiple players and unpredictable rhythms, has become ever more important. Recognising the value of workers and seeking to retain highly skilled and knowledgeable staff is no longer seen as merely a question of pay but implies providing an engaging and supportive workplace. This process is made more demanding by Simpsonians' commitment to going the extra mile – putting the icing on the cake for every single project.

It's Tuesday morning and the kitchen is intermittently abuzz with preparations for the second-floor bake-off. Amanda is concerned that the salted-caramel filling of her entry is too meagre. I tell her it looks pretty great to me, but about to be judged by her high-achieving peers, she is not feeling confident. I picture her carving time out of her evening to make these impressive dark cylinders of chocolate, which she has entered as

Figure 3.4: Amanda's bake-off entry, 'Chocolate Surprise'

'Individual Chocolate Surprise', then figuring out how to transport them to work without incident. She gets a plastic punnet of raspberries out of the fridge, grabs a bowl of hot water to warm her spoon and proceeds to melt the chocolate on the top of each cake so that the raspberries will adhere. I am impressed, as usual, by her ability to make things come together, to look good in the moment in spite of her intense schedule (see Figure 3.4). She takes about four minutes to assemble the cakes and then retreats to her desk to fire off more emails.

By late morning, Katelyn, the office wellness champion, has announced via email that it's time to chow down, and people are starting to congregate with craning and expectant faces around the three entries that have come in: 'Japonaise Fancies Two Ways' from Alexia in HR; 'Rarebit Muffins with Homemade Caramelised Onion Chutney' from Naomi in architecture; and Amanda's chocolate surprises. Katelyn locates some paper plates and a little queue forms. Lining up to eat cake in the morning, the second floor displays its youthfulness – tall and successful-looking twenty- and thirty-somethings with the odd handsomely silvery man mixed in. I'm mildly disappointed when the gathering rapidly disperses with no speeches or prizes. You fill your plate, go back to your desk and keep working, filling out Katelyn's Surveymonkey to vote: 1–5 stars for appearance and flavour for each one. Photos of each entry are included in the email for reference – a convincing performance of Simpsons' tight-ship powers.

Like all firms across the sector and, indeed, across wider UK society, Simpsons functions within an intensified labour process that offers little time for desultory activity during the working day (Boxall and Macky, 2014). As Brett, the most senior planner on the team, reflects, before the recession clients were willing to pay "for thinking time, for analysis time, for understanding". She adds that nowadays the projects are much more practical and concerned with the delivery of central infrastructure such as flood schemes: "very practical projects that are complex in terms of them needing to be done quickly with low budgets, needing to embed well in the city".

Senior planners on the team handle the intensity of their workday with élan. Their attitudes reflect a wider tendency among consultants to frame work pressure as a test of their professional skills; within a narrative based on personal choice there is nonetheless a structural subtext in which work demands can become oppressive and unreasonable (Wynn and Rao, 2020). Amanda earned her stripes for efficiency under a previous Simpsons boss who organised work around clearly defined lists of actions that had to be executed in a rapid and timely fashion. She doesn't miss this particular individual's strong character but learned to appreciate the tightness and certainty that came out of these quick-fire to-do lists. Amanda's high throughput is also a product of her 'recession planner' baggage: she tends to take on too much work out of fear that work will dry up again like it did in 2008. Sometimes, she says, this is not beneficial for her own work-life balance: "If I am not working at 145 per cent then I worry that the team might run out of work." She runs always at full capacity, getting through an impressive volume of work and never dropping the ball.

The team meeting offers glimpses of intense bursts of 'just-dropped' work with tight turnarounds; these occasions also show the unrelenting work rhythm for senior members who, embroiled in massive infrastructure projects, flirt with burnout (see Kunda, 1992, who details a similar culture in tech industry projects). It's the go-around at a Monday team meeting, Brett has an economical but authoritative tone of voice that gets to the point a little more quickly than the others around the table. She is under a pile of work and sounds rather like she is talking from somewhere within it. It is another "evil Monday", she says drily, adding that last Monday was evil too and that hopefully these will end soon.

The following Monday shows no respite. Brett's voice, as she updates us on the major infrastructure project she's working on, is very measured, like someone in the middle of a warzone who must carefully parcel out their energy. She talks about being in the report cycle and also needing to sort out her inbox of all the emails that have come in (her tone indicates that there are *a lot* of them); "So this will be a really busy week, again", she says plainly. She is also supposed to organise some meetings. "I need help because I am drowning", she adds matter-of-factly yet with a touch of wry humour. She continues, "And today at 1 pm is the recent-starters meeting. … I don't know when I will next get a lunch break", adding somewhat light-heartedly that she will grab something and eat it during the meeting.

Brett's billable work, producing the 'goodies', such as a report that a client is paying for, must be juggled against organisational responsibilities that can be something of a time sink. She wrestles with the dilemma of how to apportion time between tangible 'goodies' and managing the 'noise' of team building (both internal and external) that her role entails: "If a client's paying for me, for a report or something at the end, you've still got to deliver that with all this other stuff that's going on, so you will probably find most consultants do work longer than the contracted hours because you feel that obligation."

Simpsons' growing involvement in large, multi-player projects is placing increasing demands on Brett's skills: "You're having to always work with people, keep them on board, use bigger teams. We've got to influence more, that doesn't count as productivity, it's dealing with the heat and the noise, so we've still got to produce some goodies at the end of the day." She feels a duty to provide the product the client is paying for but is also invested heavily in supporting her own team and facilitating the cross-organisational teams that she is now part of. During one busy day of juggling, she comments:

> 'So, today, this morning, I have spent time sorting out people's challenges, people have phoned me about a call they're about to have, you know … so you're always mediating. That for me is important time to build trust, and to help people feel … but that's all internal. I've got to do some work. So, when will I be doing that work? I'll be doing that tonight.' (Brett)

Simpsonians work exceptionally hard but are also well looked after. The second-floor kitchen area, with its comfy saffron couches, signals the firm's attention to staff wellbeing. On Monday mornings, large cardboard boxes of free fruit appear for them to graze on (see Figure 3.5) – pears, bananas, plums and apples. Next to the sink a plastic stand displays a 'Prostate facts for gay and bisexual men' leaflet, a guide to lunchtime walks in the city and a pocket-sized guide to the Employment Assistance Programme. The long table, popular at lunchtime, has another leaflet stand housing the Simpsons *Live Well, Work Well* newsletter. The table is often strewn with balloons and posters for events like Women's Day, a reminder that fun, interesting stuff is going on above the day-to-day grind.

Wellbeing occupies an increasingly high-profile position in Simpsons' value system, starting with a conversation on day one of employment. At my orientation (I received part of the standard orientation that Simpsons' employees get), Alexia from HR guides me through a diagram that divides

Figure 3.5: The Monday morning fresh-fruit delivery

the staff package up into different kinds of 'Benefit' all adding up to 'Total Benefit'. Money has its place, but there are also other types of compensation that Simpsons' workers can expect. On top of the private-healthcare benefit, Alexia points out, there are frequent wellbeing perks – a masseuse recently came in for a few weeks and you can book blocks of Pilates and yoga.

Perhaps with an eye to future business, Simpsons is engaged not just in investing in wellbeing but also in quantifying it. The *2017–18 Futures Review* lauds the gains made by Simpsons' new office building in a nearby city: 'Following an investment in design for wellness at our Westborough office, the team feel better and are getting more done. The increase in wellness represents a sound business case – we are seeing social return on investment (SROI) of £214,000 per annum through boosts to employee health.'

Simpsons' senior managers have committed to tackling mental health head-on. One of them notes candidly in the *Live Well, Work Well* newsletter that he suffered from stress and has learned that going the extra mile should be the exception not the rule. When feeling overloaded, it should be OK to say, 'What do you want me to take away so I can do this', he counsels in the article. Overwork and stress are also being tackled as an integral part of Simpsons' ambitious diversity and inclusion strategy, which looks in particular at the barriers women face in the organisation's intense, project-based work culture (Lindgren and Packendorff, 2006). As mentioned earlier, the firm has hired Nadia Russell, a heavy-hitter tasked with leading the conversation about diversity, who is dedicated to creating a "burning platform" around work-life balance.

To keep the wellness conversation going at the team level, Brett has recently undergone training as a mental-health first aider.[13] At the next

Monday morning planning team meeting, she introduces an exercise she learned at the training – "I want you all to take fifteen minutes today to do this." She reassures them that they don't need to share back what they have written: "It's private but tell me you did it." She hands around a printout entitled 'Activity 2: Stress Container: What's in yours?' On a piece of A3 she draws a big triangle that matches the one on the front of the handout – it's a bucket that fills up with stresses, with a tap on the side that releases stress – this part is for sports, hobbies and fun, she explains.

This positive action around stress buckets needs to mesh with a reality in which work is intense and can land suddenly. Here, as with all high-intensity work environments, company rhetoric around support for work-life balance exists in tension with wider structural pressures and with the organisation's internal demands (Mescher et al, 2010). Earlier in the meeting, Brett summarised what she has on this week – a major environmental paper and a couple of other weighty-sounding projects. She sounds very professional and in control but also like she is at the 'don't add any more' point. Amanda helpfully suggests that she tries to face the pile of work in bite-sized chunks – "Like bite-sized GCSEs", she jokes.

The team has nurtured a culture of challenging each other when work is pushing out other important things. This is particularly important for those with more responsibility. Amanda and Brett have a working relationship in which they will let each other know if they are overcommitting to projects. Last Friday, Brett came into the office on her at-home day to get through some work on her large infrastructure project. Her presence generated a flurry of requests for input or advice on other projects and she stayed longer than expected – "She is almost too good", Amanda adds wryly. The potential for stress that stems from the team's internal workflows and rhythms is something that planning colleagues seek to be open with each other about; yet the intensity of work is also often governed by external factors that are difficult to control.

Brett's communication style when she talks about her impressive workload is an effective display of humility, power and accomplishment. She is doing gigantic things, gigantic enough that you can drown in them. Being stressed and working at high intensity (or being always on) has become, perversely, a marker of high status and power within many professional work environments (Hochschild, 2008), and Simpsons is not insulated from this.

I talked about this dynamic with Nadia Russell, who, having heard about some of our initial findings from Brett, had taken an interest in our project. Nadia, who is looking at the organisation's culture in the UK and beyond, feels that an always-on culture is endemic at Simpsons, including the need to be always contactable. She links this to a total commitment to getting the job done. She agrees with my assessment of stress as power, as a marker of high status in the firm. "We actively seek out busy diaries", she affirms, telling me that she looked at her diary today and felt "slight panic that May is looking breathable".

Nadia describes to me what she calls "the Simpsons icing". "The client comes to you and says, 'I want a pink report'", she explains, "Simpsons' response is to come back to the client and say, 'I think you want a blue report with sequins'". The point is that, in approaching a project with a client, Simpsonians get genuinely excited about the possibilities and are keen to indulge their own technical, artistic and ecological passions. She adds that they often try to bring the client along with them through a dialogue based on co-creation or co-production of ideas. This process brings its own issues because the budget remains the same: the budget is for the pink report but the Simpsonians are carried away with the excitement and have "got to get the sparkles". Nadia reckons they often rationalise going the extra mile and putting in a bit more than the budget calls for by a sort of 'last-caper' thought process – they think, 'Just this once!', and assure themselves that things will be different after this project.

The extra sparkle and gold standard of service that Simpsonians bring to projects often comes at a cost to their personal time. This is particularly the case in terms of the "intellectual wormholes" that Simpsonians pursue around issues such as walkability or climate change. Kate, the senior planner who is trying to encourage a more detailed conversation about climate change at Simpsons, indulges her passion for the topic through small windows of downtime, travel time and during quiet time in the evenings. Brett admits that many of her more interesting projects would run way over budget if she was realistic about the hours put in: "If I charged all of my time that I ever worked on something, the cost would be double."

During our phone call about Simpsons' EDI initiative, Nadia confirms that one of the chief work-life-balance issues that the organisation faces relates to getting staff to report the real number of hours worked on a project. It's a complex situation – a mix of passion, pressure and ambition that is difficult to untangle. There are twists and turns to grapple with – Nadia describes the seduction of chasing new work; the devotion to giving a gold standard of service even on small, non-lucrative projects; and, intriguingly, the dissonance between company and client values that Simpsonians cope with through compensatory work on idealistic projects in their own time.

Nadia is keen on the type of 'active bystanders' practice that the planning team cultivates, whereby you speak out when you see a colleague locked into an overwork routine. We talk about ways to subvert the organisational narrative of super-people, about how to legitimise lifestyles that are not based on being always on, about how to tune into the Simpsonian go-getter enthusiasm and make it an opportunity for the company to become a world leader in work-life balance. Recognising the tension inherent in pursuing satisfying wormholes while completing complex projects on time opens up space for discussion among Simpsonians and, she feels, is an important factor in socialising those new to the firm.

Working within the intense wider culture of the firm or, indeed, the wider profession, the senior members of the planning team feel they have made some gains for their team in protecting younger starters from the high pressures of the work and shielding them from more difficult client personalities. Indeed, as Brett says, the planning team *as a whole* does not have the kind of stressful, long-hours culture that is seen in other parts of the sector.

At the next team meeting, we are reviewing the stress-container exercise. Jack, who is one of the more junior team members, shares that he did the exercise but at that particular time found it hard to find significant stresses in his work. "Jack, tell us your secret", says Brett meditatively. Jack, who is in his late twenties, recently joined Simpsons after a stint in the public sector. He's a pleasant, helpful, quiet guy – Brett notes that he is starting to build up his reputation with clients so that they are asking specifically for him: "I'm just basically there if he needs me", she says, "but he's doing it and the client is speaking to him and he's now got that relationship".

Jack likes the fact that some of the Simpsons projects have quite long timelines so he can manage his time and his deadlines such that spikes of work don't happen. He also appreciates that, because of the emphasis on serving the client, when you go on holiday work is handed over properly and things are taken care of by others. This wasn't the case when he was in the public sector and would find a pile of work waiting from him when he got back from his annual leave: "If you took two weeks off, you were going to feel worse for having done it." His local authority was also very stretched by cuts, so benefits such as flexitime didn't seem to materialise.

Other younger team members tell a similar story of feeling nurtured and not overwhelmed at Simpsons. Xander, the artistically talented member of the team who has just been promoted, says he sticks to his set hours, 9–5:30, and has a one-hour lunch that he takes properly, going out for a walk and clearing his head so he can be productive in the afternoon. Leah, who came into Simpsons through the graduate programme, says uncomplicatedly that she has a good work-life balance. In particular, she feels protected by Amanda, who is good at guiding her not to put in more hours than she has been allocated. Leah doesn't feel that overwork will become an issue as her career progresses – she shares that she thinks overwork is a generational thing, and that her generation are less prone to it, that some of her friends have given up their office jobs because they don't like the office environment – they want more freedom and flexibility.

While proud of the fact that they are nurturing work-life balance among their current younger team members, the senior members of the team have found some of the other young hires and placement students they have dealt with to be overly relaxed, a phenomenon that, indeed, perhaps reflects wider generational shifts in work values (Twenge, 2010). As noted in Section 3.5, a laid-back attitude can be a little incongruous and confusing when work demands displays of curiosity, sharpness and hunger. Brett observes that the younger generation are often less socialised to perform a committed attitude through body language and asking questions: "The currency in the past was, if your boss took you to a meeting, you knew, implicitly, that you had to be useful in that meeting: you write notes; you behave yourself; you watch the room; you make eye contact and be engaged and involved." By contrast, she notes that in recent years "we've had issues where it's been, like, yawning, and clear disinterest". She and some of the other senior planners are committed to nurturing new team members' interests and abilities so that they can embody the animated and engaged persona needed when facing clients – this process is working but seems to take longer than in the past.

Flicking through the *Live Well, Work Well* newsletter, there is a one-page article offering a peek into the healthy-living philosophy of Alessandra Mancini, a graduate entrant from one of Simpsons' other UK offices who is pictured pumping iron and eating pizza. She is asked to sum up what she does in her leisure time: 'Outside of work, I never stop', she states. As part of a vibrant network-based culture, Simpsonians need to be comfortable with mixing work and pleasure, and this can be exhilarating. However, firms that require employees to 'put their "lives" to "work" in the creation of value for the company' (Land and Taylor, 2010, p 396) also create subtle dynamics of overwork. At the team meeting, Brett is looking at her calendar, assessing the number of office parties she needs to go to: "A million have appeared in my diary", she says, "I have to go to [nearby city] for Christmas dinner".

Decoupling stress and high achievement is especially complex in professional consultancy cultures that seamlessly blend fun and work, passion and productivity, relationships and autonomy (Muhr and Kirkegaard, 2013). Christmas can bring a slew of extra internal and external social commitments that, while fun and a bit lavish, can become a burden for those who also juggle caregiving responsibilities. Learning to navigate client relationships, following one's passions in ways that create value, managing one's own dissonance with client values and turning over stones to find new work are skills that, once mastered, bring great 'total benefits', but also require a heavy investment of emotional and mental labour.

As with organisations that are based on a strong culture, Simpsons has unwritten rules about work ethic, philosophy and attitude. For those who come in at more-senior grades, learning the culture can be harder than for those who come in as graduates or in entry-level roles. For Brett, one of the keys is finding a skill that you can utilise for Simpsons – for some this might mean something quite technical, whereas others' strengths might lie in softer, people-based skills. Having learned that all-rounders are increasingly few and far between, she tries to help team members find their unique skill so that they can flourish.

Lauren, one of the senior members of the planning team, notes that sometimes people leave Simpsons to work in a local authority and then come back. "This happens to us a lot", she says. People leave and then find out that the grass is not greener. "There are a lot of things that Simpsons does for its people that we can take for granted", she adds. For those who align with it, Simpsons' strong culture offers a secure, self-nurturing sensibility, a feeling of being part of something special.[14] As I look back over photos that the planners sent me of their workplace tea-and-coffee rituals, the images are telling: Lauren's coffee at MIT, where she was exchanging big ideas about resilience with top academics; Leah's afternoon 'cuppa' made by a colleague; Brett's mug of tea in her book-cluttered home office, where she carves out space to think, pursuing her great love of going down wormholes.

One of Brett's favourite wormholes is to think through the implications of automation for Simpsons' planners, meditating on whether, in Simpsons' consultancy model, it is possible to decouple time and money. She wrestles with the human cost that the Simpsons icing entails – the personal time that Simpsonians devote to doing their work with that extra panache. She wonders whether, by harnessing some of the benefits of automation for its own people, the company could take care of its base costs and free up more thinking time for staff, also allowing time for the Simpsonians to pursue some of their more altruistic projects and ideas during the work day. "That would be a really good future", she says.

3.7 Conclusion

Simpsons excels at client relationships and is committed to an idea of 'good' planning. The dedicated and capable team we followed were aware of the bigger societal challenges they could contribute to, and the wider company supports the development and dissemination of knowledge around these challenges in impressive ways.

There is a commitment to going the extra mile and a demonstration of skill in balancing this with the potential 'long tails' of managing projects. This comes at a personal cost in terms of work-life balance and stress, and can imply some difficult compromises. The ethics of the firm as socially progressive can conflict with challenging political and commercial environments and what is achievable regarding individual clients. It also puts pressure on individuals, creating cognitive dissonance around both work-life balance and these wider societal aims. Although part of their work adds value and capacity in the public sector, Simpsonians may, however unintentionally, ultimately support the displacement of public-sector work and employees and deny learning opportunities to public-sector workers. In sum, they represent passion and high levels of commitment to serving the public good, yet they have to juggle a series of competing interests, often leading to high-pressure work and, potentially, ethical compromise.

Our findings also point to an emerging world of large, multi-headed projects in which planners play a relatively small role and find their values running contrary to clients' wishes and the realpolitik of projects. The building and maintenance of the institutional capacity required to deliver large-scale, multi-client projects adds to the non-billable stresses of senior consultants and is of a different type and scale to the sorts of projects senior planning consultants have routinely delivered in the past. Within progressive firms such as Simpsons, individual commitment to social causes is encouraged, yet the judicious nudging and relationship-building that planning consultants have traditionally employed to pursue the public good are increasingly lost, or simply impossible, in the 'noise' of contemporary large development projects.

4

Bakerdale: a 'traditional' local authority commercialising under austerity politics

Bakerdale is a district council in South-East England. The planners there were undergoing a change management programme oriented towards commercialising their operations – charging for services – with a view to making the department financially self-sustaining. This was made possible largely by the significant development pressure created by Bakerdale's location, with good rail links to London, which had led to high house prices. We found a strong planning culture with a range of in-house planning specialists, unlike many English local authorities that had moved to buying in expertise from consultants.

We made repeated visits to Bakerdale over a period of six months, and the work we observed speaks across all our central themes, most significantly commercialisation in public- and private-sector planning. The case also illuminates the pressures austerity has exerted on the public sector, the role of politics and officer-member relations in local government and the significance of leadership.

The chapter has six sections, organised thematically. These collectively paint a vivid picture of the workplace culture at Bakerdale, the pressures of day-to-day work in contemporary local government and the realities of commercialisation.

4.1 Introduction

'I was good at geography at school, and when I was asked to think about what career I wanted to do I thought that I liked architecture so I might want to be an architect, but then I thought, "I can't draw", and in those days, architects used to draw with a pen. I thought about town planning, and I lived in Slough and our house was about one hundred yards from the green belt. It used to fascinate me that London had spread out towards Slough and then this thing called the green belt was created and it stopped the march of London. I thought, "Wow, what a wonderful idea that is!" I can look out of my bedroom window into the green belt, and it's only there because planning took control of what was happening. I found that an inspiring thought. This is what planning can do! So I went to do a geography degree and then a planning degree and I loved it; thirty-five years later and I'm still here!' (Dan, major projects team leader, Bakerdale District Council)

A commuter town, Bakerdale lacks the twee gloss characteristic of some of its neighbours. The high street feels like it has seen better days, with several of the doorways being homes for the homeless. The council offices play their part in reinforcing those first impressions. A solid-looking early-twentieth-century building faces the road, post-modern add-ons to the rear, functional but conservative. As we enter we pass democracy manifest: a large board on an easel depicting each member of the council. No political party affiliations are given.[1] They're not all old white men, but mostly.

We have some time to wait. It is quiet in the generic reception area (see Figure 4.1). Carpet tiles, ceiling tiles, a 'collect a ticket and wait for your number to be called' atmosphere. Notices pinned to green baize advertise local employment opportunities. It feels dated. Simon Wood comes to meet us right on time. He is chummy, showing us where the toilets are and informing us that there will be no fire alarms. He is in charge of the change-management programme in the planning department, introducing himself as having previously worked for a developer "and overseen hundreds of wind farm and mobile phone mast applications". We are ushered into a small, cluttered meeting room; a trophy rests on a wire shelf alongside a hard hat with a Bakerdale logo, presumably ceremonial.

Matilda Weaver, head of planning and sustainability, and Nick Alexander, development manager, arrive together, Matilda with coffee, projecting an understated competence, a performance of being busy but on top of things, capable of cutting through the crap. Nick seems more reserved, not cold but giving the impression of knowing his stuff, being analytical and capable. We describe our project: the room is nodding along until Simon interjects: "What will the outcomes be? Is it about identifying best practice?" We reply that we want to consider the whole range of what is going on in the profession, how it has changed over time. We tell them of our project's Impact Advisory Group and that we are keen to feed back to the profession through a series of reports and other outputs. Does their interest pick up here?

Speaking initially about development management, they begin to set out where in their work they do and do not use consultants. They describe a consultant they use for smaller householder applications, responding to the inevitable peaks and troughs that come with this kind of work. The consultant is a former staff member, they know he is good, reliable, gets things done. At the moment, the work they are giving him amounts to a full-time job, yet this arrangement only works because of the particularities; it is not scalable. Moving on to their interaction with bigger consultancy firms they stress that they are lucky, they have been able to maintain a good range of in-house specialists – landscape, urban design, conservation,

Figure 4.1: The Bakerdale reception area

trees, ecology – so do not have to look outside the organisation for certain expertise. While they also have a large in-house policy team, there are still several instances when they use consultancies. It has to be this way these days for advice about agriculture and green belt policy. The county council has a contract for transport planning work, but Bakerdale don't find them very good. They make a few interrelated points in relation to this broad picture. First, individual experiences are not necessarily representative of firms: "It's not who you go to, it's who you get." Second, they make a point about institutional cultures, how sometimes things gel and everything works, and sometimes they just don't. Finally, perhaps most importantly, they stress the significance of contracts, how they are written, enforced, interpreted and the importance of mechanisms for ensuring delivery and quality and for guarding against perverse incentives.

We turn to the change-management programme, a response to the suggestion from government – now abandoned – that a system of alternative providers would be introduced for determining planning applications. Bakerdale wanted to show that they are not afraid of change, that they are willing to trial new things even if they have some reservations. Matilda concluded that they needed to try and win the competition game, stressing that there is no reason why they cannot be the 'go-to' people, delivering the quality of service of commercial outfits, perhaps even better. The change programme, then, is called Go To. Given the difficult financial climate for local government, it has been seized as an opportunity for simultaneously reducing the council-funded budget of the planning department from £1.5 million annually to zero – a so-called 'cost-neutral service'. The commercialisation of Bakerdale's pre-application ('pre-app') service – whereby developers buy in-depth advice on how to make their applications successful – alongside a new fee regime, will create the revenue to cross-subsidise policy and enforcement. It is an experiment, but the signs are promising. Simon stresses that developers will be happy to pay for this service as it eliminates risk, and agents will like it too. He seems to have a different position to Matilda on the subject of profit though. Matilda explains that while big outsourcing firms look to extract a profit from, for instance, writing a recommendation, Bakerdale is different because it is not looking to make a profit. They believe they are good at what they do and the hope is that they will be left alone to do their thing, squaring the circle of making developers and members happy without compromising planning's core purpose.[2]

At the heart of the exercise is costing and accounting for officers' time. This creates difficulties around coming up with equations and models when there is no data and nobody to benchmark against. While they project confidence that Go To is working and will work, some doubts are inevitable, as they will not know whether the numbers have added up until they have added up. Members are happy to trust them and 'take a punt', but they are not interested in setting up a trading arm. They question whether that would even be desirable. Simon alludes to the "worst of both worlds", meaning that they would have to deal with all the council's HR – he seems disappointed not to have the freedom to sack people at will – while having to make a profit. It is a reasonable point though: a key part of the outsourcing model in planning involves attacking terms and conditions of employment.

We have not really got onto the meat of our project, what we want to do and when, but Simon and Nick have another meeting to attend. They discuss pushing the meeting back, which is a relief, but then wonder whether we would like to come too. It is a meeting about the change-management programme, ironing out problems. It seems like it would be relevant, a good opportunity to push on, learn a bit more – "Make a day of it", as Simon says. Decision made, we head through the labyrinthine corridors, to a wood-panelled meeting room, taking a couple of chairs to one side of the big meeting table. Nick sits with us while Simon assumes a position at the head of the table. As the officers started without us fifteen minutes ago, we are not introduced. What will they take us for? Inspectors or auditors brought in as part of the change-management programme? On the wall the public Wi-Fi password is displayed: 'Bakers11', a reference to the local football team.

The officers seem hard at it, steadily working through a document heavy with tracked changes, projected onto the wall: a 'how to' guide on advice letters. The aim is to standardise and streamline how the letters and the accompanying matrix are produced and presented. The service you would 'Go To'. The spirit seems collegial, respectful. People air differences of opinion, and I sense they are genuinely engaged in the process. Initially, the most contentious issue relates to where things are stored digitally – version control and document corruption – as it emerged that we are working from an old version of the document. There is some relatively benign back and forth about whose fault this is. Ultimately everyone agrees we need to sort it out in order to move forward. The more substantive issues seem to centre on the grey areas that are probably the reason why the system is not standardised already; the problems thrown up by reducing everything to 'yes', 'no', 'preferred' and 'maybe', explanatory codes that need to be explained in their turn. "How red is red?" one planner asks.

A sudden change of tone occurs when it seems that an officer might have been on a pre-application visit before they have been paid by the 'client'. A noticeably annoyed Simon firmly informs the room that "nobody can do work they've not been paid for". The officers, backing one another up, are at pains to ameliorate the situation. The change-management programme is a "cultural change", everybody is learning. Tensions around the process emerge again a little later when the officers give feedback on their workloads, describing being under too much pressure. Simon is more receptive to this, keen to ensure the level of resource that delivers the quality that differentiates Bakerdale's services. There are moments of light relief too. An officer introduced her own work: "It's amazing!" Nothing to change here.

Nick is sitting next to me: is he trying to read my notes?! I hope not, as I have noted that one of the officers has a mug with 'Queen of Elmsbourne' written on it and that one of the other officers can't keep her eyes open. I sympathise. It took us a long time to get to the meat of the meeting. It seems like we have been here a long time. It is a mercy, then, when Nick suggests we go and find Matilda. Making our way back through the building, he explains the contention caused by the move to hot-desking. He points out the various bits of the building, noting when they were added on, and laments the fact that the planners are no longer in the offices with the nicest views.

Matilda arrives. Do we want more coffee? No thanks. The hot-desking discussion continues and Matilda seems genuinely incensed that Environmental Health have been able to ring-fence some premium desks. She will be taking this up with someone, fighting the planners' corner. We turn swiftly to the ethnography, thrashing out a few next steps. Nick seems enthused about the idea of setting up a programme for a first week. "Before Christmas?" he wonders. Amazing. Then we can think about the new year. There is a debate about whether I will be here for the Christmas party; it all seems too easy. There are a number of other things I can do if we time it right: planning committee, the members' site visits, an advice surgery, stakeholder drinks. Nick says he will email, and he does, before we have even gotten back to our office.

4.2 Contemporary public practice

This account of our first full day in the field in Bakerdale serves as an orientation to the planning department. It helps to demonstrate the fast pace of contemporary practice in the public sector and the management skills needed to prevent efficiency giving way to chaos. We start to see the extent to which the commercialisation agenda has been adopted but also the contradictions and limits of this, as in a public sector operating at close to the limits of its capacity, it is an uphill battle to find the space – literally here in terms of meeting rooms – for innovation, reflection and change.

Three weeks after the initial meeting I am following a sign for Bakerdale District Council Offices directing me through the large shopping precinct that dominates the town centre. Later I emerge from the same entrance. Now running slightly late, I revert to plan A, striding down the high street at double speed and arriving at the reception out of breath. It is as we left it, except for a mother and two children who sit surrounded by bags and boxes. Nick comes out to greet me. Smiling warmly and shaking my hand, he says he thought I was arriving at lunchtime but does not seem disconcerted. There will be plenty for me to see this morning.

Nick shows me the space he has reserved for me, a rare privilege. It is in the second row of desks after you enter the large open-plan office from the corridor. There are distinct territories even if there are not designated places. Planners sit on the first row, with even more planners in the smaller office on the other side of the corridor. My immediate neighbours are building control officers. Subsequent rows are made up of the 'techs', managed by Simon Wood, who support planning and building control. Nick uses the half hour before his meetings to create a loose schedule for me, and he pulls up a chair so he can talk me through it. Activity is largely structured around the planning committee meeting on Wednesday evening. Much of Tuesday will be taken up by the members' site visits, when they pile into a minibus to see the applications they need to consider, accompanied by officers who can answer questions. Several standing meetings happen throughout the week: a planning surgery where officers can ask in-house experts for their opinions on particular issues; and the development-matters seminar (DMS), where any planner can add a tricky item to the agenda and solicit the advice of Nick, Matilda and John Richards, the strategic planning manager. Around these core activities are a number of site visits with planners and meetings with developers. Now that I am here, this morning is going to be busy too, several management meetings in quick succession.

The first is about Go To. It is held in the kitchen area, separated from the rest of the office by a glass partition. Simon leads the meeting, which seems to involve a lot of managers and team leaders, although not exclusively. He introduces me, and I introduce our project. Simon adds that the research is for my PhD. I clarify that it is not. The meeting is organised around reporting on a series of flow charts – 'end-to-ends' – that are on a big notice board entitled 'Agile Wall', a physical manifestation of Go To (see Figure 4.2). Simon tells us what is on them because there is no way you could read them from the seats. There are other notice boards in the kitchen. One given over to trade union matters and another with everything else, including a quotation attributed to Stephen Hawking: 'Intelligence is the ability to adapt to change.'

Simon mentions that there are sixty Go To projects. We hear about the more important ones, starting with P-Zeros. P stands for priority. Zero is an innovation, as some projects turn out to be more important than P-1s. The big P-Zero is about printing and scanning. The development management system used at Bakerdale was designed before email. This means people routinely print emails and attachments before scanning them back onto the system, a truly ridiculous situation we also observed in Southwell (see Chapter 2). Thankfully, there is now a plug-in to enable dragging and dropping. They can start rolling this out immediately, but setting it up is a bit fiddly and they will arrange a group training session if everyone feels it is necessary. They do. Simon stresses that he will "flip out" if anyone asks Rowan, his right-hand man, for one-to-one training. This will save Bakerdale a salary, he thinks, quite possibly two, "and I'd much prefer those staff to be re-allocated to other work".

Another end-to-end is about discretionary planning advice. The discussion is about ways of streamlining the service, inserting recursive loops rather than whole new processes. It is simpler and quicker. Cost implications have caused some disquiet, so Simon clarifies when clients should and should not be charged for things. He feels that sometimes clients try to bypass costly

Figure 4.2: The Agile Wall

steps before amending things later; part of his rationale is to cut this out. It enables Bakerdale to charge clients the full cost of the service they receive. There is no problem giving discretionary advice to those who have already paid for it. Those who have not should be sent back to the beginning or told no.

Simon tells us about changes to the website. Making this clearer is a key aspect of the project as less time will be spent explaining things and correcting mistakes. The latest changes are all ready to go. This good news story is swiftly derailed by someone from the communications team. She says they are not quite ready to go because the changes are not disability-accessibility approved. Simon just about keeps on top of his annoyance, making a joke about there not being many visually impaired architects submitting drawings. For us, he reiterates, it is a done deal.

Meeting over, Nick whisks me to the small meeting room. This is referred to as Matilda's office, although she rarely gets to use it as such. Two arboricultural officers are here, a woman and a man, with Deborah Wells, their team leader. Simon arrives. The meeting has an acronym but nobody can remember what it stands for; it is about how the tree officers are engaging with the commercialisation agenda. Bakerdale intend to offer a premium service whereby people pay not to worry about their trees. This not only includes working on the trees but also insuring them. Bakerdale can add trees to their insurance without increasing the cost. "We can never undercut Bob the Chainsaw, whose blokes wear flip flops", says Simon, so the premium, whole-package part is important. The kind of clients mentioned during the meeting are schools, housing associations and hospitals. Of prime importance is "getting the info into English and onto the web".

A central concern of the meeting is to free up the officers to deploy their expertise. A pie chart shows how they currently spend their time.[3] Admin is a big chunk at almost 20 per cent, as they now spend time plotting trees on maps. The technicians who used to do this have been cut. Everyone agrees this is not an efficient use of tree officers' time. Simon says that the technical support team, now under his command, have the capacity to take this task back. Time is also spent doing things, "for the community", which means looking at trees that members of the public are concerned about. For now, there is no suggestion that this will be commercialised. The million-dollar question, though, is whether they can ever turn a surplus. It seems that as the actual tree surgery work still has to be sub-contracted, the bulk of the money for contracts will go elsewhere. They missed out on a contract for a housing association recently, which provokes some hand-wringing. Simon stresses that they need to capitalise on their monopoly position and that they are trusted. The meeting closes with praise for the officers, who have committed to engaging with the process. Simon has given them less time than he has given others and is really pleased with what they have done.

Nick tells me to stay in the room. There is not space for everybody who arrives, so we have to stand around the walls. Presumably, then, this meeting could not happen in the relative open of the kitchen. Later, from consulting the organigram that Nick gave me, I realise that this is a team leaders meeting. They discuss resources and share news. Unfilled posts are mentioned, as are new starters that are joining and problems with sickness. It is a short meeting. Everyone leaves except the more senior managers, who have their own brief catch-up, airing their worries and frustrations.

Afterwards, I head out for lunch. The mother, her children and all their worldly possessions are still waiting in the reception.

4.3 Commercialisation

The description of the Go To training session in this section develops understanding of our overarching themes, looking directly at Bakerdale's commercialisation agenda. It provides insight into how the machinery of local government and the planners themselves respond, where they are able to be accommodating and where there are resistances and blockages, whether these are quasi-structural (for example, HR protocols) or rest in the professional sensibilities of the planners themselves. This episode is also illuminating about the ways in which New Public Management has been enthusiastically accepted within UK planning – for instance, through the valorisation of 'efficiency' – and where the acceptance is more grudging.[4]

The Go To training session is in the council chamber. Simon sits in the middle, the planners around him in the chairs where the members would normally sit. He is explaining the rationale for why developers will pay for pre-app advice. Without pre-app advice, what they need to do is unclear and the process is longer. With pre-app, it is clearer and faster. Anyone who thinks it is expensive should think again – for developers, if it saves paying an architect to do another drawing then the money is well spent. This introduces a recurring theme: "Have faith that you're worth it!" Of course some people will push back, they won't like it. Fine, it is not for them, it is a discretionary service after all. Simon recalls his time working for a developer. He would have really valued this option. The initial advice would not have been to nail everything down but to avoid the pitfalls that waste time and money. For planners, it is an opportunity to explore motivations, which is useful for helping applicants produce something acceptable.

There is a question. We might think about it this way, but 'clients' think they will be told whether their scheme is OK or not. Simon gives an example about a huge site – you cannot ever know for sure what line the members will take and so on. The questioner comes back; she is not talking about big schemes. The planners are mainly dealing with householder applications. Here Simon gets quite forceful in speaking about the website. A lot of work has gone into this and it is now crystal clear; these people can get everything they need to know in a very straightforward way from there. The question moves towards when in-house specialists should be consulted. It seems that some of the planners consult specialists when, it is felt, they do not need to, and this is frowned upon because it wastes the specialists' time, which is more expensive. It is clearly contentious. Simon stresses that he wants people to feel comfortable and it is important to strike a balance so that confident planners can assert their knowledge while others can find support. Quite a few people speak up on Simon's side, stating that it is perfectly reasonable to tell people who have paid for pre-app advice what you think while stressing that a specialist will be consulted as part of an application and that they will take their own view. The questioner asserts that people think they have paid for this advice as part of the pre-app. Simon challenges her: "It boils down to you thinking the pre-app advice is too expensive?" No, she thinks it is about professionalism and being professional. Simon does not engage on this point. Ultimately, he would "rather you don't use specialists' time if it's not been paid for". Again, "Feel confident, you're worth it!"

Another question. This is all fine, and especially for rational customers, but we all know that some customers are not rational, those are the more difficult situations. This allows Simon to agree that everybody knows that some customers are irrational. It also allows the point to be made again about stressing the bounds of engagements. When you pay, you pay for a service. You are not paying for a permission. This is what I can say, this is what I cannot. Sometimes it is fine to say you don't know. Simon recalls the time-versus-influence chart that is central to Go To's rationale. We are getting in as early as possible to exert the biggest influence and add as much value as we possibly can. He links this to the need to have a sustainable business case for the model, introducing the fiscal uncertainty in local government more widely. It is in everyone's interest to show that Bakerdale is good, that is the best way to protect everybody's jobs. Deborah asks a question about what the planners can do to assist the process, she references how-to guides in particular, which have been especially problematic. Simon takes an interesting new tack: "Don't beat me so hard I don't want to come to work". He goes a bit dewy eyed. Keeping the Go To train moving has clearly put him under considerable strain.

Some other paid-for services get referenced: a 'Do I need a planning permission' service and a planning history check, cashing in on the timid and the lazy. There is an interesting aside about photocopying. Simon asks if we know how much more expensive it is to do your photocopying at Office Depot rather than paying Bakerdale District Council to do it? Can we even begin to guess? Bakerdale's planners are a third of the price! Simon is outraged. He has been to war with someone "upstairs" who can't see the problem, someone with the temerity to suggest that it is good for citizens to be able to access cheap photocopying. "Those days are over. We're going to be a *premium, premium* service!"

4.4 The product, the planners and the public

Here we witness a mid-career planner on a site visit for a householder application. The episode provides insight into the day-to-day tasks of development management, part of the bedrock of planning work and by extension here of the commercialisation agenda, as the householder has become a paying client. While this points to an increasingly complex client/customer/public nexus, it also shows how certain elements of day-to-day work endure in spite of Go To and perhaps also the programme's limits. From here, the episode develops our understanding of how planners interact with members of the public and the extent to which the public understand planning.

Juliet has arranged to meet the applicant on site; he has been refused once and has now paid for pre-app advice on an almost identical scheme. She explains that this would almost certainly be refused again, but under the auspices of Go To she has come up with an alternative that might fare better. On the way to the car Juliet has to stash all her belongings in a locker. "I could do with a trolley for all this", she laughs. As we drive she tells me she has been at Bakerdale for four years. She has moved around on account of her husband's job, which is also why she took a break to have children. She left just before the National Planning Policy Framework (NPPF) came in, so coming back was quite challenging as things had changed a lot. The other big challenge was coming into a green belt authority. Interestingly, she always wanted to be a planning officer; she really enjoyed human geography and a careers officer steered her towards planning.

When we get to the site, a large plot with one modest house, I can see why the applicant wants to develop it. The applicant wants to put flats to the rear. There are two storeys of flats to one side but they are arranged around a cul-de-sac so they have road frontage. Apart from its overlooking and overshadowing these flats, the proposal is not in keeping with the character of the area, and there is a bit of an access issue, with people going in and out to one side of the current house. We stand in the cold, waiting for the elusive applicant and chatting. Juliet's suggestion is to demolish the current house, thereby better situating some flats nearer the front of the plot. Unlike less-confident colleagues, she likes working in this pro-active way, giving a more acceptable alternative rather than saying no. All meetings like this one now happen on site. Juliet is enthusiastic about change; getting good buildings built is what it's all about and Go To helps that to happen. There are colleagues who are less keen. Again, the planners have various perspectives, with some feeling like they have already seen too much change. Juliet is pleased Simon has come in from outside. She says that previous initiatives have been undertaken by secondees from within the council and it makes things harder; insiders are too embedded in the culture.

Still no sign of the applicant. Juliet rings the office as sometimes folk assume that meetings happen there. The office say no, so Juliet decides we will wait in the car for a bit longer. She speculates about what will happen in the event of a no-show – they are rare – will the applicant have to pay again? No sooner have we decided to head off, however, than the phone rings. It is the office, the applicant has turned up. Juliet's short on time because she needs to pick her kids up from school, but we go back to the office. On arrival our guys – I assume a husband and wife – are hidden behind a pillar. When we eventually find them, we all shake hands. Juliet explains that we will duck into an empty meeting space. As we have now had a good look at the site, Juliet says, she appreciates that it's large, but given that the new proposal is pretty much the same as the last one it will likely get the same treatment. She explains her idea, but they insist that they do not want to demolish the existing dwelling.

At this point someone appears outside. They have booked the room. The applicants are happy to finish our chat in the reception. I quite like them. They are clearly not professionals, just hoping to cash in on their massive garden. They are also not very au fait with planning. A lot of character terms – urban grain, massing, road frontage – seem to pass them by. They have brought a photo of the flats next door. The ones they want to build will look just like these. Part of me thinks this is a reasonable point, as there is nothing extraordinary about the area, which mainly consists of 1960s semi-detacheds in largish plots. Juliet calmly explains the policy reasons for the decision. The applicants equally calmly nod along. Juliet outlines a few options. They can appeal a refusal if they want, it will not cost them anything, and they can put in a revised application, too, if they like, to keep things moving. That is pretty much that. Back in the office Juliet suggests that they did not have a very good grasp of planning. A fair assessment. Later I check out the fees page of the website; it seems they paid £450 for this advice.

4.5 Planners and their clients

We see a quite different type of client in this section, as Rogers – a major housebuilder – come to Bakerdale for a meeting. This shows how negotiations play out between local authorities and major housebuilders, who have a near monopoly on new housebuilding in the UK and, in light of government housebuilding targets, significant negotiating power.[5] We see that this can have significant implications for the provision of important social infrastructure, in this case a primary school.

The meeting with Rogers, a major housebuilding firm, is to discuss a site in Elmsbourne – key to meeting housing targets in a district constrained by the London green belt and designated area-of-outstanding-natural-beauty (AONB) – where Rogers hope to build 250 houses. Polly, the case officer, goes to collect the Rogers people; I go with Andy Wilson – team leader for infrastructure and projects – to the meeting room. Dan, Polly's team leader in development management, will also be in the meeting, mainly taking minutes but also contributing. There are two people from Rogers: a middle-aged guy with a tweedy jacket and a signet ring on his little finger, and a slightly younger woman, who seems a bit less high-up and more engaged with the day-to-day of this project. There is also a planning consultant, with cufflinks and a big watch, and a middle-aged guy from Gavin and Mince – a large property consultant – here "just to listen" on behalf of the landowner.

There seems to be quite a lot of filling one another in, with carefully negotiated questioning in between, and as I've not been briefed it takes a while to work out what's going on. We begin with an update on the local plan, moving rapidly to an update on the infrastructure capacity document, timeframes and schedules. The necessary assessments, particularly around transport, are unlikely to be ready until next year. It is clear that the developer is keen to move things along as quickly as possible, but Bakerdale cannot make other agencies go any faster. A Housing Infrastructure Fund (HIF)[6] bid will support the development. There is a lot of discussion about junctions and where Rogers envisage them being. Andy asks about Rogers' modelling and whether it can be shared with the council. Perhaps it could be shared, in confidence; the developer has paid for it and would not want to find it coming back to bite them. Public consultation could potentially happen in March. It is a tight timetable but it seems they could potentially work towards September for a committee date.

Mr Big Watch asks about the "headlines", and the officers seem a bit wary. Schools are an issue; the developer has offered to build a school but has proposed to put it in an inappropriate place, there has to be discussion with the local education authority. It becomes apparent that Bakerdale are keen for higher densities on the site. Rogers say that the proposal is driven by the market and that they are happy to share their research with Bakerdale. They stress that it is a robust methodology. Andy pushes on this: "How do they know that people won't buy three-storey houses?" A good question. Tellingly, Mr Signet Ring answers that people won't buy flats. His colleague follows up with an affirmation of Rogers' product, which they know people buy. The site needs to embody the brand.

We move back to access and a bus route through the site, a particular bone of contention. Rogers suggest that if layouts are too conducive to buses, irresponsible motorists can drive through sites very quickly; they wonder whether these questions could be dealt with under reserved matters. Bakerdale are not keen, and Dan stresses that once a master plan is on the record it can be referred to. The developers give a bit here, suggesting the master plan could be tweaked. The officers push a bit more, advocating for joining up their thinking; if technical issues come up at reserved matters it's too late. This leads to more questions about what can be shared and when, the importance of getting everyone around the table. Again Rogers stress the centrality of their brand, "for people".

We move onto the Planning Performance Agreement (PPA) which is supposed to set out process and expectations on pre-application discussions. This is now attended by a fines and charges regime; Dan introduces this as coming from on high within the council. Rogers sense an opportunity to gain the upper hand here, stressing that fines and charges are all well and good but they need a strong timeline; they have already spent a lot of money and don't have an unlimited pot. For them, a committee date is key. The school is slowing things down. Everyone agrees that each party has their pressures. Polly will send a draft PPA to Rogers. Rogers take the opportunity to say that they can draft things if it will move the process along quicker.[7] Mr Big Watch gives a precis of where we're up to, again pushing for timescales, Bakerdale again saying they can't commit to a deadline yet. The guy from Gavin and Mince makes his only intervention of the meeting to say that the timescales are the critical bit. The meeting ends with Mr Big Watch saying that we will get a good write up regarding exemplary public/private-sector relations. Everyone shakes hands.

Polly shows the Rogers contingent out, and on the way back to the office Dan highlights the different tactics of developers: some use persuasion while others use a sledgehammer. He says that they do not necessarily appreciate that the council are reliant on other statutory stakeholders and timescales that are out of the planners' control. He also observes that landowners aren't particularly helpful here; they have a "get the permission and get building" mindset and don't appreciate the complexity and knock-ons inherent in the process.

Once she is back in the office, I am also able to get Polly's thoughts. She highlights the discussion about density/methodology. I observe that when asked about three-storey houses Rogers responded about flats. She agrees, they evaded the question. What can they do about it? For now, keep applying gentle pressure. Once the local plan kicks in and the densities are set out, they will have more clout. The thing is that Rogers want to bring forward their product, which is what they do. The school is a big sticking point. It's great that they want to build one but their suggestion is totally in the wrong place. Negotiations will continue. Polly contrasts Rogers' approach, which is based around careful negotiation and respectful engagement, with that of another developer who doesn't want to contribute to infrastructure and is pursuing a confrontational, legalistic route, which can also get very personal.

4.6 Workplace cultures, leadership and change in the public sector

This section explores how the planning culture at Bakerdale has developed over time and why it matters. Two largely verbatim extracts provide exceptionally rich, first-hand descriptions of senior officers' experiences: the first shows how a collective understanding of innovation and receptiveness to change provides a strong foundation for the current commercialisation agenda. It also focuses on the question of how young planners are enculturated and how frustrations and anxieties have emerged as statutory planning has changed. The second, illustrates how leadership is central to the planning culture at Bakerdale. Matilda expects her planners to work hard and trusts that they will.

> *Her story provides insight into the development of the commercialisation agenda at Bakerdale, while also betraying a markedly different orientation to change. It suggests that historically change was something that planners felt able to drive; it is now experienced as something that will happen anyway and as being largely out of their control. The trick, it seems, is to react adroitly.*

Something you quickly learn at Bakerdale is that a lot of the planners have been working here for quite a long time. A testament, they openly acknowledge, to its being a "good place to work", with competent managers. Nick tells me that he joined the council in 1987:

> '1987 through the 1990s, to me, is a golden era because it was exciting, there was a lot happening. I was interviewed by several managers in a big round-table interview and they were telling me all the things they were doing and it just sounded really interesting. So I moved down intending to do a few years and then move back north. I never intended to stay, but after I'd done a couple of years they moved me and promoted me. I did a while in the rural area and then I did the urban area and then I moved into the enforcement team. It was a career-grade position, which we don't seem to have now, but it was great. The purpose was to give you experience across all aspects of planning. You actually had a rota, so you would spend twelve months in one area and then you'd be moved and one of the other career planners would move round, with a view to giving everybody a rounded knowledge. And because it was good we attracted people from all over the place. From Glasgow, from some of the Welsh councils, from various planning schools; we all turned up together, so there was a really good social life and camaraderie. A work-hard-play-hard, culture. People were working ridiculous hours back then. I can remember a Friday night, looking up at seven o'clock and half the office is still there working away.
>
> A lot of that drive, it came from the chief planner. The council brought him in and he was determined to make us the best district planning authority in the country. Not an easy man to get along with but my god he got results, so the people that were coming here were the people who really wanted to get on and do well. He drove out the people who had been there for years and didn't really want to buy into his new ethos. So you end up in a room full of planners and they've all got really good ideas and it's exciting. "We're losing appeals on amenity space, how are we going to fix that?" "OK, well we could have balconies on flats". "OK, so we need evidence". So we draw up a questionnaire and we go and survey people who have recently moved into flats and ask them about how they are using amenity space. You build up that data, then we write a policy saying that we want balconies on flats, and

suddenly all new developments have balconies. You forget that that's not what it's like everywhere else, but it's so valuable. A little bit of space just to go out and get a breath of fresh air or sit out or put a plant on just to look out the window. It makes such a difference, and it was always like that, always pushing a bit further, a bit further.

We created such a fantastic atmosphere that you end up with people working away on a Friday night because we've got so many applications to deal with, but we're happy to do it because we know we're getting results. Eighty per cent in eight weeks was the target back in those days, and the boss was very driven about that. He went to the planning inspectorate, and they had a whole series of keycards and racks; each rack was a week, and as the appeals went through the system they moved them on a week, on a week, so they could see the ones that were out of time. He loved this, so we had this on the wall of the department, eight weeks and then a row at the end. Woe betide you if your application ended up on that row at the end because he'd come out of his office, pull all these cards out of the system and he'd wander round the office, throw the card on the table and say, "What's going on? Why has this gone out of date?" You had to have a good excuse because he was absolutely determined that we were going to meet all these targets and be the best authority. We didn't believe him at the time, but in hindsight we probably were the best district planning authority. Others, people who'd come from elsewhere, felt it was really good. We called it the Bakerdale way, the Bakerdale way of doing things, and it just meant that we were trying to get the best out of every single site. One I can think of, we had three public inquiries; we refused it, had an inquiry then they came back with a scheme that still wasn't good enough. We did that three times before finally they came with a scheme that we liked and they built it, and it won awards.

As I said, it was a golden age. What you had to do was quite achievable. Whereas over the years every time something happens the government says, "Oh, planning can deal with it". Transport, flooding, ecology, anything: "Oh, well, we'll just bolt it onto planning". It has become more and more difficult to deal with all these things, which are often conflicting. I feel sorry for the planners that are coming in today because the vast range of things they have to consider makes it really difficult. They don't have the same breathing space that we had to discuss applications and the room to manoeuvre. It's all very regimented and there's such a strong legal system, you're under so much more scrutiny. You're publishing everything on a website and groups who take against the scheme will do everything under the sun they can to try and frustrate it, so it is much more difficult. It was definitely, in my mind anyway, a lot easier back in the 1990s.' (Nick Alexander, Development Manager)

In outlining his experience, Nick is no doubt right in his assessment that planning has changed remarkably over the last twenty or thirty years. The culture he described at Bakerdale endures, however, continuing to be characterised by strong leadership and a desire to be at the forefront of change. In the present, and while she has been in post for a relatively short five years, Matilda believes strongly in the importance of planning and tries to nurture the planning culture. Matilda tries to absorb as much of the turbulence as she can, shielding her people so that they can get on with their good work. This is balanced by a no-nonsense pragmatism in relation to both planning's diminished influence and the budgetary impact of austerity. As noted in Section 4.1, the Go To programme emerged in response to moves in 2016 by the Conservative-led government to break the perceived 'monopoly' of the public sector within planning by legislating to allow 'alternative providers' in the private sector to process planning applications. Matilda notes:

> 'Bakerdale planning being Bakerdale planning, we thought if that's what the government is going to do, we've got to get with the programme; there's no point sitting here and saying this is dreadful. So we managed to get into some of the very early conversations with civil servants and one of them used us, because we're conveniently close to London, to get his head around the planning system. Because, of course, civil servants never know their subject, they are generalists by definition! That was really helpful because it gave us huge influence. We were receptive to his ideas and then took him out on site and showed him how it works. You could see him realising just how complex planning is. One of the conversations was, "Why do you need to do a site visit? Why can't you just use Google maps?" So we explained there might be a window in the flank wall and you don't know about the extension opposite and whatever. He said, "Why can't you just insure against that?" So if you make a decision that is wrong, the person claims against you and you just insure it. So you don't actually ever care about doing the right thing! Anyway, that was where his ministers were coming from.
>
> But we had the opportunity to show how it would work, and he was talking to other councils as well, and we went to a number of seminars in London. As things moved along this put the idea into my head: why can't we be the best planning authority? If other people are going to be able to determine applications in this area, why can't we be the one that they would go to? That's a bloody good thought! That's where it came from. We spent a year waiting for the government to decide whether it was going to do this crazy thing or not, and then they kicked it into the long grass. So at that point we said, "We need to prepare for competition because we don't know if this is coming back or not. If it's coming, we've got to be on the front foot, we've got to be ready for it".

Of course, I could only do that because people were receptive. Right at the beginning, at our next staff meeting, we had some workshop sessions about what the government's proposals meant and what we could do. The feedback was amazingly positive. It was all about how can we make this work. Not about why it's crap. I was quite staggered by that. I'd only been here a year or so at that point and I was really impressed that front-line staff weren't spending the time sitting there moaning; they were actually writing up on their flipcharts the practical things that they could do. I learned that the staff could, by and large, cope with the idea of doing something that was not in the mainstream of the way local government goes about change. So we decided we're going to do this, we're going to become the go-to provider, because why can't we be the place that gives people great service, good value for money. If somebody else can do that, we can do that.' (Matilda Weaver, Head of Planning and Sustainability)

A refrain heard again and again from the planners is that 'the only thing that is inevitable is change', and they express – outwardly at least – a desire to be at the forefront of change. Historically, for example, before initiating the Go To programme, they explored the possibility of setting the planning service up as a mutual company. The result would have seen the planners working at arm's length from the council, and the politicians would have shifted from being their masters to their clients. Ultimately this was a major sticking point as the members were uncomfortable about losing control. The Go To programme avoids this problem and others – such as a range of HR-related headaches – but similarly has roots in Bakerdale's desire to safeguard its work. As Matilda puts it, this introduction of free-market logics to the spaces of public planning was "just such a horrendous idea", but it is notable that it could not be challenged at a fundamental level as being inimical to the very reason for having public planning. Rather it had to be beaten in practice, on its own terms. This might be read as a symptom of Mark Fisher's 'capitalist realism', according to which he argues: 'Over the past thirty years, capitalist realism has successfully installed a "business ontology" in which it is *simply obvious* that everything in society, including healthcare and education, should be run as a business' (Fisher, 2009, p 17). That most planners went along with this new order, despite personal misgivings, might indicate a certain cynicism within the profession (see Fleming and Spicer, 2003).

4.7 Specialist advice in public-sector planning

Bakerdale is quite unusual in having kept a broad range of planning experts in-house. While most of the planners we have encountered so far are the archetypal generalists of local government, they are able to draw on the expertise of urban design, conservation,

Figure 4.3: The kitchen at Bakerdale

ecology and arboricultural specialists. This contrasts with many local authorities that now buy in this expertise from consultants. This is possible partly because of the development pressure within the district, but it does show the importance that is placed on this advice by the planning department in Bakerdale.[8]

Catching up on my field notes one morning, Andy Wilson comes over to ask if I would like a coffee. Yes, please! It turns out there's a real-coffee club, chipping in to buy real coffee as opposed to the instant stuff and then making up a cafetiere and sharing it around. I offer to help and while we're in the generic local authority kitchen (see Figure 4.3) making the coffee we chat about the project. It's reassuring that the planners get it, deeming it an interesting area to research at an opportune time. Andy wonders whether I might be interested in joining some of the planners who are going out for a drink and maybe a pizza later? Of course, thanks! I also get as close to dissent on Go To as I ever do at Bakerdale. Andy says he's fed up with it, but there's a caveat: when you think about the alternatives and what's happening in some authorities he loves it: "Go To? It's fantastic!"

Later on, I am able to attend the planning surgery. It sees the experts – arboricultural, ecology and conservation officers that Bakerdale feel privileged to mostly still have in-house – consulted on complex applications, clarifying how they will need to contribute to them, so they can be processed within the relevant timeframe (see Figure 4.4). The first application is in a rural location

Figure 4.4: The endless development-management decision-making process, with paper still in evidence despite digitisation

backing onto a river – the relevant planning officer comes in with drawings to introduce it – it seems to be a notorious historical location; previously there had been an ill-fated scheme for a care home on the site. Eventually that was written off because the applicant stopped engaging. A fresh application has come in for some flats, with parking, bin stores and so on. Things they need to think about are trees, conservation and ecology, and the right experts are brought in. It seems that the Environment Agency – presented as a law unto themselves – have identified some potential flooding issues for the site, and it is also speculated that a sustainable-drainage objection is probable. The conservation officer doesn't really have any concerns, suggesting that it's a pretty nondescript, scrubby area. The ecology officer steps in here – light-heartedly – to describe this as a habitat. He would like surveys of bats and badgers.

The conservation officer stays in the room while others are sent for. He is standing in temporarily – having previously worked for Bakerdale for a very long time – because the actual conservation officer is away on a long holiday. He is a consultant now and suggests Bakerdale is good to work with while many other authorities are terrible, particularly in London: all the good staff jump ship, leaving young planners with little experience and no clue. Phones ring forever; nobody gets back to you. He has one tall tale of a phone being answered: "How the bloody hell did you get my number?" is hollered at the caller before the phone is slammed down.

The next item is someone who wants to create a couple of ponds on their land in the AONB. It is land adjacent to a dwelling that previously was a manège. On the face of it, the ecology officer thinks it is not a bad thing, but there are some issues around people turning agricultural land in the AONB into a sort of designed garden. More emphatically, however, there is a suspicion that the applicants are trying to create a swimming pool by stealth. The cross-section that the applicant has helpfully supplied does indeed have a shallow end, a deep end and a jetty. It's not at all clear why they want to create these ponds – a contemporary craze for wild swimming is referenced. So the question is: When is a swimming pool not a swimming pool?[9]

4.8 Planners in the clubhouse

In this section, we witness interactions between Polly, a Bakerdale planner, and a private-sector counterpart as they visit a site together. This kind of constructive pre-application advice is not new to planning, but it is central to the Go To project. Accompanying Polly on this visit also provides us a chance to get reflections on the earlier meeting between Bakerdale and Rogers. Finally, we are able to see the planners in a more relaxed mode, as they get together for a drink after work. This gives a sense of the more informal ways in which workplace cultures and relationships are created and sustained.

I head out with Polly to a pre-app meeting where the applicant is paying for advice. The client in question is a golf club and they want to build a reservoir. The idea is that they will store water to help maintain the course during dry weather. On the way, she tells me about studying planning at Newcastle from undergraduate level. True to form, a careers adviser suggested it. Polly liked the vocational aspect, the idea that it would lead to a job. Her dad worked in construction, which she thinks might have been an influence. Her husband is also a planner, so they have a lot of planning chat at home. I also get some further background on the site. They recently built a driving range, which involved a lot of earth-moving, trucks coming in and out and has left local residents tetchy. She thinks the reservoir plan won't involve anything like that but we need to be braced for some local concern. The site is in the AONB, but given that it's already a golf course she doesn't think it's likely to be an issue.

In the clubhouse, Polly picks out the agent straight away. A smart older man in a burgundy tank top. She introduces me as a colleague from the university spending the week in the planning department. The agent gets the coffees. He has done planning applications for the golf course before and knows his stuff, talking us through the idea, where the reservoir is placed, why it makes sense. "Do you play golf?" he asks, before explaining that fairways shouldn't be too dry. He wants to keep the application as slim as possible and doesn't go in for unnecessary box-ticking. They've done some soil testing as there is a former landfill slightly up the hill, but there don't seem to be any problems. He's got an engineering firm to draw a helpful cross-section of the new reservoir. These can go in, but he stresses again that he's not a fan of "all the guff" you frequently have to put in these days. Polly thinks a slim application is a good idea too. She asks about landscaping around the site. He's keen to have plenty of nice planting to soften the effect and to pay a little more to create a habitat if possible – "A bit of seed costs nothing but can have a big impact." Polly gets reassurance about the impact of the works – there will be no earth coming in or out, just some plant on the first and last day.

There's some chat about this pre-app process. The agent thinks the fee is steep, much more than he was expecting. Polly alludes to the new process having been mandated from above. The client didn't really see the point of the pre-app but the agent thinks it's important to build relationships, to get a dialogue going rather than dropping an application on the planners out of the blue. Before we go out for a walk around he asks me who I am, what the project is. He gives me the benefit of his experience, which broadly aligns with our findings thus far: experienced people departing local government, leaving young planners out of their depth; too many cuts means planning departments are under-resourced. He describes some of the difficulties he's had in other authorities: stringing him along for ages and then refusing the application; waits and delays. He says Bakerdale are good. Somebody will give you some advice and you know they're sound. They've got their members to think about, of course, but if they know their committee and can give some indication of what way things might go that's much appreciated.

It's a beautiful day on site. Some trees have been cut down, presumably where the reservoir will be, and some left around it. We look from a number of angles. It's already an engineered landscape, they're just engineering it a bit more. The agent is personable, bantering with a golfer out on the course. Polly asks him if he used to be a planning officer. No, he was a chartered surveyor and became a partner in a firm that they sold to Abbey National; he stayed for five years but seems to have had some disagreement with management and gone out on his own, taking his clients with him. That was twenty-five years ago and he's never advertised for work; people come to him. It emerges that the council own the freehold for the golf course and that many years ago the local authority ran it. The agent describes a difficult climate for golf clubs, the need for everything to be first rate. Everyone seems satisfied that the application is going to be straightforward. If they send a few documents tomorrow Polly should be able to get the advice – on the new matrix – out sometime next week. Everyone shakes hands.

On the drive back we talk a little about the application. Polly supposes it is in the council's interest for the golf course to be successful, given that they own the freehold and the golf course will bring more money into the area. We chat a bit about changes in Bakerdale and planning education. I mention that most of our students now want to work in the private sector.[10] For the

Figure 4.5: The Bakerdale planning office

money, she supposes, and doesn't blame them. Polly likes the idea that she's providing a public service, and the pension is still good. She's sure that will disappear soon though.

Back in the main office (see Figure 4.5) – again, it's quiet – I have a bit more time to catch up on my field notes before Andy drops by at 5:30 pm. At the pub, we find some others already there. Leo, the urban designer, Sam Harris, Tina and Matilda. I try to get a round of drinks but nobody will let me, no doubt due to the impression I give of impoverished studentship. Matilda is relaxed in the presence of her planners, and they are relaxed with her, with no discernible difference in the tone of the conversation before and after she leaves, having bought a round and finished her sparkling water.

She and Tina – a policy planner – have been at a mediation day. They feel that they have accounted for themselves well and the developer has done himself no favours, an older man refusing to admit he ever got anything wrong and escalating things where he should back down.

People ask a little about my background, having done the planning master's and not become a planner – "It's never too late!" Matilda says. Andy buys a pizza and insists that everybody else has a slice, having chosen toppings in line with what folk said they did and didn't like. At first we are sitting in a courtyard area where the planners point out a bricked-up door in the adjacent listed building. Installed without permission by the taxi office that used to be there, the planners made them brick it up – victory! Moving inside, we discuss the planners' favourite budget supermarkets and note the conflict with the 'town centre first' policies they are in favour of at work.

4.9 Planners and politicians: the member site visits

This section explores the roles that elected members play within local-government planning, and adds to our sense of how planning is understood within local government more widely. It documents an additional facet of the culture at Bakerdale: that it prizes good relationships between officers and members. Considerable time and resources are given to facilitating these relationships and to keeping members well informed. It is also an opportunity to better understand a weakness of the Go To programme, whereby regardless of how much clients pay, the planners cannot guarantee that the members of the committee will vote in line with their advice.

As with all local planning authorities, regular meetings of the planning committee are at the heart of Bakerdale's routine. On the day preceding the monthly meeting, a minibus takes committee members to visit each site that will be under discussion. The case officer for each site attends too, to talk members through the proposal and their own report before answering questions that arise as the members look to gain a street-level understanding of the potential development. In the austerity era not all local authorities have a bus trip for members, but Bakerdale feel it is important.[11] As such, on my second full day in the field I find myself with a committee agenda, preparing to board the minibus. It is a useful opportunity to observe how the members and officers interact, and how they understand both their roles and the process.

As we cross the car park, Nick explains that many committee members do not come on the visits as they are at work. Some turn up in their cars for the bits they are interested in, as do local ward members who are not on the committee. True to form, then, the assembled members are mostly past retirement age, all white, all men. They seem cheery and I sense that they enjoy their outings on the bus. Nick introduces me and our research, pointing out that it is government funded, as it is felt more understanding is required into the role of the commercial sector. There may be a nod to the political composition of Bakerdale here, which is controlled by the party currently in power nationally. As only two local authorities are being looked at in detail, Nick suggests they are lucky to have me. The members take this as a sign of Bakerdale's planners being first rate, and congratulate Nick. Will we be looking into the role of developers? Nick says that the principal interest is in commercial planners but that he thinks we have quite a broad interest. I agree, asserting that while Nick is right, we are interested in the roles played by all the actors. I will later discover that some of the members have issues with developers.

Juliet is accompanying us in the minibus for the first application. She jokes that she hopes I don't get travel sick, the first couple of sites being in the district's far north and involving driving down some winding country roads. She chats away with the chair of the committee about her children. There are clearly good relationships between officers and members, who as we drive ask questions about what is happening with this or that site. I get a couple of dinner recommendations. Once Juliet has managed to convey to the driver where she wants to stop, she stands up to provide her introduction. The routine is always the same. The officer stands at the front, they hold up a big copy of the plans and they talk the members through why they have made their recommendation. The members ask questions, we get out and have a walk about, chatting and conferring.

On this site, which falls within an AONB, a few years ago the landowner put in an application to build a stable for horses. They built somewhat beyond what the plan suggested but nobody noticed. Now they have applied to convert the stable into a two-bedroom house. The planners told the owner that as their initial development was too big it does not have permission, so their current application would be treated not as a conversion but as a whole new application. Unfortunately for the planners, however, the owner was able to get a certificate of lawfulness to say that the building had been there for four years or more. As such it now must be treated as a conversion. The reasonable consensus from members is that the owner knew what they were doing; they are increasingly suspicious because more and more of this kind of thing seems to be happening. The members are displeased, not angry but keen to "close the loophole" if they can. Nick steps in to say that it is not a loophole: the legislation has been purposefully designed this way, this is what the government wanted. Do the members read between the lines to see the criticism of their own political party as they were clearly meant to? One of the councillors says that we must not give up and must try to oppose this sort of thing: "Don't let them get to you Nick!"

Walking around we get a closer look at the stable, which has a cavity wall and several windows. No sign of horses. Juliet says that officers ask more questions of buildings like this now. A member says that Bakerdale's new plan will look to increase the length of time a building like this would have to stand from four to ten years before it could get a certificate of lawfulness. They wanted to say twenty-five but the planning inspector said no. We notice some other stables on the far side of the field, they look a lot like this one. "There'll be a whole housing estate before we know it!" One member asks me if I have anything to do with architecture. He is disappointed with my answer because in his opinion buildings are awful these days – everywhere is being made horrendous!

Sites two and three are in suburban Bakerdale. While relatively minor in the grand scheme of things, these two applications, just a couple of doors apart, have caused a great deal of consternation. The street is of semi-detached and detached houses with garages, built in the 1960s or '70s. One application is for the addition of a pitched roof to a garage, the other for an extension to the side and rear. The pitched roof is contentious as it will be the first one on the street, setting a precedent and in the eyes of the residents being out of character. Issues with the second application revolve around its effect on neighbours' gardens. The councillor for this ward has turned up. We have been asked to go and stand in the various gardens so we can better understand. The members struggle to see the point of this but agree that it should be performed for the public. Half go one way and half the other. From the rear it is clear that nearby houses also have prominent extensions. While it might be understandable that some locals are fed up with this, it also seems unlikely that it can be stopped now.

The bigger extensions might not have been approved in the past, before permitted development (PD) rights were extended.[12] A member of the public engages Nick. He has a list of things to get off his chest: frustration at another local development; annoyance that some travellers have parked up nearby; and anger that someone on the street is allegedly running a car-repair business from their garage. While much of this is outside of the planners' remit, Nick listens, being the face of the council. I sense that opposition to these applications could be a channel for a number of local and personal resentments. On the way back to the bus I'm able to have a brief chat with Jane – one of the planners – mainly about what I'm doing, how long I'm here. She says she has been a planning officer "for a million years", at Bakerdale for four. It is a good local authority, with good managers who know what they're doing. I am yet to hear a dissenting voice.

We drive towards site four, which is on what was once a council estate, although most of the homes have now probably been sold via the right to buy. The chair of the committee is talking about growing up in the area; he points out the school he went to and the route he walked. It seems, once again, that there is some public concern with this particular site. It is on a cul-de-sac, currently a three-bedroom semi-detached house with a drive. The houses are arranged around a small green with a tree on it. The effect of this is spoiled by the cars parked wherever there is space, car ownership having clearly outstripped the original design. Coming from a city I have been struck by how in Bakerdale it is assumed that a household will have at least two cars.

The proposal is to turn the house into two three-bedroom flats – potentially doubling the number of occupants in the building – and pave over the front garden for more parking. There is a lot of concern among the members about this proposal. The upstairs flat in particular will be very small. The size of the open-plan kitchen/living spaces lead them to believe that the applicant may hope to create two homes in multiple occupation (HMOs). While concern about HMOs is high in Bakerdale, here there are also design concerns. Downstairs a bedroom is underneath an upstairs living room/kitchen, and another bedroom is up against the new parking spaces, its window close by the stairs to the upstairs flat. Winston, the case officer, is sympathetic to their concerns, but unfortunately these are not planning matters. A question is asked about the minimum space standards coming in the new plan – these are nationally determined standards that councils can choose to write into plans. Bakerdale's new plan also has a policy to ensure common rooms in HMOs. The proposed flats would meet neither of these standards, but the new plan is yet to be adopted. A discussion ensues about the potential for removing PD rights to prevent the conversion of the flats into HMOs, reinforcing the sense that this kind of proposal is not what members like to see. As the discussion continues I begin to wonder about whether there is a dark side to the heartening focus on quality around atypical families and Eastern-European immigrants.

Today's final site is adjacent to what were once watercress meadows. En route we pass a recreation ground and see some large houses on a ridge opposite the site. One of these is occupied by a former councillor. Residents are unhappy with the proposal to situate forty lodge homes – high-end static caravans – opposite their houses. The land is owned by the council. Way back it was a waste disposal site, then for many years allotments, until it was discovered that the soil was badly contaminated. High levels of lead are mentioned. This leaves the council in a bind over what to do with it. Their commercial section are currently offloading assets and have put in this application for what they think is an appropriate use, assuming the site is capped with 60 mm of concrete. This puts the planners in an interesting position as, in one sense, the council is negotiating with itself. The main concerns have been around crime, particularly around an old railway-line-turned-footpath that runs along the back of the site. This means that the designers have been prevented from making a through route, which could give criminals an easy get-away from either the lodge homes or the dark and secluded footpath.

There are lots of queries. About the contamination: How bad is it? How safe is the capping? The answers: pretty bad, very safe. Can they create a condition to make the park homes for over-fifties. "Not a planning matter", says Jane, but whoever buys the site could impose that condition if they wish. Furthermore, as you can't get a mortgage to buy lodge homes, it would probably happen anyway. One member asks whether the council could house all those currently living in bed-and-breakfast accommodation here. Nick answers this, saying that they are currently bringing forward other sites for this purpose and this out-of-town location would not be ideal. I'm left impressed by the members: they are engaged with key issues, both within Bakerdale and within planning.

We get off the bus for a walk around. It seems that the former councillor, now an angry resident, could be trouble. The chair of the planning committee asks if I'll be going to the committee. "Perhaps you could sit in the gallery with a stun gun and deploy it at an opportune moment?" We walk around the back of the site and some way down the former railway line. A councillor points out a former sewage works that is now covered in high-end Barrett-style homes. Another councillor interjects that it was also a paper mill, "not *just* a sewage works". The members seem pleased with the new estate and question how dangerously secluded the path can really be. Jane says part of the issue is the difficulty of escaping if you're attacked. On the way back to the bus I ask a councillor how long he's been on the committee. Twelve years; it's interesting but difficult. He says he lost his cabinet seat because he was in charge of bringing the reserved sites forward a few years ago; colleagues were not very happy. You can't please everyone.

We head back to the office, where I attend the committee chair's briefing, a short meeting to ensure everything is in order. The main business is for the officers who will service tomorrow's meeting to brief the chair and the planners on who is speaking when – objectors, applicants, agents – tomorrow there will be someone speaking on every item. Everyone seems to be dreading a long meeting, but they also seem to relish it a little bit, as a one-off chance to perform and share in both working hard and being irked. I also sense that they think this is what it is all about, keeping the wheels of local government and the planning machine turning.

Discussion also covers which items are likely to be contentious, factoring in the mood of members on the bus. The meeting is informal, including gentle jokes, particularly about the former councillor and the lodge homes and one or two particularly pompous citizens, frequently imagined as being angry about something else but venting via the planning process. The young guy providing admin support is considering having a back-up plan in case the gallery fills up. Everyone tells him not to bother. Something will be on telly or it will be raining and in the end we will be lucky to have four or five attendees.

4.10 Planning and local politics: the committee

This section complements the last, moving from observing officer-member relations in a more informal mode, as local politicians begin to make up their minds on site, to observation of how those relations and decision-making processes are performed for the public. The section speaks closely to our interest in the purpose and nature of contemporary planning work, particularly what has endured and remained the same over time. It also raises important questions around the commercialisation agenda, however, as given how planners' room for manoeuvre has become smaller with their diminished political influence and the wide acceptance of managerial and neoliberal logics, we might see that the buck stops with decision-making processes in the context of local government. From here we might wonder whether local politicians now stand as final guardians of the public interest and ask what role will be left for planning expertise and judgement.

The Bakerdale District Council chamber is pleasingly retro: green baize, polystyrene ceiling tiles and red brick; a picture of the queen looks down on us. Everything is well amplified, a number of screens and projectors are available showing pictures from the sites. I sit with members of the public, more than twenty of whom have turned out. The first item on the agenda is the splitting of the three-bedroom house into two three-bedroom flats. Winston introduces the application, then the public objector speaks. He has three minutes and is objecting, he says, on behalf of many people with concerns. While the building is not officially an HMO, it seems they feel that it is operating as one at present. They believe that this is also the plan for the future and have concerns about parking and sewerage – the drains have already been blocked once, apparently because they are not built for this level of occupancy. Nobody speaks in support of the application.

One of the ward councillors has come to speak, and does so, largely in an incoherent fashion about Sir Walter Raleigh – the building is on Raleigh Close. When the committee members take over they are concerned about the creation of bad housing and also about the HMO issue. There are references to "proper families" and "family homes". At one point, I hear a member of the public ask their companion, "What was he on about?" They snigger. Parking is another big issue; they speculate about two people inhabiting every bedroom and twelve new cars appearing on Raleigh Close. The design is bad and one member dubs it "unfit for human habitation". Winston reacts to the discussion, clarifying that if the new plan was in place this would not meet the space standards. The vote is to defer, going back to the applicant to review the design. Perhaps when it comes back the new plan will have been adopted and they will have more teeth to reject it.

Next up is the stable. After Juliet's introduction, the objector also states that he is speaking for himself *and* for other concerned parties. He speaks against brazen applicants but is cut off mid-sentence when his three minutes are up. To make the case for the development, the applicant and her agent share the three minutes between them. The applicant stresses that she has lived in the district her whole life and that she and her husband plan to downsize, moving into the development themselves, freeing up their current house for a family. The agent stresses that there is technically nothing wrong with the application. Members are concerned, but worry that there is little they can do about this in planning terms. One member stands out by taking a different line from his colleagues, telling them that they have had their powers curbed because in the past they would reject perfectly sensible development. This means they now have to support this sort of thing. He thinks it is high time they started positively developing rural areas where people are keen to live. He is countered by a colleague who refers to this as "development by stealth". There is a proposal to refuse, which is carried ten votes to one.

At the halfway point we take a break. The chair approaches me for a chat. He says his aim is to draw out the relevant points somewhere during the discussion. He thinks they should have just refused the flats that they deferred, although it does give the applicant a chance to rethink. He also suggests they will get an appeal on the stable application. I agree. He does not mind; they will have done everything they can and then it will be up to the inspector.

The contaminated allotment site with the 'park homes' is up next. Two objectors share the three minutes. The former councillor is first. A big guy with a northern accent, he shouts out his objection, arguing that the proposal is totally inappropriate and has dangerous traffic implications. He gives the impression of enjoying being back in the chamber. His neighbour is more measured, introducing the points she is going to make – largely policy oriented – as if debating at the Oxford Union. Again, however, and to her irritation, the clock runs out. A couple of the members withdraw from this debate because they have conflicting interests. It's not clear what these are. Those that do speak are worried about the contamination but feel there are no other options for the site. It seems like a sensible proposal. They add a design condition before voting by a majority to approve the application. The former councillor is grinning and chortling as he walks out. No doubt he expected to be voted down.

Next up is the pitched roof. It seems that most of the people in the gallery have come for this item – they have had a long wait – and are presumably interested in the following item too. Both the objector and the applicant speak; the applicant is an articulate Asian woman with a headscarf. There is a lot of restlessness when it is suggested that other houses on the street have been changed and modified, and the folk in the gallery are vocally annoyed when the pitched roof is unanimously approved.

It doesn't get any better for the assembled citizens as we move on to the extension application. The argument is familiar: other houses have been extended, this house can be extended. There is discussion among members about the gap between the properties, it should be at least a metre, but their measuring suggests it is 80 cm. Winston gets a ruler out, he confesses he has not measured it on site and makes it 90 cm from the plan. A metre is not a hard and fast rule, so this would not be a reason to turn it down now. A member says he was concerned about this extension but when he went into the garden and saw how big some of the others were he felt powerless to stop it. The applicants from the previous application have stayed in the gallery and are clearly amused by their neighbours' consternation. The extension is approved unanimously.

Walking back to my hotel, passing the surprising number of rough sleepers in Bakerdale, I think more about the divide between the councillors who want to develop and the ones who want to conserve, about how fissures emerge in outwardly politically homogeneous authorities and the possible implications for planning and commercialisation. Perhaps a big part of making the Go To agenda possible is the fact that members, who want to be enfranchised to refuse development they think is unsuitable, need good relationships with knowledgeable officers who know their patch. No doubt it would be harder with a Theta planning robot (see Chapter 2).

4.11 Charles Street, plannerly pragmatism and negotiation in contemporary public practice

This extended episode documents our engagement with Charles Street, a mid-sized development that we follow as it develops over a period of months, and with Lee Strong, the senior planner taking it forward. As well as adding to our understanding of the scope and limits of the commercialisation agenda, it is an opportunity to see interactions between local authority planners and the development sector at close quarters. This provides a nuanced account of how negotiations can work around larger schemes, and points to the meaning of 'pragmatism' in contemporary practice.

I

"What's your shoe size?" Lee Strong asks. We are heading to Charles Street, a sizeable development in progress that he thinks will be interesting to follow. I have a few minutes to look over the plans while he finds me some appropriate safety footwear. The development is in a conservation area on the less posh side of town, at one time the industrial district. Part of the site is being preserved and part rebuilt to provide 230 one- and two-bed flats. The design makes a virtue of the industrial heritage. Feeling almost like a real planner in my newfound hard hat, boots and hi-viz, Lee briefs me as we walk. We are going to meet Amber, from the developers. There are some conditions related to demolition that they might not have been following, starting to knock something down before they've done something else. The conditions are stringent because the site is in a conservation area.

At Charles Street, only a huge red-brick industrial building remains. The site manager shouts over to us. We sign in; Amber isn't here yet. Some roof slates are on the table for Lee to look at: samples of the old tiles, which tend to shatter when they're taken off, and of the ones they want to replace them with. It looks like a pretty good match to me. The site manager arrives and asks if we want to have a walk round. He is from Leeds and works for a big demolition company. While this work goes on, he lives on site in a caravan. His hands are black with dirt, and he's wearing an enormous gold bracelet on one wrist and a diamond earing. He is a good talker, explaining what has been knocked down and when, issues to do with retaining walls and the like. We walk over to a building that used to house interesting little artisans and clubs. The side of it is missing and soon the rest of it will be too. Lee explains that the council are developing a bespoke space the former tenants can move to if they want. They have had some problems with people breaking into the site. Some homeless people – who used to live here – got in over the back wall and started a fire, which inadvertently spread to some boxes. "To be fair to them, like, they rang the fire brigade." To try and keep a lid on this kind of thing all sorts of sensors and cameras have been installed.

Amber has arrived but she's not dressed for walking around so goes to wait for us in the canteen. We head into the building; they have had to clear out a lot of stuff from the squatters and drug users who were in there before. The floors are now big empty expanses, ready for the next important job: making the whole thing watertight. We get all the way to the roof via a complex of ladders and stairs. There's an impressive view of one side of the valley from the top of the building. Lee is unsure about the merit of the red-brick, former council houses that comprise most of it though.

We head back down and meet Amber. She's a character: straight talking, wicked smile, so posh she doesn't care. She clearly enjoys bantering with the demolition guy and he clearly enjoys bantering with her. When Lee makes a point, she often follows up with "That's true" or "That's correct". They talk about how things are progressing and the processes for moving them along, the conditions that they've maybe not been following, and there is some amicable debate about how to interpret the detail. The developer wants to play ball, now at least, and there is a discussion about how to go about approving the tiles they've chosen. Lee says it looks good to him. Amber wonders whether there is a process for signing these things off after the job is done. Some of these things have to be based on trust, Lee says, with the caveat that if it wasn't right and somebody noticed there would be trouble.

They discuss the process for making a big Community Infrastructure Levy (CIL)[13] payment that is due soon, another one that has perhaps been expected already but not arrived. Amber asks some questions about the CIL payment, what it goes on and such. Lee explains the process, how there is a bidding procedure within the council for things like road improvements that folk think will be useful. It emerges that normally the annual CIL fund is about £4 million. Amber laughs; her scheme will be contributing about half of this. Based on some of the other developments in Bakerdale, though, I think they could be expecting quite a lot more than £4 million this year.

The next stage of the project will be delivered under a system called design and build, which Lee hates. Amber is curious; it works well for developers. The system means that somebody bids for the work, providing a price for the materials and delivery. Obviously people want to put in the lowest bid possible, but this makes them prone to cut corners later, providing a lot of headaches for the planners. A way around this is to specify the materials in the contract. The demolition guy asks about when he will be able to progress to the next stage of construction. Lee explains that once he gets confirmation of what tiles they will use on the roof he can turn it around in a couple of days. It's an eight-week process, he says, but he doesn't work in eight-week processes; when it comes in, he'll send it out. Everyone's pleased about that.

Lee is happy with how the meeting went. The important thing is that they know that he knows what is going on and that he conveys that they must not start excavating for drains yet, which they've agreed. As we walk, Lee points out recent developments, quite a lot of them on the council's land, which they are steadily disposing of. We take in 'the Containers'. The clue is in the name: shallow foundations, which are cheap, shipping containers sat on top and renovated; they're about six wide and four high at the minute, still being done up and made suitable for habitation. The rents will be low and enterprises displaced by the Charles Street development will get first dibs on a space. The idea is to incubate start-up businesses and support community groups. Lee says it's good that things are starting to happen on this side of town, development that will bring more development in its wake. He seems proud of his job in helping to facilitate this. A dyed-in-the-wool pragmatist. Getting the Charles Street development going did involve giving as well as taking on the part of the council. I push him for specifics but he doesn't really go there, although I guess that it might be affordable housing as he mentions how they hope that the flats will be more affordable for people on account of not being on a premium site.

//

Around a month after our site visit, I attend a meeting about Charles Street's PPA. I head over to meet Lee, who is pulling various papers together – a performance of being a bit disorganised that belies the fact that he's on it. We head out to the reception to meet Amber, who is accompanied by her architect. Lee must sort out a pass for them to get into the staff car park, so

I show them up to the meeting room. It is good to feel useful, but I am glad that Amber has been there before. After a few minutes Lee arrives. Now Amber will need to move her car. I volunteer to be helpful again. On our drive around the corner she tells me that she sits on a conservation board which is currently looking at a lot of development the council is bringing forward themselves. "It's a conflict of interest, isn't it? Deciding their own planning applications?"

Back in the meeting room Lee and the architect are discussing bricks. Some of the materials are fine, but the bricks are not. Could it be a dud sample? One of the conditions is that larger sample panels will be available on site. Lee begins saying that he could meet them on site to look at this before stating, "Actually I can't". This is a reference to the elephant in the room. He's not yet been paid. Amber assures him that it will all be fine by the end of the meeting today. We move on to drainage. Lee has been chasing Thames Water and the Flood Authority. Presumably this chasing will also be grinding to a halt if some money is not forthcoming. Next up, the mast for the antennae that will need to be temporarily relocated. Lee has found out that this will need planning permission because it is twenty-five metres tall. "Good to know", says Amber. He advises they get a temporary permission for two years: "With the best will in the world there might not be a building in eighteen months." This is a reference to the fact that the antennae will be transferred to the roof of the new building once it is finished. "Who should apply?" Amber wonders. She should, although there is some discussion about whether a slightly shorter mast might not need planning permission. Amber seems taken by this idea but Lee seems to be of the opinion that getting the permission for the temporary mast is not going to be a huge issue, so it might not be worth their while to try and source something else. We move onto the atrium. This will link two buildings and is another contentious aspect of the development. There is debate about fire regulations and design issues. There are cost implications and ventilation requirements. Amber is concerned about the fire people agreeing to it. Lee suggests that it will be fine to give them a sort of ultimatum – this is our proposal, if we've not heard back from you in so much time, we will assume you are happy with it.

Next, we talk about conditions. Amber thinks the definitions of a lot of them are "a bit vague". There has been confusion around how the developer shows that things have happened, driven by the county council signing off an archaeological survey without Bakerdale knowing about it. The developer had assumed that the district and the county would be talking to each other. This is not so, and Lee stresses that Bakerdale are the planning authority and everything needs to be sent to them too, as Lee needs to ensure that things are signed off on. One plan the developer currently has is to fill a void with concrete, and there is a worry that the void is not within the "red edge" (the red outline that determines the site in the plan). In a way it is reassuring that they are concerned about this, as Lee points out that most developers would just say yes, it is inside the red edge, and get on with it.

Finally, that elephant resurfaces. "I know you're due some cash", says Amber. "Overdue some cash", says Lee. It is coming. Somewhat outlandishly her boss insists on signing all of the cheques himself, which is why there is a delay. Now it is clear that this means Lee will stop engaging, Amber will be able to hurry him along. Part of the issue is that the boss thinks the cost is high and doesn't really understand what he's paying for. Amber asks how the fee is decided. Lee explains that it's agreed at the beginning and the signed documents exist to show that the developer has approved it. From now he won't do anything until they have paid – he suggests he probably shouldn't be having this meeting. He's good at generating goodwill by cultivating a slightly freewheeling persona. Amber asks what seems to be a jokey question about whether he has to cost his time in ten-minute slots like a solicitor. "Five minutes actually", Lee says. They are shocked. He explains that he has two time sheets. One for when he gets in, goes to lunch, comes back and goes home. Another in which he logs everything he does all day; the smallest segment is five minutes. If an application comes in and he assigns it to someone in his team, that's a five-minute job. "Interesting!" Amber says. "We want to know what we spend our time doing", says Lee. And, presumably, how much everything costs.

III

The following month we return to Charles Street, and Lee updates me as we walk. He had to down tools for a while, but the developer has paid so meetings can resume. Yesterday he was at a conference about good placemaking and delivering high-quality design, but he will be on holiday for most of next month: "I've been here twenty years now so I'm going to have some time off."

On site, the issues around payments don't seem to have soured relationships. There is handshaking and banter about the roof, which is on but still covered in red plastic protective covering. "We're thinking of leaving it red", says a guy from the developer who is accompanying Amber and the architect. Heavy set, he has a northern accent and gives the impression of being hard-nosed but also liking a joke; his favourites revolve around cutting corners and making savings on the development. White uPVC windows are mentioned. Lee has a good line in counter-banter; it is fine for them to leave the roof red as he'll be able to pick it out easily when he's watching them from his garden. He is going to be off next month, he says, mainly pottering around the house.

The discussion focuses on details: the atrium, where glass will cover the stairway at either end but the middle will be left open; the effect of the louvres that will be in the stairwells: a fire precaution to prevent smoke collecting. The northerner cannot see the sense in this: with walkways running the whole length of the building and the middle of the atrium open, you are not going to choose to go down the stairs at the end where the fire is. We look at some brick samples, textured ones that are an improvement on the last ones we saw. Also paving colours – about which everyone has a different opinion – and ornamental-tree pit sizes. They are waiting to hear from the flood authority. Amber asks about the site over the road. Lee explains that he has reduced the time they will have to start the work from three to two years, to "kick them up the arse". Amber approves.

There is some salty discussion about PD rights. The northerner says they are converting some offices and Lee pretends to spit on the floor. The developer feigns outrage: "We've won building control awards for our PD!" "Building control! But does anyone want to live in them?" Lee retorts. The developer says that in his opinion PD can be done really well but "the cowboys have ruined it for everybody". This forms part of wider discussions around market issues. Developers are feeling the pinch. They talk about a metal fence that Lee doesn't seem keen on and some changes to the car park, which was to be two storeys and is now one. They are happy for Lee to hear the rationale around cost savings, but it won't really look any different so it is probably fine. "How do we formalise it?" asks Amber, making sure to nail down what she can do to move things forward.

More banter follows about responsibility for the road alongside the site. "There are council street lights on it", they tell Lee. It is not in a great state, however, so the council are clearly not keen on taking responsibility, presumably hoping that those developing the buildings on either side will sort it out. After running through Section 106[14] and CIL details and the relationship with the county council, we turn to the telecoms mast that the developer is still trying to sort out. This is slow and painful; the latest idea is that they can temporarily move it to the roof of the hospital. We wrap up with discussion about the contamination work they need to do. This is very important for Lee; they can't just start digging because there's a risk that they will contaminate the main aquifer. The developer side have a brief chat among themselves about how they have said they will do some sampling. If they have promised to take a sample from under the building, says the man developer, somebody is getting sacked. Another joke? Do it properly is the message from Lee.

On the way back we dissect the meeting, how the developer-side want to appear to be pushing their luck sometimes and not others and the strategic implications. Lee seems to appreciate this as a kind of shadowboxing in which everyone has a role. He says he has key things that he needs to get across, particularly today around contamination. They will have to send the proof that they have had the work done properly.

4.12 Conclusion

The commercialisation of the planning service at Bakerdale colours much that happens there. Contrary to our initial thoughts, it has been executed sensitively and in broad terms, especially regarding larger developments, is fairer in its execution than it first appears. A new and clearer website is a key supporting feature, providing readier access to easily understood information. Nevertheless, there is confusion created by the new matrix of client and customer types. As noted in our introduction, the gap between planning's normative justifications and the outcomes realised through its day-to-day practices has perhaps always been wider than some might like to admit, and it is hard to see how further capitulation to neoliberal logics can do anything but entrench this.

As such, it is worthwhile to look more closely at the wider implications of the Go To project and Bakerdale's culture of embracing, and leading, change. A history of good leadership in the planning service is underpinned by certain values and a desire to do 'good' planning, to look out for issues of social and environmental justice. This progressive approach softens the edges of commercialisation processes, ensuring a degree of public interest is retained. On the one hand, commercialisation might not be seen as either good or bad but rather judged on the details of its execution and the ability of officers to retain a degree of discretion around the rules. On the other hand, we might not only point to what is lost in consistently giving way to neoliberal, ideological impositions on public-sector planning, but also to what it tells us about the UK planning profession in the early twenty-first century. If planners in the past could set the terms of debate, or at least give the impression of doing so, this is no longer the case. In Bakerdale we can see how this is driven at both smaller and larger scales in planning's diminished role within the state, in its political marginalisation and in the widespread acceptance of this, including appreciation for managerial and neoliberal logics, at the level of individual planners in particular workplaces.

By way of proof, we must sadly also note that Bakerdale Council is no more. It was reorganised out of existence a year after our fieldwork ended as part of a drive for greater efficiency, merging with a larger authority. We hope some of the positive aspects of its culture survived the merger, as might the deep, useful, local knowledge held by its planning officers and councillors. Our account provides evidence that efficiency savings might come at the expense of a range of less-tangible things that in the long run it might not be in the public interest to lose.

5

OIP: the 'regular' planning consultancy

OIP is a medium-sized, wholly UK-situated planning consultancy. The northern branch where we did our research has a strong regional presence and some specialisms, such as strategic planning, which serve a national function for the company. It is an organisation very much staffed by professional planners, in contrast to our multi-disciplinary case documented in Chapter 3.

We spent several months following the core team of planners. The chapter explores the realities of organisational ethnography in planning. It connects to our central themes of privatisation and commercialisation of planning processes, including business practices up close, and the nature of planning work, focusing particularly on how different knowledges are deployed in planning work and the contribution of the private sector in this regard. The case also sheds light on issues of work-life balance, the role of age, class and gender in the workplace, the value of 'banter' among colleagues and in wider communities of practice and the significance of organisational culture. In short, it allowed us to see close at hand 'everyday' planning work from a private-sector perspective.

5.1 Introduction

OIP's offices are in the Suffusion Centre, a soulless newish development of the kind Owen Hatherley (2010) described as the New Ruins, on a busy road on the edge of the city centre. We are on the ground floor and the windows are grubby, which we point out as a misjudged icebreaker to the receptionist. It seems to do the trick: she offers to make us tea, a deep-brown, no-nonsense brew.

We are ushered into a room off reception (see Figure 5.1). This is a fairly generic office environment, in common with most of the others we encountered (see Chapters 2, 3 and 4), and while we wait for David a series of projects roll past on a screen, some big, others small; some look great, others pretty standard. Later, David describes a varied mix of work, perhaps less 'exposed' to housing than other planning consultancies. Underneath the screen nestles a presentation pack of OIP Beer with a glass, commissioned from a local brewery owned by a relative of an OIP employee. It's harder to imagine Simpsons doling out bottles of beer to clients.

Figure 5.1: The OIP meeting room

David arrives, replacing our primary contact, Stanley, who has been at the high court longer than expected. In his email, Stanley described David as 'one of my directors'. In his late thirties, his accent is hard to place. We outline the project. David has looked at our website and seems enthused.

The meeting is friendly, constructive. Midway, I notice a window cleaner arrive. David agrees that OIP fills a gap in our case studies. We suggest general shadowing plus some 'episodes' to follow. David's suggestions overlap with Stanley's: an appeal at Overwood in a couple of months and a scheme with Alison, at Undercliff, going to planning committee soon. David consults diaries on his laptop as he makes the list. They have a weekly team meeting I can attend next week to kick everything off and finalise the episodes.

For a moment David has a predatory look in his eyes when discussing projects. Another time he mentions the "goalkeepers' union" of planners (see Chapter 2) – united against the NIMBYs (not in my back yard) and politicians. We pick up some exasperation about local authority planners.

5.2 Commercial consultancy as seen from the shop floor

The first day in the field at OIP provides a grounding in the day-to-day life of a private-sector firm. As well as providing insight into the substance and rhythm of commercial work, we encounter the relationships between staff, the culture of the organisation and the importance placed on traits such as agility, initiative and work ethic. We also note the challenges of doing ethnographic work in such environments.

I arrive for 9:30am, with time for a tour and introductions before the 10 am team meeting. On arrival, Sophie, the receptionist, says she's expecting me, shows me the kitchen and says I can put my lunch in the fridge. This seems odd as I should only be here for a couple of hours – there's the team meeting, then a chat to pin down projects to follow and get dates in the diary.

We move into the main office, a big space with four rows of desks that houses all the staff. Sophie is trying to announce me to the room; it is not really working. David says he thinks this is better done in the meeting. He shows me to a desk. Have I brought a laptop? No. I start to wonder: am I being invited to stay all day? Did the email suggest this? I play along.

David introduces the people sitting around the table. Olivia, who runs the office, and Tony, the regional director: "I float around", Tony says. "Not a nice way to describe yourself", David grins. I sense that the banter might flow thick and fast in the commercial sector. It is now 9:35 am, and while most desks are occupied, it is very quiet in the office. The rows are set up in the same way as Bakerdale but there is more permanent stuff around – folders, files, kids' drawings. David has his trainers under his desk. I notice a desk plan has been provided to help me understand who's who, but it is hard to orient myself. I assume I am on the desk labelled 'hotdesk'.

Hot by name and nature – the office is like a greenhouse. Olivia has an umbrella up to shield her from the sun as one of the blinds is broken. As I acclimatise, we inch towards 10 am. I wonder how we will all fit into the small meeting room. One guy in the office is dressed very casually compared to everyone else – T-shirt and jeans versus smart and business-like, although there are no ties.

We shuffle into the meeting room. Some people head into a different room to talk about something else though, which suggests there are more important things than attending the team meeting. I sit next to Dan: young, fresh faced, probably a recent graduate. We are tightly packed around the table, people arriving later bring chairs with them. Olivia leads the meeting, inviting me to introduce myself. There is gratifying nodding as I do my spiel. Then we go round the table, first with people saying where projects are up to, describing leads they have picked up on. It is quick, hard to follow, description being limited to the name of the place and a sentence or two. Some projects are small fry and people are glad a couple have fallen through, particularly some Velux windows in a conservation area. There is a clear distinction between the younger and the older planners.

We move on, sharing diaries. It feels like looking busy is the name of the game. Dan has a handwritten crib sheet to make sure he doesn't forget anything, while others are a bit more laid back, expressing their busyness through wincing and yearning for holidays. We go around again to talk about tenders, discussing whether some of them are worth it. Sophie and one of the young female planners also fill us in on marketing. One of the things everyone must respond to is networking. Dan seems pleased to be going to Junkyard Golf, a joint social between the Royal Town Planning Institute

(RTPI) Young Planners and Women in Property under the header 'Aspire, Succeed, Inspire', sponsored by Savills, Bouygues UK and Linden Homes.

As the meeting draws to a close, David stresses that this is the only day Stanley is in for some time, "so if you need him grab him". I feel the tone relax. Dan and David have stayed up late to watch *Game of Thrones*. Others panic about spoilers, while the uninitiated wonder whether it's worth it. We move onto some fish that live in the office. They have taken to jumping out of their bowl. Olivia, laughing, says that they were supposedly the low-maintenance option. Sophie, in charge of the fish, comes into her own, describing how one jumped behind the fire extinguisher. Dan came to the rescue but dropped the fire extinguisher on his foot.

The directors have a supplementary meeting. As I loiter in the corridor David asks me what I want to follow. I am put on the back foot, as I could hardly tell where one project ended and another began. I mention the ones we already discussed – Undercliff and Overwood. "Yeah, grab Alison and Stanley for those". "Stanley is in there", he points to the other meeting room. Grabbing doesn't come naturally to me, however, especially as I'm still not sure who Alison and Stanley are. I feel apprehensive as I return to my seat to look at the seating plan and wait for Stanley. After a while, I conclude that I might have to be more assertive in finding stuff to follow. I go over to the row behind me where the younger planners sit.

I rehash my precis and ask whether anyone has anything I can follow. Prolonged silence. Eventually, a planner called Henry kindly offers up something he is taking to planning committee in a neighbouring authority next week: it's been a prolonged application, a listed building, "lots of little things". I am effusive: "Brilliant. Amazing. Perhaps you could talk me through it later, if you've got a few minutes?" He agrees and I return to my seat, pleased to have got an episode to follow.

But what to do now? I check my emails, turning off the second, extra-large screen. I think again about whether planning resists ethnography, a kind of work that is hard to follow because if you are not in a meeting or on site you are typing. But is that any different to other office-based work?

The directors' meeting is over and they are back at their desks. David does a tea round, I offer to assist. Henry has told David that I'll go to planning committee with him, presumably asking permission. David thinks the application is interesting; no big issues but things keep going wrong with it. We talk briefly about five-year land supply, about Overwood. I notice that David laughs a lot – sometimes out of nervousness but mainly from the absurdity of it all – he has a dry sense of humour and is adept at carrying multiple cups at once.

Back at my desk, I am unable to grab Alison as she is on the phone. A few minutes later, I notice her striding out of the door, coat on. Am I out of my comfort zone? More so than at Bakerdale? Is it a private-sector thing? The

Figure 5.2: Stanley's desk

need to perform your worth? Time moves on and I am both struggling to look busy and getting hungry, Stanley and whoever else is in the meeting room have been in there for two and a half hours so I leave to get lunch.

On my return, I am happy to see the meeting is over. I sit down, assuming Stanley, who I have still never met, will come over and introduce himself, or David might introduce him. After a while I look at my seating plan, I glance over my shoulder and realise that the guy in the casual clothing must be Stanley. I think about the stress that has been put on 'grabbing people'. Deciding that perhaps I should do just that, I walk over. Stanley stares steadfastly at his screen (see Figure 5.2).

"Hi Stanley, pleased to meet you". Stanley continues to stare at the screen for slightly longer than I think is polite. "Hi", we shake hands, "I was going to get together with you when Biff gets back". Biff is another person I don't know. Stanley seems like one of those middle-aged men who can steadfastly only focus on one thing at a time; if they try to think about something else they pinch the bridge of their nose, sigh and then they give up. "Of course, yeah, no problem".

I return to my desk and think about the absurdity of earning a living acting awkwardly in other people's workplaces. David is making more tea so I go in for round two. He makes a joke about making tea and I'm able to reference the myriad ways that planners organise tea making (Schoneboom and Slade, 2020). He is not a fan of the 'every man for himself' approach, "I hate that, all a bit mercenary." Olivia comes into the kitchen. She criticises the fact that teabags are still floating around in mugs to which he has now added milk. Olivia says she's too old to drink bad tea and we spend some time calculating how many cups she will drink in the thirty years she hopes to continue living.

Back in the office, a hush descends. Sophie comes in with a birthday cake, liberally covered in candles. Everyone starts singing, I join in but my voice feels much louder than everyone else's. I hope it becomes obvious whose birthday it is before I must sing their name. And I hope it's someone whose name I know. Thankfully, it's Sophie, who takes two goes to blow the candles out. There are a lot of them. A joke? Sophie jokes that the cake is covered in wax. The fun over, it is finally time for my meeting with Stanley and his team.

Stanley gives me an introduction to his strategic planning team. As well as Stanley there is Biff, Charlotte, who is probably mid-twenties, and another woman, maybe a year or two younger and a bit quieter, whose name never comes up. They have built expertise in creating solid evidence bases that stand up to scrutiny at planning appeals. Stanley refers to this as "the sharp end of policy formulation". They work for both public and private clients, not quite equally, probably a 40/60 public/private split. Because of people being all over the place, this team meeting does not happen as much as they would like. They have printouts listing their projects and they go through them, where they're up to and what is to be done. They stop from time to time – not all the time – to explain things for me.

First up, work for a group of London borough councils on land supply. It gives Stanley an opportunity to refer to the housing situation in South-East England as "fucked". The modus operandi, then, is informal: they relish winning the argument and are confident about it. I detect a slight anti-local-authority undertone; councils are preventing the houses people need getting built. "That's why if you own a house in the South-East you're winning", says Stanley. The changes to the methodology for calculating housing need are referenced, as well as the fact local authorities had eighteen months to submit a plan based on the old methodology, which many are rushing to do and, therefore, doing badly.

Next they discuss work for a district council in South-East England. OIP are redoing their land-supply statement because a planning inspector rejected it. They tell me they have a 100 per cent success rate so far. Elsewhere in the South-East they are lined up against councils arguing similar things; it is keeping everyone busy, meaning no houses will get built anytime soon.

The pace of the meeting is quick, a lot of plates spinning at once. An inquiry comes up, with a focus on evidence and projections. This is Overwood. Charlotte is going to be away. "There goes my weekend, then", says Stanley, who will now draft the proof. He seems almost pleased to be working hard and long. Others do too. He says he had a whole weekend off last weekend, before remembering that he spent four hours driving around sites. "But because I was in the Lotus it felt like fun!" Everyone smiles approvingly. I put the date in my diary. Stanley says I should get Charlotte to talk me through it.

They have three planning inquiries and one informal hearing on the horizon.[1] As in the Simpsons case from Chapter 3, the chat about these reveals a willingness to pick up small projects with little profit, as you never know where they might lead. Biff comes into his own when unpicking local authority evidence; all too frequently local authority planners just don't get it. He clearly relishes the scrap, proving that he has the bigger brain. Even so, he is reserved, likeable. The (sub)regional focus of the office means he also has local knowledge, and we discuss one of his pet sites. It is close to a good road junction and well away from any potentially annoyed neighbours. In the plan currently being consulted on, it is designated as a new settlement. The landed gentry who own it are not keen on selling, though; they have apparently moved through the range of 'how to keep hold of your estate' activities: weddings, holiday lets, open gardens, brewing, cheese making. Everyone around the table agrees that cashing in would be their best option.

The meeting closes rapidly, Stanley getting up and leaving. I try to talk to him on the way out about Undercliff – it seems pinning down details is not his thing. He's clearly on his way somewhere as he has a suitcase.

Finally, I have a quick chat with Henry about going to committee next week. We go into the meeting room and he shows me the site. Village location; an old farm; the client wants permission for twelve houses and to sell the site on to a developer. It is a listed building, which is one of the issues, alongside a main road, another of the issues because of potential pollution. I can see a colonnade, which is being preserved. He describes the site as "bashed around". There's a pumping station next door, which they needed to prove isn't noisy. These are the kind of issues that have kept coming up, hence why it has dragged on for two years.

Henry will drive to the committee and give me a lift. A great opportunity to chat, but driving seems nuts given how quick the train is. I ask how long he has been at OIP. Just over a year. Before that he was at a smaller consultancy for four years. He asks me about what's come out of the project so far and I tell him about the various work packages, that some of the strongest voices talking about resource problems in the public sector are consultants. He nods.

5.3 An inside view of a planning committee, where public and private sectors wrestle in plain sight

All our case studies demonstrate the importance of local authority planning committees. Here we see their operation from the perspective of the private sector. We also further our exploration of contemporary planning practice to illuminate the realities of planners' working lives in the private sector – their rhythms, frustrations and anxieties, alongside challenges and opportunities. We gain further insight into the resource imbalances between public and private sectors and get a private-sector perspective on both public-sector spending cuts and local government commercialisation processes.

I arrive at OIP an hour before we are due to leave for the planning committee, as Alison and David have agreed to talk me through Undercliff. David references the Undercliff local authority planner's report being out and notes that Alison is excited. "Or is that nervous?" Alison smiles, nervously. She has a few things to do before our chat. Fifteen minutes later, she presents me with the report: "Give me a shout if you've got any questions when you've read through it."

"OK, thanks." It is sixty-five pages long. This was not really what I had in mind but I play along, spending ten minutes trying to get as much as I can from it before asking some questions. The application seeks outline permission for ninety residential dwellings on private land. Fourteen pages summarise representations from the public who have been using the land for recreation, who understand it as having environmental value and who enjoy the view; but it is private land and not green belt. The bulk of the report is given over to discussion of policy. The authority is in the difficult position of not having an up-to-date plan and are unable to demonstrate a five-year supply of land for housing. While the proposal conflicts with a whole range of policies, the report concludes that it represents 'sustainable development', providing housing and public open space. The officer recommends that planning permission be granted subject to conditions.

I grab Alison. So what does she think of the report? She thinks it spends too much time on, and gives too much weight to, old policy. She talks about the housing supply issue, there not being a plan because of how difficult it is politically to deliver one. She refers to the case officer, "Quick Ken", and the fact that he has been stalling for a long time – the application went in about two years ago – but says that the authority cannot justifiably do this any longer. She thinks the likely outcome is a committee rejection, but says that they have been able to come to agreement on lots of issues with the council. This will place OIP favourably for an appeal. The land is owned by a land promoter who will be happy to fight it, although Alison notes the cost of doing this and that it's not that big a site. To reject it, she thinks the members will end up tying themselves in knots. Not only is the local plan out of date but most of the things the public are upset about are irrelevant. As such, it will end up coming down to landscape objections, which Alison describes as being 'subjective', and they might throw in transport too. "Then again", she says, "you never know".[2] Alison will be on annual leave on Tuesday, so Stanley will speak at the committee on behalf of the applicant.

In the car I talk some more with Henry (see Yarrow, 2019: 24 for a similar observation on car journeys as useful ethnographic sites). After he graduated there weren't many planning jobs, so he did something else for a couple of years before working for a small planning consultancy. He normally goes to work on public transport and there is a real age split in the office between the older planners, who drive all the time, and the younger ones, who don't. We talk a little about the weirdness of planners playing a key role in encouraging people out of their cars while also being drivers by necessity and as such possibly having a driver's mentality. He thinks mentality is key for changing people's outlook.

He's ambivalent about the culture at the commercial coalface – getting the applications in and then getting them out again, high-turnover, quick turnaround, 'paper pushing'. At the smaller consultancy he was closer to the applications and engaged earlier on, allowing him input on design. By way of illustration he says that OIP don't have a plotter so they can't print to scale. He queried this and got some blank looks. "If the scale is wrong, we blame the architect". Henry talks about a high turnover of staff at the more junior levels at OIP, while the directors are steady. He also says there is a heavy workload, but that it is manageable. Again, this is increasingly the case the higher up you go; David is always in when you arrive and when you're going home, and Stanley works 24/7. Henry is hoping for deferral of the decision today, partly so he won't have to do the public speaking. He doesn't relish this and has spent the morning writing a script.

We park in a gloomy underground car park. "I'm glad you've come with me", Henry jokes. I loiter outside the council offices to eat my sandwich while Henry goes in ahead. When I go into the reception, I tell a customer service person that I am here for the planning committee, she looks confused. "Do you have an appointment?" I'm thrown off balance slightly by the fact she doesn't know what the planning committee is. I notice a booth over to one side where somebody sits giving off a more old-fashioned local authority air. I try my luck there. She knows what the planning committee is. She takes my name and writes it in a big book. She gives me a sticker and directs me to some seating. Someone will collect me. A minute or two later a planning consultant joins me. A minute or two later still a man opens a door: "Who's here for the planning committee?" He takes us through a door that is ordinarily locked and into a lift, which he operates. Once we get out of the lift he leads us into the council chamber, there is tea and coffee in the corner if we want it. I go and sit by Henry in the public gallery. The chamber is big and round. The acoustics are bad and the councillors are incapable of speaking into the microphones. There is also not much of a view. I can see one councillor, two if I perch on the edge of my chair and lean left. If I lean right, I can see the committee chair and a few officials.

We're item three on the agenda. At first, things move quickly. The councillor I can see is anxious about trees. I note that people get five minutes to speak. On the second item, the chair tries to move to the debate too quickly. After they have asked questions of the public speakers, the members want to ask questions of the officers, *then* have the debate. There is some discussion around biodiversity offsetting. A more vocal member speaks up about the importance of things being provided on site; he says that too often they take the easy route of getting a cheque.

Quite rapidly, we're up. An officer with a boring voice introduces the application. It's in the green belt, a conservation area, a departure from the plan, and as such hinges on the public benefit. He notes that elements of the current site are listed and in a bad state of repair, "falling into the road". The parish council have raised some issues, particularly around pollution and traffic. It is quite a unique scheme, being enacted to a high standard and with *only* a 17 per cent profit for the developer, so there will be no Section 106 (s106) contributions. The plans are up on the screen by this point, the officer highlighting that the design tries to recreate a 1950s look.

Afterwards the officer, a local person, speaks in support. He has Parkinson's disease and apologises if his delivery is slow. He says that villagers are happy about the dilapidated site being redeveloped but are concerned about traffic. People drive through the village too fast and it is dangerous; they want the 40-mph limit reduced to 30. A councillor asks him to confirm that they do support the scheme but that they want their significant traffic concerns addressed. This is right.

Next, Henry speaks. He opens with a polite introduction and, with a halting delivery, talks about the history and negotiations around the application, how they have been able to overcome initial concerns and will be protecting the assets on the site. Councillors ask about the traffic concerns raised by the resident, the fact that the village assets are all on the other side of the busy main road. There is no crossing. There has not been a traffic study. There is no footpath. Would the developer go further? At this point, an officer steps in to say that there is nothing the agent can reasonably do about the speed limit in the village. Henry is conciliatory: in relation to the crossing, viability for the scheme is tight and Highways have not raised this issue. Similarly, with the traffic study, it has not been raised. He says that in relation to the speed limit they would be more than happy to write a letter in support of a proposal. There is a further question regarding air quality and Henry talks about the findings of a study that says it is satisfactory; he highlights that the methodology for the study has been jointly approved by the developer and the council.

After the speakers have been grilled, the members turn to their officers. Or perhaps more accurately, turn on their officers. First up it's development in the green belt: this is justified because of the dilapidation. "Ok", says the member, "but why has it not been looked after?" I can see the back of the officer's head. His ears look very red. He talks about the bad location and the difficulty in carrying out work, but there is no discussion of the council not having the resources needed to do proper enforcement. Next up the ward councillor speaks. He is one person I can hear very clearly. This proposal, he says, is delivering nothing for people, there is nothing to help them cross the road. Where is the highways officer? Sick, comes the answer. An officer says that there will be a new footpath to the bus stop. But what about the crossing? Highways have ruled it out because building it is too dangerous. The councillor points out the evident absurdity of this.

The chair intervenes to say that we are straying from the point. The member doesn't think so, and things gets tetchy. An officer says that there are mitigation options such as reducing the speed limit, it is just that planning cannot make this happen. He highlights the assumption that most people will come and go from the development by car. Another councillor suggests deferring so they can get the highways officer here. Somewhat melodramatically, he adds that he won't go on a site visit as it would be much too dangerous.

The head of planning, obviously keen not to defer, suggests they get a different highways officer in to give more general advice. In the five-minute break during which we must wait for the other highways officer, I go to the toilet: two councillors are side by side questioning the response from their highways department. "We've got an officer that's too lazy to stick their neck out!" I wouldn't say he is shouting, but people don't ordinarily talk this loudly in toilets.[3] Back in the chamber, the highways officer arrives. There are knowing glances between officers. Hypothetically, a councillor asks, if a developer were happy to finance a crossing, where do we stand? The officer says there is no way you could have a zebra crossing. If a signalled crossing were safe and justified, however, it could be considered. People begin to question just what the hypothetical crossing is for. The local member gets angry: "it's to the bus stop and everything else in the village!" Clearly, the debate is heading nowhere. Someone proposes to defer so they can talk to *the* highways officer, someone else seconds this and they vote for it.

Poor Henry had to speak and it gets deferred anyway. During the break he chatted with an older guy who I assume is the owner of our site. I introduce myself. He is amiable, and seems very much like the kind of person who would own some farm buildings. Neither he nor Henry seem annoyed. For Henry it is par for the course. The owner just thinks it's a circus. Henry says later that the client is in no rush as he plans to sell the site on once it's got permission. They have a quick chat about what might happen next, how nothing is likely to change given the constraints and how they will likely be in the same situation in a month's time. Never mind.

On the drive back Henry is sanguine about the committee. He references his nervous delivery as a good way of buying sympathy. He says I will see a very different approach from Stanley, one of sticking it to them. Henry also references the freedom that comes with the client's plan to sell the site on. They can agree to anything, it won't be their problem.

As we drive, we chat about OIP, the networking you have to do, which Henry isn't keen on. He did a lot when he started, now probably two events a month. It could be worse but it's hard on the liver, a bit of an old boys' club. He says it's weird that you see the same people all the time; they start to almost feel like friends but of course they're not, you only ever talk to them about work. He says Alison is a networking demon, which is probably why she's a director already. She does it right though, not staying until the end. The events are often put on by local law firms. OIP gets a lot of work this way. Their marketing, he thinks, is "crap". They don't have a newsletter, it's just a bit of social media, a bit of LinkedIn, the odd advert. So it's the networking, a couple of big conferences and their reputation.[4]

Henry works extended hours so he can have Thursday afternoons off for childcare. He doubts he works more than a public-sector planner, probably forty hours a week, including the networking. The only thing unquestionably better in the public sector is the pension. The work is what you make of it at OIP, and the directors work hard because they want to – they could employ someone else if they wanted to do less[5] – but you have to *perform* working hard. He feels that he should go back to the office for an hour now rather than going home and doing his emails there, even though it would amount to the same thing.

We also have time to talk about pre-application consultations (pre-apps) and moves towards commercialising local authority planning.[6] Henry refers to this as "naughty". He says pre-apps are expensive and generally not worth the money, as they hold little weight. He thinks councils should be funded properly and their advice should be free.

5.4 Private-sector knowledge

This section demonstrates how knowledge is generated and used in the commercial sector, in this case in partnership for a public-sector client, and how this fills a knowledge gap in planning. In doing so it shows a pseudo-privatisation of knowledge on the back of a void created by the decline of public-sector (sub)regional planning. The episode also speaks to the UK's uneven developmental geographies, particularly the implications for house building and responding to climate change, and data and technology in planning are again seen to be lacking.

I arrive at the suffusion centre behind a man in his late twenties wrestling with the intercom system. On gaining admittance, he too goes to OIP's office and introduces himself to Sophie as having come for a meeting. "You're here for a meeting too?" She asks me. Yes. We wait in reception. The guy introduces himself: Eddie, from a big planning consultancy. He explains that his meeting is about an employment land review for a nearby authority. I can see some of the directors are assembling in the meeting room, while others aren't getting ready for the team meeting as they would ordinarily.

David comes into reception. Would I like to observe the employment land review? Of course! Although I'm unclear just what that means. David introduces himself to Eddie, who explains that a colleague is slightly delayed. In the meeting room we realise there won't be enough chairs; I go to find one with Tony. I ask how he's doing. The usual aches and pains, he says laughing, "All self-inflicted!"

In the room with Eddie are Alison, Stanley, Biff, David and Tony. Eddie explains that the review of strategically important sites has been jointly commissioned by the local authorities of the city region. It's been hard to get this project going as it was difficult to get data. They have been able to make a proper start now and are looking at sites of five hectares and above and thinking about economic sectors. At this, Eddie's colleague Ruth arrives. Clearly more senior, formally dressed, with an indistinct middle-class accent as opposed to Eddie's local tones, she takes over the introduction and things become clearer. There are two parts to their brief: a more strategic appraisal for the city-region, involving several local authorities, and a further one for the urban core. They are here today as a listening exercise, picking OIP's brains, although Ruth does explicitly refer to OIP possibly wanting to promote sites on behalf of clients. Eddie has a presentation that he could show, but you cannot link wirelessly to OIP's big screen, which runs off a PC. OIP don't seem embarrassed by this. It is suggested they can just 'busk it', getting the sites up on Google Maps, but Alison goes to find a USB stick so that we can at least attempt Eddie's presentation. Ruth explains again that it has been "a nightmare getting consistent, usable data". "Been there done that", says Stanley. Alison's USB stick isn't working; Google Maps it is.[7]

We start with Stanley telling them about OIP. He stresses the broader contextual understanding and knowledge that OIP have, which makes them different from others. Tony joins in to say he feels that local authorities tend to have an insular view. Stanley comes in again to stress what I guess is the OIP line, emphasising the importance of quality sites rather than quantity. He refers to the large number of brownfield sites in the region that authorities might look to repurpose: "They were good for water and coal. We're not doing that anymore."

Eddie circulates maps so we can look at sites. OIP start on their own big-ticket item, a high-tech manufacturing park, which allows them to emphasise what they feel are the main issues. David gives the overview, conveying OIP's depth of knowledge of the market and of sites across the region; the heart of what they are and what they do. Stanley joins in, highlighting how high-spec the sites have to be. For instance you need incredibly deep foundations for the machines to work accurately. You can't just stick that anywhere in the region on account of historic mining.

Build out rates have been higher than expected. David is emphasising the fact that if you make it easy for these people you will be rewarded. Stanley takes over, these clients value the "campus style" that they have been able to create: "It's not a biscuit factory, once they're here, they're here." David comes back in: "But in the first instance they said, 'We want this site or we'll go to Croatia'." He pivots to 'translational research': researchers might discover things and not realise their significance. In the campus environment someone can pick that up, realise they can save two grams on a part and save trillions of pounds.

Looking at a key site together now, Tony notes it is constrained by the green belt and a golf course. Ruth asks about the green belt and Stanley explains that it is pretty comprehensive around here. The golf course is municipal, Tony explains. "It could be moved, then?" Eddie speculates. David says that the golf course is not such a bad land use here – maybe some of the employees like it – but there are some other fields that could give way in the shorter term nearby. In contrast to the more corporate consultancy world detailed in Chapter 3, OIP don't have to present a united front; they slickly pass the baton but are quite happy to take different perspectives. The impression is of dynamic thinkers who won't bullshit you. We move onto the competition in places like this – essentially good motorway links – whereby more interesting proposals give way to 'Amazon-shed-type' uses. In turn, this feeds into some bewailing of Highways England's being difficult whenever you want to develop something here. Air quality is the big problem, but road capacity is also an issue.

From here, we jump around various areas in the city, starting in the north, a neat segue by way of motorway junctions. Alison points out a good site. Stanley talks about the lack of a clear vision for this area, again with issues around road traffic. Next, the city centre, particularly the provision of offices. Alison says that local agents will have a better idea of this but that grade-one, quality offices are hard to find. Tony thinks the council have been particularly bad in this area, with no clear strategy for decades. Stanley backs this up with OIP's own experience of moving office a couple of times and struggling to get places that are good, well located and accessible. There's also a discussion around people acquiring offices to flip to residential use. "Meaning students", says Stanley. Maybe not, thinks David, highlighting that they tend to be one- or two-bed flats. Stanley agrees, but says that it tends to be students moving in. The purpose-built student stuff, then, is a competitor for space in the city centre. A race to the bottom around permitted development (PD) rights is mentioned (see Clifford et al, 2019).

What's the solution, then, the guests wonder? Has the horse bolted? A clear strategy for the City's approach to offices is Tony's answer. He talks about a key arterial road. Currently there are a lot of brownfield sites here and a lot of not terribly good uses like car showrooms, which are already starting to relocate. Traffic is terrible. Stanley highlights that there is a lot of very small-scale manufacturing, much of it very long standing. The term 'grey economy' is used. It's important stuff, but if you try to relocate it, it dies, and older business owners take the money and retire (see Imrie and Thomas, 1992).

This introduces an important issue, with OIP highlighting land designated for employment that 'should' become residential. Alison shifts us geographically to an industrial estate in a distant suburb. She says much of the site has been vacant for years, one large unit has recently become vacant and there is little interest. The road network is past its best. It would be much better off repurposed as housing. Tony references the master plan that brought the industrial estate and surrounding housing estates into being forty or fifty years ago. It made sense then, not anymore. We briefly discuss an adjacent district, hearing more of the quality-over-quantity argument. "Putting old employment sites back into a plan is more of the same", says Stanley. Stanley and Alison leave at this point. Sophie comes in with hot drinks. Tony refers to his "usual mug", positioning 'Mr Greedy' so everyone can see him. Ruth and Eddie move us along, apologising for taking so much time, saying it has been "really interesting and useful". They are still keen to talk about other authorities.

Biff comes into his own now as a "local lad", as we look at some big ex-industrial, coalfield sites. "Hi-tech renewable energy" is mentioned, an apparently long-term strategic vision that OIP are sceptical of; Ruth and Eddie don't question this scepticism. Carbon capture is mentioned, again in a sceptical fashion. Ruth summarises: "What you're saying is, it's the right location for warehousing and logistics?" David: "Yeah, we're talking big sheds not hi-tech low-carbon." I realise that this feels a bit like what people might imagine planning is about, deciding what different things you are going to put in different places. A strategic view of the region seems to be emerging – the brain is in the big city; in one direction we've got some light manufacturing, in the other logistics. This includes an airport, which David sees as strategically important: lots of space for expansion in this area, while others nearby have none. This could bring a lot of jobs and the visitors are warned not to let short-term fixes hold back this longer-term vision. Simultaneously, David takes care to introduce some "brownfield sites in the green belt" that are coming forward. Not mind-blowing stuff but potentially significant, seems to be the message: Don't overlook it.

David has to leave for a meeting, with Ruth and Eddie saying how grateful they are for everyone's time. Only Tony and Biff are left now, and they stress that they have found it useful too. Tony makes a reference to doing "proper planning". He thinks sharing intelligence and ideas is the name of game, "doing things properly", the strategic thinking that the UK has been bad at. He refers to the reason people become planners in the first place: to make things work. "It's not all about making money", he says, which sets him up to do a favourite gag about his teenage kids bleeding him dry. He also makes a reference to the green belt being a dated policy. He sees no problem in developing it sensibly if environmental benefits can be ensured elsewhere, and mentions us all needing to walk, cycle or take public transport within twenty years.[8] Eddie makes a reference to Guildford, where an inspector recently overturned the council's plans to develop in the green belt. Tony corrects himself, saying the London/M25 green belt is the only one that's still important. With that the meeting closes, we take to handshaking and thank-yous and goodbyes. Tony heads in one direction, Biff in the other. I need to find David.

He is near the printers. It has been a hectic couple of days as a former client got in touch yesterday to ask about their permission expiring, when they need to start work and when they need to discharge their conditions, which turns out to be this Thursday! I express shock that they would take their eye off the ball like this and David agrees. OIP told them six months ago that they were running out of time, but they were unmoved. They have subsequently remembered a second site in the same situation and David has been frantically chasing local council officers to try and sort things out, all part of maintaining client relations: you never know where the good will might lead.

5.5 Planning work and planning culture

Our afternoon with Caroline provides insight into routine work in commercial planning. It also highlights some contradictions of contemporary planning, the differences between commercial firms and the implications for employees. Most importantly, however, it allows us to further explore ideas of knowledge, expertise, and 'evidence' in contemporary planning.

Since I was last at OIP I have been to what I thought was the planning committee for Undercliff, only to find that it had been deferred. To find out why, I grab Alison in the kitchen, where she is protein loading on fish and hard-boiled eggs. It turns out the officer's report had lots of errors in it, as per Alison's initial assessment. She thinks the committee will now be in July and will keep me in the loop. I've had more success in arranging shadowing of Caroline, a newer OIP recruit: some site visits today and a conference call she and Biff are having tomorrow. Advertised as "a flavour of development management culture", Stanley is concerned that the site visits might be a bit boring, but I'm more than happy to tag along.

It is a hot afternoon and Caroline is keen to stress that I can head off whenever I like. She says that the work has been commissioned by a client who wants to develop a site on the edge of the city. The client wants to show that the council a) don't have a five-year housing land supply, and b) that the supply they do have has an abundance of student and one/two-bed flats in the city centre rather than 'family homes'. OIP have got the council to send their land supply data and now they will check it. Caroline says the council don't have the skills to do this and maybe only review things every five to ten years when they are doing a plan. Isn't that a resource issue rather than a skills issue? Sort of, although Caroline stresses that there are some quite complicated calculations involved once you have got your data, and you need to know about build out rates and so on. The numbers change constantly, as once someone is living on a site it is technically no longer part of the supply. Caroline has a map of sites and a printout of the council's data with a box for notes. She will take pictures using her phone. Her list includes expired permissions as checking on these tests how accurate the council's data is.

We start with two office-to-residential conversions above shops in the city centre, perhaps PDs. One of them seems to have people living in it – Caroline notes a net curtain and potted plants – the other is still under construction. As we walk, I ask what else she's working on. Caroline mentions a health impact assessment in the Midlands and some neighbourhood plan work in a seaside town. A citizens group there have got funding to help, first with identifying aims and objectives and then with writing the plan. There are finance issues in taking the work forward, and OIP have pointed them towards some other funding they could apply for. Finding or creating evidence has been particularly tricky for the neighbourhood planners, with more work than they anticipated going into informing and justifying their decisions.[9]

Caroline talks about the balance of the work she is doing now: all strategic work, whereas in the role she had before OIP it was doing 50/50 with development management. She mentions that it is good OIP do a mixture of work for developers and for public-sector clients, but highlights potential conflicts of interest. You can't work on a council's evidence base one minute and then tear it apart the next. Careful thought sometimes must inform what work to accept. We are now distracted by what seems like a tiny car park site with an expired permission. "Ninety", Caroline says. Ninety units? I marvel at how tall it's going to have to be, but ninety is the council's reference number. The site will accommodate a modest forty units.[10]

We are moving out of the city centre. I speculate that developers might be keen to build student flats to avoid some of the obligations they would be subject to for regular homes and that they are confident they can convert them if they are unviable. Caroline says she thinks that the council requires them to be designed in such a way that they could be converted, but she is not convinced that they would necessarily be more viable. She also seems to have some sympathy with her client given that families can't live in them and need to live somewhere.

We walk through an island of council housing in a sea of student residences. As Caroline and another planner have recently been taken on, I ask whether OIP is expanding. Sort of, but they're also consolidating what have been disparate arms. They are also taking on people so that they can start to do environmental and landscape assessments in-house. Caroline thinks there is a good feeling at OIP; it is a community where people get on and will occasionally have a drink together. It is definitely less intense than where she worked before, a big multi-disciplinary consultancy; her role was split between two cities, and the culture was intense and profit driven. OIP feels less so, and you can go home when you should go home. Interestingly, Caroline also has experience of another large, multi-disciplinary firm which was less intense. Part of the issue was doing a lot of work for public-sector clients who did not have big budgets. In order to win the work you had to pretend you could do it quicker than you really could, which was stressful (see Chapter 3). There was a fixation on billable time, and at one point the profit they had to make increased from 10 to 12 per cent, making a bad situation worse. It seems that the experience nearly put Caroline off consultancy, but there were no easily commutable public sector jobs – she had done commuting before and never would again. OIP were advertising and she is relatively happy; their fees are cheaper because they are smaller – the pay is good – and they charge clients for the hours they actually work.

We are now looking at a derelict building that has permission for residential use over several storeys with business use underneath. I speculate about this being PD, and we discuss the most recent PD scandal – windowless flats – which Caroline has tweeted about. Unsurprisingly, and rightly, she thinks it is terrible and makes a mockery of the planning system.[11] Would OIP work on similar schemes? She is unsure but would feel bad about it if they did. Caroline's struggling with her OIP phone camera by this point, which has very low storage. She fishes her own phone out of her bag and mentions that she turns the OIP one off when she is not at work.[12] Caroline talks about the line-management aspect of her new role. As Biff and Stanley are often out of the office, some of the more junior planners sometimes feel a bit directionless, and Caroline is going to sit in the middle, making decisions when Stanley and Biff aren't there.

We're on the edge of the city centre now, a formerly industrial district, and Caroline is pleased to see that some of the permissions include houses and that not everything is for students. She asks how I feel about the regeneration here, as she has recently had a debate with a friend on this topic. I'm ambivalent: it's not the most pernicious kind of gentrification, but I still think some things are getting lost and that it could be done better. Caroline is enthusiastic about it. It was the red light district and now people are living here! She heartily recommends a restaurant she has visited recently.

Caroline is struggling to orientate herself, understandably given that there is so much building going on, and on a couple of occasions I wonder whether we are taking pictures and making notes on the right site. It's been a sweltering afternoon and Caroline is heading home, checking out more sites en route. I say goodbye, heading in a different direction, although will see Caroline at OIP tomorrow.

5.6 Interdisciplinary working and more realities of 'PlanTech'

The conference call witnessed here adds to our understanding of contemporary planning's contradictions while also demonstrating how varied commercial work is. Furthermore, it shows one aspect of planning's current relationship with the legal profession, alongside the difficulty planners have in clearly explaining the substance and implications of their work, even to other professionals within the development sector. It shows the private sector forensically looking for weaknesses in local authority arguments and how financial resources distort planning processes.

I am listening in on a conference call for a resident's group objecting to a site allocation in a local plan; a large green belt site – almost two thousand homes. They have mobilised a lot of opposition and a lot of cash: a crowd-funding page, showing individual donations of as much as £1,000, has allowed them to approach OIP and engage Queen's Counsel (QC). The group's leader is herself a retired solicitor, well placed to get her voice heard. It is an unusual project for OIP, and if the residents did not have a case they supported then they would not be doing it. Does this suggest they would work for developers if they thought they didn't have a point, I wonder. Either way, OIP think the local authority have not used their evidence well. OIP will be tracing how the evidence has been translated into policies and arguing that the council have made the wrong calls. A connoisseur in these matters, Biff says it is a badly written plan.

In the meeting room, there are technical issues with PowWow, the conference-call apparatus. The telephone console isn't recognising the security pin code. Biff tries several times. Caroline tries. I notice Caroline helpfully suggesting potential solutions that Biff ignores. Eventually Caroline goes into the other meeting room to try in there. It works straight away so we head through. I have not been in here before; there is a picture of a student village on the wall. The QC, Martin, is on the line, as is James from OIP's southern office and Claire, the resident co-ordinator. The QC chairs. There will be three topics: the strategic assessment (SA), the green belt and the five-year land supply.

We start with SA, Martin mentioning some case law and stressing the importance of making it easy for the inspectors. This is James's domain, and he says the options consultation the council did was very constrained; they did not properly consult on a full draft plan and made decisions before having a full suite of evidence. There was no mention of strategic priorities in advance and no chance to consider alternatives. The duty to co-operate is central to the plan, the idea being that the council can agree that another council will shoulder some of their housing burden. Claire asks about a relief road which is going to be built regardless and presumably represents some reason why the houses are going here. Martin starts to grill James, who has been somewhat unclear. I think he has also written a report that is, to Martin's mind, somewhat unclear. Martin says that the local authority has a simple task, to make decisions based on some evidence. It is perfectly fine for them to make actual decisions at various stages in the process so long as they have reasons; he asks James to say whether the council had reasons. James says that they rejected some sites too soon, before a big piece of evidence was put together. Nevertheless, it is not unlawful to choose at an early stage. Are there reasons why they have done it? The real crunch for this happening is at the REG19[13] stage, and James says there should have been another SA at this point.

Claire interrupts, mentioning a site on the eastern edge of an adjacent town, which could prevent the houses being built in her backyard. We go around this quite a lot. The QC says that the authority need to meet *their own* need, but Claire thinks it is a duty-to-co-operate question. The other site is actually quite small, and Martin is anxious that they don't end up saying that the need is actually greater than it is. The QC is not going to give them any respite: it is not a question of whether it is the best plan possible but whether it is good and sound. They need to know why other options were rejected. He tells James that it is a straightforward process. James thinks the reasoning is not clear. The QC says the council have gone for major settlements in their strategy; we're debating one of these. This leads to a breakthrough: OK, it makes sense as a site, but why such a high number of units? Why not spread them out and mitigate the impact? The QC is happy for the other points to be made, but this needs to be the focus.

At this point Martin is cut off. Once he's back, Biff asks a question about the other options. "This is the nub of it", says the QC, "this is how we have to attack it, why 1,600 on this site, why not spread it?" Can we show that there are alternatives? Lack of co-operation between the authorities is key. We get cut off. Biff strides out into the office. It turns out that everything has gone down, all the phones and internet. Caroline tells me that this currently happens several times a day. The provider dug up the road outside and ever since there has been nothing but problems. Eventually everything comes back. The QC thinks that another part of the argument is that green belt release is premature because a merger of several councils is in the pipeline, and subsequently the authority will be looking strategically in the other direction.

We turn to housing numbers. Biff leads us through this as he has written the report, which provokes nowhere near as much interrogation from Martin. The council has a lot of errors in their numbers. A neighbouring authority taking some housing should reduce their requirement, but they do not show this properly. There has been a change in the framework, meaning that they should use a new methodology. In using old data and cooking it incorrectly, they end up with a higher requirement. Biff also says that a site this big will not get built until at least year six of the plan, so it is not five-year supply.

Finally, we discuss the green belt, which Caroline leads on. She gets a harder time than Biff, but not as hard as James. This may have something to do with the fact we are running out of time, however, as the line of questioning is similar. What are we trying to show? Identify the central point and attack that. Martin: "We need to get to the essence of our criticisms". He asks Caroline if there are any bits of the green belt assessment she doesn't agree with. Not so much, but it is not clear how the assessment leads to the choices the council have made. Martin summarises: the council need a more robust approach for a big green belt release, and the fact they have not done a proper job raises big questions.

I sense that people are keen to wrap up but need to tie up loose ends. Claire wonders what she can do to help. Not much. They have commissioned two landscape assessments and discuss whether to use one, the other or both. Biff says one is better as discrepancies between them would be problematic. They will give the one they won't use to Kathy – who wrote the one they do want to use – so she can add anything that is helpful. Martin, the QC, is cut off again, and doesn't bother ringing back. We discuss the wider plan, especially from Claire's point of view. It uses up parking space in the town centre to create retail space; to her mind this will actually further diminish the prospects for the town centre. Biff says calculations on this are very formulaic – so many people will spend so much money and therefore need so much floor space.

After Claire hangs up, the planners stay on the line for a debrief. Biff laughs, "Do you need a lie down, James?" They think the QC doesn't quite appreciate why some of the context is important from a planning perspective, but he is good at what he does and they respect his approach. Getting serious, they say that they need a strong executive summary on each document. The memoranda of understanding between the various councils in the area on their duty to co-operate is mentioned – it seems there are often weaknesses to exploit here. As we leave, Biff and Caroline note how unusual it is for a group of residents to be able to set themselves up to challenge a plan in this way: "Concerned about losing their Waitrose and creating the market for a Lidl!"

5.7 The 'bragfest': inside a business development meeting

This episode shows the private sector at its most informal. It reinforces the importance of networking, providing unique insight into business practices in planning and key elements of the cultures that the commercial sector creates and sustains, notably the importance of rituals around sport and drinking, othering of the public sector and a wry, rather cynical counterpoint to the gallows humour of the public sector. It is illuminating regarding the age and gender dynamics of certain workplaces, and sheds light on wider issues of work-life boundaries.

I am in the OIP conference room with Stanley, Biff and David. Biff is a bit surprised by the prospect of a meeting; he is one of only two still working at 5:45 pm when I leave, and I get the feeling he could have done without this. The meeting is with a law practice which does planning work. They have sent three people: Robert, the lead, about forty, with a dark suit and an open face, tall with dark hair; Emma, early/mid-thirties blonde with a spotted dress and glasses with dark frames; Michael, mid-fifties with an incongruous short-sleeved shirt and a pinstriped suit. The OIP folk are more casual: one in a white shirt, tie and jeans; another in a red-and-blue Ben Sherman check shirt and blue trousers; the youngest, David, is smarter in a black jacket, grey trousers and white shirt.

The purpose of the meeting is unclear, and the first twenty minutes is pure banter. Emma doesn't speak once, and it is a bit 'blokey'. Tales of 'crap' local authority planning are exchanged as common currency. I feel some of this is for my benefit after Stanley introduces our project in a particular way.

Business begins proper, with Stanley leading. Emma is starting a planning branch in the law firm's local office. The meeting is to see if any collaborations might be arranged between the two firms. Stanley hands over to David to explain what's happening in development terms in the city. David says the city centre is "doing well" in terms of private-rented housing: there is lots of university investment, but still no local plan. He moves on to neighbouring authorities noting quite a lot of green belt release. Stanley chips in to say that for five years they were "spending a lot of time with them [the council]" to get sites out of the green belt, arguing for a few medium-size sites. "Everyone got a bit of sugar", he says.

The talk focuses on student housing, noting how a nearby city missed out previously and is now firmly "in the crosshairs of the development industry". There is "space galore" in that city centre starting to develop. Another nearby city has approved a large tower block which the law firm confirms they worked on with another planning consultancy who have "some good young boys". There is then some laddish chat about drinking, Robert says that "a floor [of the developer's office] has a sun terrace ... six fridges permanently stocked ... you know what they are doing from 3 o'clock on Fridays".[14] Developments in this city haven't been easy; local politicians were nervous about such a big development. David chips in with regard to a similar development: "[I was] really annoyed, I was threatening to punch people in the throat." It appears councillors blocked his application, wanting an independent assessment of both sides' existing independent assessments. Emma still hasn't said a word.

Biff gets us on track with what OIP are doing: a large tower, private-rented sector; despite Brexit gloom people are still enquiring. OIP have a wide client base of landowners, universities, local developers "for quite a way in all directions". London investors are coming back. Biff talks of "gutter fighting" and it being "not as crazy as it was". Stanley notes that the developers who survived the 2008 recession are more professional: "They know to use you sooner."

Robert pitches in: "Did that job come to anything that came from my rugby mate?" "No, he didn't come back to us", comes the response. "I'll see him in couple of weeks when the season starts", he replies.

Stanley notes that they also work quite a bit for local authorities, which leads to both sides talking about local authorities and shared services (Clifford, 2018). Biff notes that local authorities tend to shed senior folk after plans have been prepared, but they need them for implementation. The lawyers agree, with Michael saying he knows someone who did five or six local plans, spending nine to ten months in each, but left no legacy. Stanley says they have done triaging for local-government planners and will sense-check their evidence for them, "strategic assessments and site selection processes being a happy hunting ground for us". Underlying this is basically a plea to keep knowledge in local government, that tacit knowledge, why policies are what they are, which is lost with a purely commercial approach to policy preparation and this creates costs for the private sector too. The contradictions in their criticisms of local government aren't noted, but then much of the anti-local-government banter feels ritualistic; shared bonding, loosely based on fact.

There is an interesting lack of technology here: no laptops; three people have notebooks and pens which are barely used, the others nothing. The only thing on the table prior to the meeting was a stack of RTPI regional event leaflets.

A discussion on crematoria as a growth area for planning starts up in which there is a degree of sensitivity, with folk sharing experiences of the need to allow privacy and time to grieve at a funeral, although perhaps this accords with a market logic that dictates you will need more of them if you have more sensible, longer timeslots (see Madell et al, 2021). Biff notes he is working for a community group, presumably opposing a proposal for one. Michael says crematoria planning is much like retail and that the big players in this market mirror the supermarkets vying for developable land in the 1990s. Emma then makes her first intervention, slightly more cynically than might come naturally in order to blend in with the laddish banter, which then breaks out again in earnest.

Stanley somehow segues from death to near-death and starts talking about retirement homes. OIP are modelling the economic impact, the high rate of job creation – for carers, gardeners, café staff – especially if you open it to the public. Michael notes that it's lots of unskilled work, which usefully provides work for unskilled folk where you need it. Biff mentions the need for retirement homes to be walking distance from housing for employment and the flexible opportunities this provides for workers. For five to ten years Biff has thought the senior-housing sector is going to take off, but it hasn't quite. He says something revealing about fifty-five-year-olds not being fifty-five-year-olds anymore (which reflects his own approximate age) and thinking they are still thirty-five; OIP model based on seventy-five-year-olds' needs.

Stanley, apropos of nothing, mentions that they secured a large green belt site for a university-led development. This provokes more othering of public-sector planners and members: "When they want it to happen" things can go quick; "Some officers are proactive [others] can't find their backside with both hands."

Despite the anti-local-government banter, it turns out Robert is ex-local government. He deploys this knowledge to commercial advantage, and lots of personal relations are on display along with some discussion of who knows who: "Darryl, yes, I know Darryl." Biff too has local-government experience. There is some discussion of flooding, Stanley humorously notes that they got two hundred extra houses allocated through a local planning process and that part of the argument was "You will be up to your ankles on our site, you will be up to your knees on others."[15] At this point, Biff, possibly making up another appointment, excuses himself, noting on the way out how the law firm "caused me to pull my hamstring playing cricket". Michael notes that planning is "a small and incestuous world".

There are more 'worst reasons for refusal' and 'poor defences at inquiry' stories to cement the private-planner social capital by othering the public sector, "I'm in full attack mode at this point", Stanley says at one stage and then relays a story about "the standard method" and a local authority: "Plenty of work for all of us if that carries on", he concludes.

David pitches in with some information about air quality being a significant new material consideration. English Nature[16] sets nitrogen limits for all local authorities in the New Forest, and councillors are using this as an excuse to refuse all housing. They are now rerouting traffic and relocating car parks with £3,250 per house under Section 106 to pay for it.[17] This meets with disapproval: "If our planning system operated sensibly with unusually competent officers, we'd have to find something else to do for a living", says Michael. Robert warms to the planner bashing: "Clear out the deadwood and find me a Section 106 officer who can add up", he says in reference to some issues he is having with a local-government merger.

It's wrapping up, business cards are exchanged; Emma asks "if you can get me on any mailing lists?" Stanley says they occasionally have events in the office and makes one last sales pitch, noting things beyond planning that the company does. They ask a bit about our project and I say a few choice words. "Like an academic version of *The Planners* on TV?"[18] one of them asks. "Yes", I say, "that's pretty much it, though almost certainly with a smaller audience".

5.8 The planning inquiry

This extended section observing a planning inquiry speaks to a number of the book's themes: the realities of contemporary planning practice, highlighting especially the resource imbalances between public and private sectors; differential understandings of citizens' importance to planning processes; increasing legalism; the nature of planning work; and the implications of a 'housing crisis'. The section also speaks to the status of different kinds of knowledge and expertise. These coalesce around planning's abiding role (and self-justification) in serving the public interest and the open question of whether, and how, this is realised through contemporary practice.

It is Friday and I am in the suffusion centre to meet Charlotte about Overwood as the inquiry is next week. We start at the beginning. Another agent put in the first application, for three hundred units on the edge of a nearby town, which was refused. OIP were engaged to resubmit. Through negotiations with the council, they got seven reasons for refusal down to two. At this point Charlotte gets Hannah, as she will give a better overview.

I've not met Hannah before. An associate director, she is friendly and unassuming. She explains that they had to submit a second application rather than go straight to appeal because too much time had elapsed since the first. She highlights how much work went into finding common ground with the council. The sticking points are: first, the scheme's impact on an air-quality-management area – there has been a dispute between the environmental health officer (EHO) and OIP's independent consultant, particularly around methodology; second, policy issues, principally the impact on a 'strategic gap' that the council want to maintain between settlements. OIP's argument is that the site is outside of the strategic gap and that evidence suggests the policy is out of date anyway.

We look at Google Maps. Charlotte describes it as "low-grade agricultural land", accessed to the north-west. There is an additional argument related to five-year land supply, but Charlotte says this is a backup and really it will hinge on the other two. She is pleased the council have agreed that land supply does not represent "a limit on development". It seems OIP are less confident making arguments about land supply now following a decision at another inquiry. Overall, OIP think the arguments are straightforward.

The agent for the initial application was more of an architect-planner, which may be why they struggled with the complex planning issues here. Charlotte and Hannah say the local authority planners have been "reasonably

OK" to work with on agreeing to common ground. They have got over some fairly large highways issues, also issues of sustainability and archaeology, involving expensive trench digging and artefact removal. They say it has been complex – this has been said of everything I have seen at OIP – but a good project to work on overall. They think it is a sustainable site and makes sense in planning terms, describing the feeling you get straight away as to whether you are working on the right project or not.[19]

Hannah is confident that they will get the right outcome, although who the inspector is makes a big difference. They hope to be able to accompany them on the site visit. You cannot direct them, and the council planners are there too, but you can answer questions. As we zoom in, I am struck by how small the site is for so many units and remark on this; it turns out this second application was for just 150 units, although presumably a smaller site. Charlotte says that ground-nesting skylarks were found and that their habitat is being maintained, which constitutes betterment. A circular walking route is being created.

I ask about the inquiry itself. Charlotte says that the submission of evidence is the stressful bit for her insofar as you must ensure you get everything in punctually. The inquiry itself is quite easy, involving digging out documents or looking things up as directed by Stanley. For a development-management planner like Hannah, planning inquiries are a bit of a rarity, while the strategic team, which Charlotte is in, do five or six a year.

I ask about the public reaction to the proposals. "Horrendous!" One hundred and thirty objections, and six hundred signed a petition. A local councillor lives adjacent to the site and galvanised local opposition. Charlotte explains that the properties nearby are all bungalows. "They'll be dead soon anyway!" Hannah is more sympathetic, even if their objections "aren't planning matters". Some residents are even selling up and threatening to sue if they do not realise what they think is their property's former value. "But they don't own the view!" Charlotte thinks that people who really want country views should buy houses in the middle of nowhere, not on the edge of a settlement. When putting up the notices, Hannah could see curtains twitching, and Charlotte mentions another site where residents took down the notices and tried to delay the inquiry by claiming that they never went up. Hannah was sure to take photos of them in place.

Day one

While the town feels somewhat 'left behind', the town hall is grand. The committee room has wood panelling, an elaborately painted ceiling and high-backed leather chairs, and the room is laid out as per government advice (see Figure 5.3). At one end, nine members of the public face the inspector;

Figure 5.3: The recommended public inquiry layout

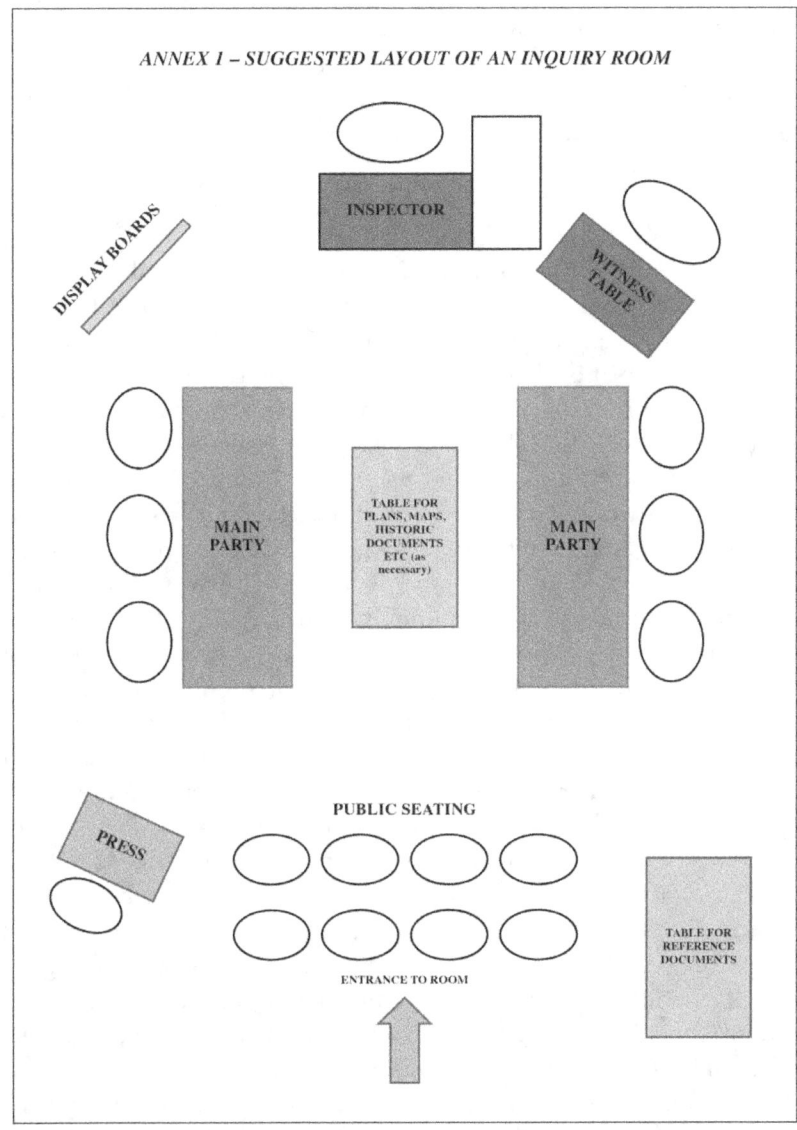

Source: Based on Planning Inspectorate, 2016, https://www.gov.uk/government/publications/setting-up-a-venue-for-a-public-inquiry-hearing-or-examination. Contains public-sector information licensed under the Open Government Licence v3.0.

OIP, their barrister and experts to one side; the council and their barrister to the other. Stanley is in his chalk-stripe suit next to the youngish-looking lawyer, Max Benn.

The Inspector is in his early forties, with a rugby-playing vibe. The advocates confirm who they will call for evidence. The process is explained to members of the public: there will be opening statements, and then evidence; people will be able to ask questions of the experts, if they get the inspector's attention they will be brought in. The inspector summarises the five main issues as he sees them: whether the policies are out of date; whether the borough has a five-year land supply for housing; the principle of development; whether the development would compromise the character of the countryside; and air quality.

Max Benn opens, stressing the need for a holistic view of the development plan. He brings up the strategic gap, which prompts some head shaking. He pauses to check we can hear him. "Only just!" He speaks up. He says that the broad principle is for sustainable development. As some policies are out of date, a five-year supply of housing land isn't demonstrated and given various bits of the National Planning Policy Framework (NPPF), the positives of the development outweigh the negatives and it should be approved. He moves to specifics. If you follow them back, the open-countryside policies originate in a twenty-five-year-old plan, which made provision to 2016; they are "seriously out of date". He says that the council has expanded their rejection on the question of the strategic gap, which is not precisely defined. This seems to be an important point, as he is no longer reeling off policy abbreviations. He says that the council has chosen to ignore a report that they commissioned a consultancy to produce and which said they could maintain a strategic gap while bringing some development forward on this site. Limited weight can be attached to the emerging local plan, which would define the gap. He reiterates that it is not clear, in any case, how the development would harm the gap, as none of the 'experts' identify harm.

Moving on to the five-year land supply, he claims the council can only show a two-year supply and have a 25 per cent shortfall. The council maintain that they have more than a six-year supply based on the new methodology. The methodology is important, as the change is part of the argument for the plan being out of date. Stanley's evidence is going to be crucial here, and Benn quotes the planning minister's instruction "not to take your foot off the gas" (in terms of having an adequate land supply for new housing). On air quality, he argues for the method of OIP's expert, Dr Gill. He says that in promising electric-vehicle charging points the appellant is demonstrating "best practice" and mitigating in line with council policy. He turns on the council's EHO, saying that he has undertaken no modelling and misunderstands both the policies and Dr Gill's method. Up for particular ridicule are the EHO's arguments regarding the age of the vehicle fleet locally: he "doesn't quantify" and makes "unsubstantiated assertions". The site is sustainable in being walking distance from local amenities, an argument that moves neatly into his summation: the scheme is for much-needed housing in a sustainable location.

The council's advocate, Penny Taylor, goes next. This is "simply not the right location"; the site "*is* within the strategic gap". Taylor's opening statement is pithier than Benn's. She starts on air quality, saying it is a straightforward dispute and that the EHO can show rising pollution levels. She suggests that providing charging points is nothing special these days and that people will not necessarily use them. She moves on to the planning objections, stressing that local knowledge is the reason that the consultant's *borough-wide* report on the strategic gap was ignored. She says that members know the distinct identities of settlements. The aims of the policies are consistent with the NPPF, and the local plan's emphasis on brownfield regeneration implies restricting greenfield development. As the council *can* demonstrate a five-year land supply, the standard policies apply. Her conclusion reiterates that there are no problems with this determination and points to the emerging plan, which would also look to restrict development here.

We adjourn for the first time. I chat to some residents. A man with a crew cut, strong local accent and some blurry tattoos says that this rigmarole is par for the course. They want to develop there and will do whatever they can. He stresses that air quality is a real issue. He collected signatures for the petition and people told him they avoid opening windows and sitting outside at certain times of day. He notes a discrepancy between the claim that development won't make air quality worse and their argument about providing plenty of parking spaces. My eyes meet Stanley's and he gives me a conspiratorial wink. All of the residents seem sanguine – "que sera, sera – but you've got to fight it if you can". "I'm seventy-three and not ready to stop causing trouble yet!" another resident chips in.

After the break the council's EHO gets his turn. A bald man in his fifties with a pair of enormous boots and a short-sleeved shirt, Taylor introduces him with great emphasis on his qualifications. Max Benn starts gently, but increasingly starts to harry the guy in plummy, public-school tones. The EHO, to his credit, remains cheerful. The advocate addresses him as *Mr* Glasshoughton constantly, contrasting his evidence to that of *Dr* Gill. Benn keeps disputing a point about the age of the vehicle fleet, wanting hard science as to whether this trend will continue. Obviously, this data isn't available, which he seems to suggest is all the council's fault.

The point is that if you build houses here most folk will drive to them and this will increase emissions. OIP are keen to say that their model suggests all will be well. Benn has his files very much in order and, sounding ever more upper-middle class, keeps asking *Mr* Glasshoughton to refer to documents he doesn't have: "You haven't got the document, but it is a *very* important document." The council is less well organised, perhaps reflecting the resource imbalance. Overall it seems like a lot of trouble for 150 houses. Mr Glasshoughton is getting redder and redder, he is losing. I inwardly cheer when he scores a point back but he is too eager to please, he needs to learn when to say the bare minimum. The inspector is non-interventionist, allowing the advocate to go round in circles over what you can and can't model.

No one from the public wanted to speak at the outset, but at the end of Mr Glasshoughton's roasting, my new friend puts his hand up. Benn looks horrified. Inquiries are often predictable, but inspectors do take the public seriously, grateful perhaps that someone has shown an interest. "We don't understand the fancy words being said but we do know the air isn't very good and more houses will make it worse." That was basically it. What was the point of the last two hours?

Over sandwiches I learn that OIP's strategic planners are vegetarian while the development management folk are carnivores. They seem very cross with the council for putting up the EHO, who they regard as incompetent. Air quality is a total red herring – if you build houses you will get emissions, being their line of reasoning. It explains why the advocate was trying to perform a character assassination and emphasising the credentials of his person. Stanley allows me access to their internal meeting with Max Benn, who, while we've been having lunch, has been talking to Penny Taylor about the air quality issue. The outcome is that Dr Gill will prepare an agreed statement from both parties about what was and wasn't at stake here. OIP think the council should withdraw this objection.

Max is mildly condescending as he brings us up to speed. He seems well-meaning, but I wonder if planning inquiries shouldn't adopt their own language and rules rather than borrowing them from law courts? Apparently the council were keen to secure his services but OIP beat them to it. Stanley is complimentary about the council planners when I ask, but notes they have been hit hard by cuts.

Following a recap of what's happening process-wise regarding air quality, the afternoon sees us move onto the planners. The council planner, John Morrel, seems typical: quiet, competent, self-effacing, with a penchant for full-strength coke and chocolate bars. I'd put money on him having a stock English-planner background: lower-middle/aspirant-working-class parents. He is the strategic planning policy manager and has about twenty years' experience at various local authorities.

Morrel notes that the land is in a strategic gap outlined in the local plan recently submitted to the inspectorate. Max questions how much emphasis should be placed on such an emerging policy. Then there is interminable to-ing and fro-ing about specific policies. Max goes in heavy with legal precedent: "You will of course be very familiar with Lord Justice Duff and Suffolk Coastal." Broadly, Morrel does well: he knows his brief, plays it straight and – unlike Mr Glasshoughton – doesn't get drawn off course. He does, however, get increasingly wound up by the circular questioning. At one point Max skewers him on a case he doesn't know. It's not kind and not in the public interest, but the inspector lets proceedings run. Occasionally a wry smile seems to acknowledge Max's rather outré manner.

By mid-afternoon my attention wanders and I take to admiring the stoicism of the public here, trying to navigate the acronyms and interminable nit-pickery. Stanley looks half asleep but quickly hands a note to Max when the planner lands a glancing blow, suggesting it's just his poker face.

The afternoon is much the same as the morning. The landscape assessment is wheeled out and Max makes much of the council picking one of its recommendations and not others, as if this doesn't happen for good reason all the time. Class is important here. Max is in a different one to everyone else in the room and it shows. I don't think there is deference as such, but it gives him confidence to play the plummy lawyer. We get much intricate detail, which will likely have little bearing on the outcome. Max spends hours trying to find minor inconsistencies between policies. For example, lots of time is spent pointing out that the 2006 plan policy is very like the latest one. Morrel stresses that the new policy has been reviewed by the council and examined by an inspector. They rehearse this three times. As vast tomes of evidence have already been submitted, the lawyerly point-scoring is eating up great chunks of taxpayers' money: "I think the point's been laboured", the inspector wryly comments eventually. He also chides Morell, suggesting the only three options he has are to say "yes, no, or don't know" following some exasperation at an impossible-to-answer question reframed for the third time. This feels like the inspector's training kicking in; he should really be telling Max to stop winding up the witness. As we close, the inspector asks about tomorrow. Penny says no council witness is available to talk about landscape as the authority don't have a landscape officer. A testament to the public-private asymmetry in resources.

Day two

Day two begins and the council withdraws their air-quality objection. This strikes me as a shame as there was a case to be made, but perhaps OIP threatening to pursue costs forced their hand.

First up is the council's case officer. We begin with the apparently standard run-through of her experience: after an education in planning, she has worked here for over a decade. The council's barrister runs us through the now familiar array of policies. They *are* up to date. The council *can* demonstrate a land supply. The developer's proposal conflicts with the strategic-gap policy. The benefits of the proposal do not outweigh the harm. The inspector intervenes here, perhaps resolved to be more involved. He says we are hearing a lot about conflicts with policy but that does not necessarily represent harm; he is looking to hear about *tangible* harm. The officer says that there is harm in her "professional judgement", referencing the settlement boundaries, the effect on the footpath and how this relates to the strategic gap. The inspector pushes her again: "But in layman's terms?" Encroachment of the built form into the countryside, the merging of settlements. "Are these common to all greenfield sites?" the inspector asks. Yes. Has she somehow undermined their argument? OIP are keen to suggest that this is de facto green belt policy.

Max's cross-examination: to start, his standard rigmarole of checking that the officer has all the documents he will reference. His first argument is that some policy implicitly suggests there should be development at Overwood. The barrister then moves in a landscape direction, saying that the council has no *evidence* of harm. He distinguishes between the expertise of landscape professionals – such as the one OIP are paying for – and of planners. The officer states that initially the council did not receive landscape evidence from OIP and that the council do not have a landscape function; she is exercising her professional judgement as a planner.

Next, the "character and function of the strategic gap", with Max pushing the officer to be precise about the harm, to say that it is minimal – the public are grumbling that they can't hear – the officer says she will not quantify it. The inspector intervenes here to say that she must quantify it as a planning professional. Does professional expertise amount to quantifying things you cannot quantify? The inspector, I note, is an engineer, which may suggest a desire for quantification. He is placated by "low to medium". We move on to the trigger for bringing forward housing in greenfield locations, whether this was considered at the time and what the position is now. Mr Benn says the trigger has been met. Stanley's evidence confirms this. With this questioning on triggers, the council's barrister steps in to say that her colleague is trying to have a second go at questions that were answered yesterday. The inspector fudges, saying that we should expect questions on applying policies but he does rather think we might move on.

Which we do, to the subject of weight. Particularly, in the first instance, how much weight should be afforded to delivering market housing at the current time. The inspector pushes the officer to be specific. She says medium. He wonders if she means moderate. The inspector intervenes to reframe the question. Under the core strategy target, can they or can they not demonstrate a five-year supply? The council made the mistake of including the workings-out of the old methodology in a key policy; on this basis they cannot, although on the new methodology they can.

After a break, we move to the strategic gap. Max suggests that the plan does not specify boundaries. The officer's professional judgement as a development control planner is that it does. From this we move to the landscape report, again. The line is that the consultants are qualified to exercise their expertise on these matters, while the steering group of councillors with their "local knowledge" are not. The officer agrees with this "on face value", which seems a wrong move: local knowledge and local politics surely count for something.[20] Cross-examination over, the council's barrister wants to ask just two questions. "Has the council ever used an up-to-date methodology in general but an old one for a specific site?" No. "Would they ever?" No. We have another short adjournment before it is the landscape architect, Mr Hewish's turn.

Max will not ask Mr Hewish questions on his own evidence because the council has not provided a landscape expert. Instead, he asks about the consultant's report. Hewish is asked how qualified they are to write a good report. He lists their expertise and good standing. Is the method they used sound? He waffles about robustness. Eventually the inspector intervenes to ask if there are any criticisms. No. Max asks if they could have advised differently. Yes, if they felt they had to, to achieve a strategic gap. It all seems very transparent. The advocate leads him around the evidence, getting to the question of local knowledge and judgement so Hewish can stress that members lack expertise.

We get to impact and whether assessing this should be objective or subjective. "Objective!" Hewish crows, pleased to know the answer. The council's advocate wonders if this questioning is not straying towards policy matters. The inspector asks where the questions are going: Highlighting the importance of professional objectivity, says Max. The inspector thinks this point has been made. Penny Taylor would like to ask a couple of questions. Max thinks that there is no basis for cross-examination because there is no council evidence on landscape. The inspector agrees but cannot see the harm either. The questions centre on to what extent assessing a strategic gap is a matter of judgement. Hewish knows his line and sticks to it. Before lunch, a member of the public asks whether these people have walked around the site. They all have, except the inspector, who is going to. "Then how can you argue that putting 150 houses here will have no impact?"

I head to town with Hannah from OIP for sandwiches. She thinks that the council just haven't come with a case, and feels sorry for the case officer, who she respects. She is a bit nauseating about Max's genius, proving that there is an audience for the Oxford Union debating-chamber stuff. Back in OIP's room we eat our sandwiches while Max walks Stanley through the line his questions will take later. He stresses that he is not coaching Stanley on how to reply. Hannah, Mr Hewish and I sit quietly. Foolishly, I dare to eat a peach. Max marvels at the NPPF: "I love it; constantly revealing new meanings!" Happily, for lawyers.[21]

Stanley has ditched the chalk-stripe today for a grey-green number. His hair is trying to look smart but a tuft sticks out. Max makes sure we are in no doubt about how eminently qualified Stanley is: thirty years of varied experience in town and country planning. Step by step, he is led in setting out OIP's case. First, there is the importance of setting out "clear and precise" boundaries of strategic gaps in order that you can assess their character. Does a strategic gap really not have a character unless it is drawn on a map? Stanley refers to the policy saved from the 2006 plan as a dated, pseudo-green belt policy. By being imprecise it conflicts with the NPPF. The point is made that strategic gaps are not about enabling access to the countryside; a reference to the footpath that will become stuck between two housing estates should the proposal get permission. They move on to the methodological change regarding land supply that renders the policies out of date. Subsequently, Max invites Stanley to say whether each of the important policies is up to date or out of date. "Out of date ... out of date ... out of date!" The public laugh at the pantomime.

Penny Taylor's turn to grill Stanley. First, she asks about the principle of development. She invites Stanley to say that there is no gap between Overwood and Epwell. The point is to make Stanley look absurd. She paraphrases the relevant section, "land of an open character between Overwood and Epwell", it's pretty clear, isn't it? Stanley is adamant that it is not *all* land. He does a thing where he holds his hands in the air, "Overwood is here, Epwell is here, our site is over here, it's not between Overwood and Epwell." Taylor decides they should look at a map. "Epwell is to the south-west, Overwood is to the north-east, ergo the site is between Overwood and Epwell." Stanley refuses to agree. Taylor says we are getting silly now. We get into a discussion on the importance of reading a policy as a whole; tricky, as they can both read it how they like. OIP get to argue that their site is sustainable insofar as it is within walking and cycling distance of a centre. The council get to argue that OIP's reading doesn't balance the constituent parts: regeneration, housing, economic growth and green-space strategy. Taylor talks about a "common sense" reading of policy. The public approve.

We move on to five-year land supply and then the public are invited to ask questions. "We're not clever enough", comes the reply. Max gets an opportunity to ask his witness some further questions. He makes sure the landscape report is at the forefront of our minds as he takes us through each set of Taylor's questions, reiterating the OIP line.

The inspector looks tired, perhaps fed up of all the lawyering. We are well into the afternoon and still must wade through conditions and s106. The inspector stresses to the public that this is standard at inquiries and will not prejudice the council in any way. Interestingly, the public know a great deal on many of the topics. They note all manner of local wildlife, things the inspector acknowledges surveys cannot necessarily pick up even though the planning system expects a professional survey. A win for local knowledge. Overall, the inspector suggests the council are rather overzealous with their conditions and they happily row back on many of them. The inspector suggests that some of the items are better left for reserved matters – parking and bins for instance. There is a condition regarding construction disturbance which the inspector is keen to draw the public's attention to: curfews and no Sunday working.

OIP seem keen to wave the s106 agreement through; it is all decided and signed. The inspector, however, is keen to look more closely, not least for the public. The discussion seems nit-picky. The solicitors who drafted it come under scrutiny for their erratic use of full stops. We go through a standardised list: public art, the provision of which has a policy basis; affordable housing, 'up to 30 per cent', subject to viability; sustainable drainage; nesting birds. The inspector is keen to know how figures for health will be spent. There is a document. He seems sceptical about this and makes this plain to the public; there will be money but they may well not see any of it. Finally, we are done. We will reconvene tomorrow for an informal discussion on land supply before closing statements.

Day three

Day three begins with housing and land supply matters, an informal discussion similar to that on the conditions, unlike the more formal cross-examination of experts we witnessed on previous days. Stanley leads the discussion, introducing the council's duty to provide a five-year supply of housing land. There is a disconnect between this lofty performance of expertise and the methodological realities underpinning a submitted table listing nineteen sites with planning permissions for housing. Stanley's evidence details the shortfall Stanley predicts between the projections and what they might really deliver. The council disputes this and the table also represents their position. In Stanley's defence, his proof of evidence is more detailed than the table which is to facilitate the discussion, with work underpinning it on housebuilding and planning more widely. Nevertheless, it is not all that sophisticated; it relies mostly on driving around and having a look (see Section 5.5).

We laboriously work through it site by site. While some of the sites are clearly not delivering and are unlikely to deliver – the sort of sites where some engineering works happened in 2006 and nothing since – at other times Stanley is pushing his luck. At one point Stanley argues against some town centre sites as being viable/appealing to the aspirational. Is the suggestion that the town is a bit rubbish? Another case of OIP having their cake and eating it: the town is vibrant, growing and there is immense housing need so we must build at Overwood, but it is also a dump! In either case, the council fights back. They have had several successful town centre developments; the town centre and economy are becoming more vibrant by the day; the people of the borough are cool and hip!

We adjourn for an hour so that the advocates can get their closing statements together and consult with their clients. Max is keen to ensure he gets another, shorter break in between Taylor's statement and his own. I'm not invited into OIP's room, so I seize the opportunity to speak to the inspector, who is usually adept at fleeing the room as soon as the inquiry is adjourned. He has been with the inspectorate for five years, and chairing inquiries for one. On inquiries, he mentions the ongoing efforts to streamline the process, cut down on cross-examinations, get broad agreement in advance and speed everything up. He is supportive of these. He is friendly, inviting me to get in touch if I need help.

I walk into the market square, which is reasonably lively, although the stalls themselves have a car-boot-sale feel. I find a café with a courtyard at the back. The place is full of the recently retired, some of them clearly in charge of young grandchildren. It strikes me that they are an important demographic here, having paid off mortgages that were tiny anyway and now possessing a little disposable income. They are an important demographic in the public gallery too. Do they feature in the imaginations of the planners, or is it all dreams of wealth-creating hipsters and young professionals?

Penny Taylor's summation is relatively succinct at a little over half an hour. The argument is broadly structured around the key issues identified by the inspector: the policies are up to date; they have an adequate supply of housing land; the development will have an adverse impact on the landscape; and it conflicts with the policies/plans. She acknowledges that the air-quality concerns are not part of the argument anymore, implicitly suggesting that they haven't gone away. She gives a detailed elaboration of case law and of how the NPPF works. She also says, gratifyingly, that "planning is not carried out by or for lawyers" and makes the case for local knowledge and elected representatives being "crucial elements of town and country planning in this country". Overall, Taylor endeavours to stress a holistic approach to planning and to reading the development plan.

After a short break, Max hands out copies of his closing statement. He highlights four issues identified by the inspector that are outstanding: the principle of development; the question of whether the policies are out of date; the housing-land supply issue; and the effect on the character of the site. He identifies two issues that have fallen away: air quality and heritage. I'm not sure where heritage has come from. He highlights considerable common ground between the parties, setting out in detail the concessions made by the council. I notice Morell shaking his head in disbelief at how their words are being repackaged. Max stresses the primacy of evidence and independent assessment over local knowledge. He suggests that consulting professional experts is at the heart of planning in this country. We go into every reference to case law made by Penny Taylor to hear why she has misunderstood it. Max then turns to land supply, unnecessarily going through the contested sites one at a time. He draws attention to the affordable housing the site would bring as a significant benefit that should be afforded significant weight. On landscape he gets a laugh from the public when he suggests that the scheme will bring a variety of "improvements". An hour and twenty minutes in, we thankfully seem to be approaching the end. A key closing point is his addressing Taylor's argument about planning not being by or for lawyers: Stanley is not a lawyer and there is nothing lawyerly about their argument!

The council does not get a right of reply, but Penny Taylor is keen to refer to some "factual matters". Unsurprisingly, Max is not keen, but we do have some back and forth until the inspector's patience fails. Any costs? No. The inspector thanks the advocates, says that all being well there will be a decision soon, and that's that.

I invite myself to OIP's debrief and nobody objects. I introduce myself to the developer's agent, a well-turned-out, grey-haired man around sixty. Hannah gets sandwiches, asking the agent if there is anywhere nearby that does nice baguettes. "What, here!?" he scoffs. He seems local but has clearly decided he has moved up the social ladder.

Max is quietly optimistic about their prospects. It could still go against them but they feel the inspector would have to do some work to justify this. Max says that younger inspectors like this one are being "driven hard" and are less likely to dismiss appeals as some of the older ones do. On Stanley's policy evidence they seem confident. They also think that landscape harm is key because this is where inspectors could refuse it and where different inspectors can wildly diverge. So much for objective knowledge! They think the public did them a favour by being so quiet. "Why did they bother coming?" Because you want to build 150 houses on their doorsteps maybe?

Max asks about our project, keen to be useful if he can. He is interested in academic research as he has done some. He tells me barristers cut their teeth defending councils, thereby learning their weaknesses – for instance, fearing costs – and then move up to representing developers. He thinks they did themselves a favour by not pursuing costs in this case, as it can be a headache for inspectors. Often what you can reclaim is limited anyway. The agent stresses that his client wanted to play it straight, no funny business. Filling the developer in at the end of each day, he has been stressing that it's a cricket match, not a football match, played over several days. Max refers to the process similarly as "the sport we play". People appreciate that the council are hard-pressed, but they didn't do themselves any favours in a number of respects. They are not used to inquiries so don't have the templates for proofs of evidence or the institutional savvy that some authorities might. The suggestion is also that they were doing everything very last minute, which made things hard for their advocate. Nevertheless, Max thinks Taylor could have done a better job.

Talking about the project, I refer to "development pressure". Max says they don't think in this way, they think about "housing need" – keen to feel like the good guys. Stanley says that shelter is one of the five fundamental human rights, having a nice view is not.[22] Politicians get short shrift from Stanley too; he says he's always found it odd that people elected to represent constituents who largely don't want development get the final say on whether it happens or not. By contrast, he stresses that "evidence" should drive decision-making.

Max has another night in his hotel here before his next gig. The agent is surprised he is not going home. He refers to the nice mattresses at the hotel, which you can buy if you want. Last time he stayed, there was an '80s-themed fancy-dress party downstairs, people dressed as Rambo, Cyndi Lauper: "That's just how people dress round here", says the agent. Everyone laughs.

5.9 Conclusion

OIP occupy a different market niche to Simpsons in Chapter 3. There is overlap, but OIP have a deeper long-term embeddedness in sub-regional work. They are a vital part of a place-based knowledge landscape, with a greater significance in recent years as they fill gaps in knowledge previously plugged by the public sector, especially in relation to strategic planning. This knowledge is both specific and synthetic. It concerns sites and their histories, an awareness of market demands and sets of technical knowledge regarding the requirements of specific occupiers. By synthesising this knowledge, OIP develop a picture of opportunities for development at local and sub-regional levels. This observation extends the literature on planning knowledge and where it resides which underscores a shift in power between public and private sectors: it is more likely than previously that the robust knowledge required to underpin planning work is found among private-sector planners, a change promulgated in part through extensive networking. Indeed, networking is a vital, largely undocumented feature of private-sector work that was far less present in the public sector, where austerity had cut these and other learning opportunities to the bone.

The 'public interest' focus for OIP is on providing much-needed housing but also on 'good planning' – suggesting where sites need repurposing to respond to changing conditions and unhitching local authorities from some of their 'path dependencies' in relation to them. They see themselves as providing an 'objective' view that can transcend what they perceive as inevitable local opposition to development driven by citizens' and politicians' self-interest. This inclination tends to 'other' citizens' and politicians' voices. Unless clients prioritise it, there is little motivation to drive innovation in sustainability or design. The weakness of the public sector both helps their cause, in allowing them to exploit the asymmetry of resources at planning inquiries and elsewhere, and also generates issues when fundamental data about, for example, land supply isn't available. The commercialisation of public-sector activity, such as charging for pre-application advice, also makes local-government officers remote and inserts more delays and costs into the land development process. OIP are alive to the pressures public-sector planners are under, but they also criticise them, sometimes unfairly and especially in conversations with other private-sector planners.

Meanwhile, OIP is a good place to work. Work intensification and extension exist at the director level,[23] but this is largely a choice (see Land and Taylor, 2010) and most staff find it a pleasant place to work. There is a culture of respect in the workplace, and the commercial pressures that might subvert work-life balance issues at, for example, larger employers such as Simpsons in Chapter 3 do not effect individuals here in the same way. Getting on at OIP also allows you into the "goalkeepers' union" of planners in the region, so long as you are willing to respect their understanding of the rules of the game.

6

So, just what are planners doing?

Planning is rarely out of the news these days, certainly in England. It gets mentioned in speeches by party leaders, it garners headlines in the national and local press and has been the focus of multiple reform initiatives, especially over the last twenty years. Yet, these debates largely concern the 'planning system' and its policies, targets, methods, legislation and decision-making procedures. Academic literature has also tended to follow this line of thought – seeing planning as a system that can be analysed, asking whether it meets wider societal objectives (for example, delivering much-needed housing or sustainable development) or evaluating the structural and political position of this activity in wider cultural and economic contexts. Yet, seeing planning merely as a system blinds us to the actual practices and environments in which planning is done.

This book has adopted a radically different approach, drawing on in-depth ethnography of real planning contexts to understand the everyday work of planners. It has put planners and where they work at centre stage. We have followed planners and the other professionals, members of the public and politicians that they meet with in four very different work environments. Our close attention to the work of planners has revealed distinct differences across the four cases, but also a series of commonalities that help us identify core features of a planning identity, however stretched this might be in rapidly changing environments. In rounding off this book, we present some closing thoughts on the nature of planning work in twenty-first-century England and some implications for understanding the profession, not only here but in many other countries.

6.1 What are the circumstances in which planners work?

Our aim to explore both public- and private-sector cases was very deliberate. Much research on planners and their work has focused on the public sector, with an uptick only recently in interest in the private sector (see for example Linovski, 2019). Our cases show some clear differences between the two sectors, such as the dominant part played by singular clients in the private sector and the often project-based focus of work in this sector. However, the differences are not as clear-cut on closer inspection. Southwell showed a partly privatised and outsourced public planning service where planners could be asked to work elsewhere, as prescribed in the contract with Theta. For planners, this involved the loss of expertise at critical junctures, as colleagues were removed to work elsewhere, and struggled with patched-together IT systems. However, commercial imperatives were not absolutely dominant, and planners and other staff had an engaged relationship with the locality and its people. Indeed, the number of local authorities who have fully outsourced their planning services remains very small,[1] there being political and practical concerns regarding the lack of local engagement and political control over what is often a very sensitive activity (see Slade et al, 2019).

Despite outsourcing being rare within English public-sector planning, broader commercial imperatives are increasingly structuring the work of planners working in local authorities. Bakerdale demonstrated a particularly overt attempt at introducing a more commercial mindset to the work of planners through its Go To programme. In seeking to drive income generation and efficiency, planners were both required and cajoled to change their approach to work by accounting for their time in more detail, ensuring their advice was billed for and following detailed, often computerised procedures. That the planners at Bakerdale did not actively reject this new way of working may be explained by a 'realism' that 'this was just the way things are going' shaped by a decade of local government austerity and longer-term continual 'reform' in both local government and planning. It speaks to the adaptability of planners but also raises more-concerning questions about the extent to which planners view themselves as having agency in shaping their work and what it seeks to achieve. While Bakerdale is at the sharper end of commercialisation in local authority planning, this is nonetheless a trend observed elsewhere and which is picked up in other interviews conducted for the Working in the Public Interest project (see Gunn, 2019; Slade et al, 2019). Indeed, austerity provided an ever-present background to our work, driving cost-cutting and efficiency initiatives that often hindered the capacity of planners to do anything other than the most basic work to keep the show on the road. As has been seen, and will be discussed in Section 6.2, austerity also came at personal cost to planners in terms of work intensification and uncertainty. However, the relative silence of planners surrounding the commercialisation of local authority planning is concerning as it points to a profession unwilling or unable to confront change in the environment in which it works (see Fisher, 2009).

While local-government planning has seen significant changes to the environment in which it works, private-sector work has shifted too, albeit in more subtle ways. The two cases of private-sector consultancies in this book demonstrate the close, though different in each case, ties between these companies and the public sector. Private-sector planners were acutely aware of austerity in terms of its shaping the context of their work, both regarding opportunities for supporting stretched local authority teams and also in relation to the frustrations of engaging with poorly resourced councils. Simpsons framed itself as an ally to local authority planning departments, bringing not only technical expertise to the public sector but also an increasing awareness of public-sector cultures and practices structured through ongoing work with councils and tactical work with ex-public-sector planners. This, however, was not always plain sailing, with Simpsons' planners being drawn into tensions between different actors, both public and private, in contentious projects. This points to a wider change in the private sector towards working in increasingly large, multi-actor teams. No longer are simple client-consultant relationships the mainstay of work in such large, multi-disciplinary consultancies, and planners often manage relationships with significant numbers of often powerful stakeholders, including fellow consultants. These larger projects provide more-sustainable long-term income streams (see Linovski, 2021), but for the planners who work on them, they also face dangers of longer tails, greater complexity and even ethical compromise.

On the face of it, the smaller OIP consultancy was engaged in more-traditional client-consultant relationships, advocating proposals for developers and promoting land for clients. Their work was mixed but dominated by work for private clients. Nonetheless, they had to navigate local planning processes stripped back by austerity, often to their frustration. In some ways, they turned this to their advantage, developing their in-depth knowledge of local planning debates to fill a strategic-planning knowledge void. In becoming the major source of planning knowledge in an area, this brought them into partnership with other consultancies looking to share this knowledge, information which in a bygone era may have been in the public domain, collected by the local planning authority. This presented in a rather ambiguous relationship with local authority planners, sometimes spilling over into frustration with councils and their lack of knowledge of things such as land supply on their 'patch', which we discuss in Section 6.4.

6.2 How do planners work?

We have highlighted the ways that planners work, how they organise their time and activities and how they work with one another. A great variety of working practices were observed, from deploying highly technical specialist as well as generalist advice to clients to engaging extensively with the public, sometimes in ways more akin to those of therapists or social workers (see Hoggett, 2006). However, a highly dominant strand, and one that is rarely talked about in literature related to planning, is that of work extension and work intensification. One of the lazy stereotypes used about planning is that public-sector planners have few incentives or much willingness to work hard. An infamous article in the *Daily Mail* in 2010 was titled 'The Great Inertia Sector: A whistleblower's account of council work where staff pull six-month sickies' (Walker, 2010); it sought to portray local authority workers as playing online poker and being constantly on sick leave, and claimed that 'the culture is very much one of getting minimum done for maximum pay'. Our observations showed this to be very far from true, with significant work pressure and long hours in both the public and private sectors.

Within the two public-sector settings observed, thinned-out teams as a result of austerity, combined with a shifting policy and regulatory context, meant that planners were often significantly stretched. This was combined, noticeably in Bakerdale, with a more-commercial approach to managing staff time – such that planners were recording their work in five-minute increments – but also with a desire to keep specialist skills in-house. In Southwell, the outsourcing model also necessitated more flexibility in terms of planners' work, such that they could shift their work between localities, covering gaps elsewhere and generating income for Theta. This was often stressful, necessitating the management of institutional and technical complexity while staff were still required to produce work of a high standard. Indeed, this commercial approach was developed in order to retain resources, as a buffer to local-government cuts, showing the complex relations between the drivers of work intensification within a neoliberal public-sector environment. Managers were alert to the pressures, with those in Bakerdale seeking to retain a team ethos amid the wider changes, and a positive work culture was also present at Southwell.

Many of the same pressures were notable in Simpsons and OIP, though this presented differently in the context of client relationships and the winning or retaining of business. Working days were often stretched, with additional hours taken up by more informal 'business-development' activities, receptions and networking events. In Simpsons this was particularly acute, as planners sought to demonstrate their 'hunger' for up-to-date knowledge by attending and presenting at workshops and undertaking additional research and reading in their own time. However, dealing with more complex, larger projects also increased the amount of time spent on them, requiring planners to find ways to manage the long tails of projects and demanding clients. For some, the always-on culture was symbolic of high status, though some more-junior planners failed to embrace this culture and were consequently seen as lacking 'hunger'. Memories of the property recession of the early 2010s instilled in some planners a desire to keep the work and clients flowing, reflecting the 'austerity planner' identified elsewhere in the Working in the Public Interest project (Slade et al, 2019). However, the implications of such work intensification were also apparent, and partly recognised (especially in Simpsons), with planners feeling less able to deliver high-quality work or do the broader thinking as well as experiencing impacts on their family life and mental health. That trade unions were not much present in any of the workplaces (though they were more apparent in the public sector) may indicate a wider reluctance to counter work intensification and a feeling that this is part of the new normal of working life. While issues of work-life balance and intensification might be dismissed as generic issues that don't have particularly distinctive features for planning, our research showed them to be significant features that hindered planners' abilities to effectively plan and develop new ways of approaching the challenges that planners profess to tackle. The resistance among more-junior planners to such pressure and their attempts to maintain a better work-life balance hints at positive change to come, at least in the sorts of private-sector workplaces we encountered.

Leadership within the workplace was an important dimension for understanding work intensification and planners' belonging within an organisation more broadly. The relatively strong and traditional hierarchy in Bakerdale enabled the chief planner and senior colleagues to generate cohesion and trust in their team, even while significant change in the form of the Go To programme was ongoing. Their vision of Bakerdale's planning department as being one of the best in the country necessitated the retention of in-house expertise, resisting a wider trend in which local authorities have lost specialist officers. Meanwhile, in Southwell, the lack of cohesive senior council leadership combined with an outsourcing model meant a more fragmented approach that left the planning team unable to set a long-term agenda for how work was done and unable to define the planning priorities that they sought to achieve. Leadership in the two private-sector cases was different: less traditionally bureaucratic in form, but nonetheless significant. At first glance, Simpsons had quite a loose and flat leadership structure, promoted through team workshops, independent learning and an emphasis on taking the initiative. However, the workplace culture was also carefully managed through small teams and the setting of expectations by more-senior staff, who at times were disappointed, as mentioned previously, by the lack of 'hunger' among junior staff. OIP was smaller, and while all staff were expected to contribute to networking, the senior team members were key for representing the company and generating work. Their technical knowledge combined with an understanding of clients meant that they were trusted by more-junior colleagues, who were able to access support when needed but who could ideally work independently and with a minimum of fuss.

A final aspect of workplace culture is one that is rarely mentioned in planning research and involves the physical spaces in which planners work (though see Beauregard, 2015). This not only matters in terms of the ability of planners to work effectively but also has symbolic value in reinforcing particular cultures and expectations. Universally, planners worked in open-plan offices. Hot-desking was dominant in the public sector and in Simpsons, while OIP staff tended to retain their own desks (and thus have a 'home' within the workplace). There was a corporate feel in all the places observed, with standardised signage, furniture and IT equipment, and offices in relatively modern buildings. The workplaces were anonymous, and the planning offices could have easily been home to another council department or consultancy. The stereotype of planning offices with plan libraries, map chests and proposal maps pinned to the walls seemed to be a thing of the past. The exception was perhaps Simpsons, which is housed in an old industrial building tastefully converted into offices, with breakout spaces and kitchens, replete with free fruit and flowers at the reception desk. This contrasted significantly with the reception areas in Southwell and Bakerdale, which were functional and used by a wide range of the community, giving a more democratic feel to the workplace. Despite much talk of 'PlanTech', the IT used in planning offices was often basic and creaking, using patched-together systems and frequently causing frustration to the planners. The exception, again, was Simpsons, where technology was more smoothly integrated and mobile, emphasising the flexible nature of their work but also enabling work extension.

6.3 Whom do planners work with?

One of the notable features of the planning work we observed was the constant nature of managing relationships with other professionals, politicians and the public. Planning is not a self-contained, technical profession but rather one that requires planners to carefully negotiate their role in relation to others in multiple settings and over a diverse range of issues. Planners often framed this as 'balancing' between different interests, but this perhaps displays too much confidence in the power of planners to actually balance between often powerful groups. Instead, much of the work of planners involves negotiating relationships, both in the sense of mediating between different groups but also of finding their way through difficult situations. Learning to navigate this institutional complexity is as key in local authorities as it was historically (for example, Healey, 2010, especially Chapter 3), and dealing with it is a major feature of Simpsons' business model.

A key group with whom planners work are local politicians. Both public- and private-sector planners appreciated the significance of politicians in the planning process. The majority of the engagements with politicians were in set-piece events, such as planning-committee meetings or consultation events, though more-senior officers tended to spend more time with politicians in briefings and other more informal occasions (see Kitchen, 1997). For planners in the private sector, set-piece events were often the only opportunities to engage with local councillors, and certainly in OIP this may have shaped a rather negative view of these politicians. A view expressed a few times was that planning would be better without political 'interference', that politicians are predisposed to be anti-development due to their reaction to very local public opposition to development and that their lack of expertise should preclude them from having a final say. For others in the private sector, including in Simpsons, a key skill was having their ears close to the ground to pick up local political soundings. At times Simpsons relied on officer insight to help them navigate local politics; at other times they worked with ex-public-sector planners to guide them. Within local authorities, planners were often frustrated with local politicians, though more-senior planners saw it as their role often to guide them to make the 'right' decision. The low regard in which politicians are held by planners can be seen as a potential problem for planning and the profession, leading many to ignore their input. Our cases showed that, at times, councillors contributed valuable insights based on local knowledge, common sense and a sharper appreciation of the values underpinning decisions. Planners tended to be somewhat trapped inside their own 'professional world', shaped often unconsciously by the current pre-occupations of the 'system', rather than asking simple questions such as where the occupants of new housing might shop (see Chapter 2).

While planning is often cast as a public service with a public-interest orientation, engagement with communities was not a particularly dominant part of the world of planners we observed. For those who worked in local authorities, particularly in development management, direct relationships with the public in the form of applicants and objectors were, however, a significant element of their work. At times, this required sensitivity to place concerns and an understanding of different interest groups as well as skills in communicating with those not versed in planning policy and processes. Sometimes, as in Southwell, the public were talked about fondly, and in small interactions were treated with respect and understanding. However, for many planners, particularly in the private sector, engagement with communities was not a significant element of their work, aside from at more formal events, such as public inquiries and the odd consultation event. Communities were often one step removed from their day-to-day work, being drawn into their world in the form of consultation responses and speeches at planning-committee meetings rather than through any form of direct engagement. How planners construct 'the public' was fascinating, with many supporting the principle of public engagement, but bemoaning the participation of a small group of self-selected 'usual suspects', while in locations such as Bakerdale they were presented as 'customers' and contrasted with 'clients' who were applicants for planning permission. The presentation of applicants as 'clients' was not questioned, with one Bakerdale planner noting: "I think, generally, we should be more like a consultancy. I find it hard to argue against it really. Ultimately, someone gets planning permission, that's a private benefit. Why would you pay for that with public money? So, I think we should be billing for everything."

When presented this way, in terms of customers and clients, relationships tend to be individualised rather than conceived as multiple and often overlapping.

Thus, when communities as diverse groups engage with the planning process, this model of singular relationships is disturbed, and perhaps planning becomes worse at understanding the public with which it is engaging.

Clients were a particularly significant feature of the work we observed both in the public and private sectors. Within the private sector, clients shaped work fundamentally. Winning and, often more importantly, retaining clients was a big part of the work of consultants, though this tended to fall on more-senior shoulders. Client power was apparent, though planners recognised the limits to this. In Simpsons, the mantra of 'only advise' sought to protect their planners from being embroiled in directing decisions, though some clients sought to push the limits of this, particularly in seeking to shape recommendations and analyses. Planners found this challenging, and talked of ways to navigate these tensions, though there were few examples seen of consultants actively walking away from projects or commissions. More apparent, and linked to the discussion in Section 6.2, was a sense of not wishing to disappoint clients, with planners going the extra mile to retain them and thus working beyond contracts and briefs. The creation of 'long tails' was often a bugbear of work, with some planners priding themselves on how they managed clients and projects to avoid this. However, as noted earlier, the rising complexity of multi-team projects was found to be increasingly challenging, particularly as partners were often highly knowledgeable professional players themselves.

A final, but important point, was that of how planners talked about each other. The substance of work and the cultures of workplaces were similar across public and private sectors, but planners often typified those working in the other sector. At times, particularly within the private sector, council planners were talked about negatively or condescendingly, perhaps resulting from frustration in dealing with often stretched local authority teams. However, public-sector planners were often also clients for private consultants, and some excellent working relationships were observed. Indeed, Simpsons sought to cultivate these relationships, seeing local authorities as significant clients who often came back for repeat business. For planners in the public sector, views of private sector planners were often more mixed, with some having experience of working in the private sector and some acceptance, as we have seen earlier in this section, that they felt they should act more like consultants. In reality the stereotypes were often reversed and it was the public-sector planners that were working longer, busier hours with their time more heavily monitored and accounted for, while the private-sector planners might be spending the afternoon in the pub, ostensibly on the grounds of networking and developing client relationships. The point is that such preconceptions are often outdated, and the realities of contemporary planning work take myriad forms in which public/private distinctions no longer apply in ways they might once have done (Steele, 2009).

While they might stereotype each other, planners spend much of their lives in relatively small worlds where each others' strengths, weaknesses and strategies are well known. Some consultants, for example, were trusted by public-sector planners to do 'good' planning work, while others required the deployment of various strategies such as non-engagement, the use of silences and various other forms of skilled negotiation practices. What has been less commented on historically in planning is the particularly classed, racialised and gendered nature of relationships within the sector. Social events, networking and business development often revolve around alcohol and socialising in pubs and bars, often outside core working hours. These rituals are sometimes firmly embedded in the culture of the organisation, from out-of-hours socialising and social groups to in-work rituals such as tea making (Schoneboom and Slade, 2020). In noticing rituals and wider aspects of work, our ethnography was sensitive to areas often dismissed in more-formal writing about planners and their work. Meetings, in particular, were good places to observe the micro-politics of everyday planning work. Humour and banter were significant parts of the working environment, whether this involved gently mocking an applicant or the telling of jokes about the public sector when private-sector planners got together. The humour and banter were not accidental but were important ways of building in-group identity (and, of course, of othering and excluding some groups) and getting through an often pressured, frustrating day.

6.4 What do planners know?

Over forty years ago, reporting on the last significant ethnographic study of English planning, Jackie Underwood and Patsy Healey noted: 'Any claim to "expert" status … would seem to require an association with knowledge and skills which have some specificity, some universality and some technical intricacy. The knowledge and skills that were displayed by the planners studied here hardly satisfied such requirements' (Healey and Underwood, 1978, p 121).

We would not go as far as Healey and Underwood in saying that planners demonstrated a lack of specific skills with universal applicability. However, despite more-specialist appraisal and design elements, much of the planning work we observed did not generally require deeply technical and codified knowledge and skills. While planning consultants might seek to demonstrate their technical skills to attract clients, much of the planning we observed was of a more 'generalist' nature, involving advising on planning applications and proposals and supporting policy work. This required planners to have a good understanding of national and local policies, precedents and the wider landscape of bodies that engage with the planning process. It also required tacit knowledge of the institutions and places in which they worked, enabling them to advise on how a proposal might be accepted or a policy might be interpreted.

Knowledge of places was particularly significant, though used and appreciated differently. Public-sector planners generally demonstrated a deep understanding of their localities, in geographical terms as well as institutionally in terms of the local politics of development. They also showed a deep affinity with their place of work, this often being the same locale where they lived and frequently where they were born. This sometimes extended into a deeper understanding of local citizenry, being aware of community dynamics and showing sensitivity to ethnicity and class. While this might not hold true in some local authorities, such as those in London where rapid turnover of staff may hinder the development of local knowledge, in our two public-sector cases there was more stability. This led to many local authority planners having significant, often decades-long experience of work in a place. For some in the private sector, this was sometimes seen as local authority planners being 'stuck in the mud' and resistant to change, though evidence from both Bakerdale and Southwell showed that planners were generally very flexible in terms of institutional and policy changes.

The nature of private-sector work sometimes militated against strong attachment to place; nonetheless, consultants sought to understand local planning dynamics, often using their networks and events to learn about what was going on in different markets and using this to identify opportunities and generate new business. OIP's regional engagement and understanding of local land markets, policy frameworks and opportunities for development in some ways filled a gap left by the decline in regional planning, replacing knowledge previously held by public-sector planners. Indeed, their status as experts in such areas as housing targets and land markets brought with it a technical know-how that was pragmatically applied through appeals, public inquiries and so on. While technical elements of planning, including the development, evaluation and critique of evidence bases, are nothing new, an increasingly adversarial planning system, in which significant money is to be made from development, heightens the value of such knowledge. And while much government rhetoric over the past thirty years has taken aim at 'red tape' in planning, we might see a growing requirement for evidence as part of a 'regulatory capitalism' that emerges in a neoliberal space and relies on regulation to constitute markets and socialise risk (Levi-Faur, 2005). Consultancies such as OIP might be seen as beneficiaries of this trend (Inch et al, 2022). Nonetheless, other forms of knowledge were downplayed in the move to commercialise planning. Southwell's outsourcing model required public-sector planners to do work in locations distant from their workplace, raising the prospect of a thinned-out version of planning in such places where local knowledge was replaced by computerised information and remote forms of access. The potential for the introduction of planning/design codes and the use of PlanTech to orchestrate knowledge and more-automated decision-making may further diminish the extent to which deep and engaged local knowledge is a feature of planning work, with consequences as shown in Chapter 2 and the use of Google Maps in the 'murdered hedgehogs' example (also see Chapman et al, 2020).

Beyond the local knowledge that is important for planners, a wider set of more generic skills are frequently deployed, key among them communication. The range of actors that planners encounter in their day-to-day work requires the best to be highly effective at writing and speaking to different audiences. Within the private-sector cases, particularly Simpsons, project-management skills were prized, often being brought into everyday work to try to manage individual workloads and share information. These project-forms of working are increasingly apparent, as planners move away from more traditional, bureaucratic modes or the simple provision of advice to a single client. In turn, planners need to rely on a range of networking and people-management skills, from dealing with micro-aggressions (for example from clients) through to handling silences and gaps in communication. While Healey and Underwood argued that planning shows little in the way of specialist expertise, our research showed instead a distinctive set of ways in which expertise was pulled together and deployed. The fragmentation of institutions, a changeable policy environment and the increased complexity of how the built environment is produced and managed means that planners require some agility in how they develop and deploy their knowledge. This can be seen as a particular form of technocracy, though one aligned within a distinctive neoliberal environment (Raco and Savini, 2019). It also, however, points to an imbalance of resources, skills and capacity between the public and private sectors, particularly after ten years of local-government austerity. Training budgets in local authorities have been severely cut, and opportunities to learn and network have diminished, meaning that the private sector is now the repository of much 'authorised' knowledge in the sector and is more alive to emerging issues, be they new areas of demand, such as crematoria (see Chapter 5), or changing global policy debates over, for example, the walkable city (see Chapter 3). In hosting events, they play a more dominant role in the profession (and in the Royal Town Planning Institute (RTPI), in particular) and gain from an increased profile and greater opportunities to share knowledge. While some of this knowledge is in turn bought in by councils contracting companies such as Simpsons, this is limited in scope, and the potential for a knowledge asymmetry between public and private sectors is apparent.

6.5 Who are planners and what do they believe in?

Healey and Underwood's quote at the opening of Section 6.4 indicates a belief that professions require some substantive, expert and codified knowledge, something that the planners they followed did not display. While there was no one form of or approach to knowledge displayed by the planners we worked with, it was apparent that there was a shared community of understanding around planning that might be seen as a more significant facet of professional endeavour than knowledge alone (Vigar, 2012). The planners we talked to generally saw themselves as professionals, albeit with some having doubts (see Slade et al, 2021, for example). In the private sector, professional identity was particularly significant for drumming up trade, holding one's own within a multi-professional company and working with other professionals. In the public sector, professionalism was less instrumental, but was significant in defining planners' terrain as the key profession focused on shaping places. Despite this, the RTPI was not a dominant part of the professional lives of those we worked with. Membership of the institute was strongest in the private sector, and there was some engagement with regional events, but its status as an organisation seeking to promote and protect the profession was rarely discussed. Instead, prior experience of planning education was seen as a more significant common denominator among many of the planners we talked to.

While professional identity was quietly demonstrated, largely around a form of shared community or communities of practice rather than through particular skills or knowledge, most planners cleaved to a vision of planning as serving the public. The public interest was talked about by many planners (perhaps because of the name of our project), but often in rather diverse and sometimes contradictory ways. We have mentioned in Section 6.3 the invocation of 'customers' and 'clients' within Bakerdale, perhaps presenting a rather thin and individualistic approach to the public. The involvement of local politicians as democratic representatives of the public was not viewed as a particularly strong way of invoking the public interest; indeed, politicians were often seen as getting in the way of 'good' decisions. Nonetheless, planners did recognise the distinctive and significant role of local politicians in defining and representing local priorities, even if they disagreed with them. Certainly, within the public-sector settings we identified a continuing public-sector ethos among planners who sought to serve the locality with integrity and accountability. However, the extent to which this can be sustained in a context of increased commercialisation and fragmentation of roles and work is questionable, this and may provide a distinct challenge for planning as an activity that has already faced sustained critique in the past twenty years.

As an alternative, some planners sought to define their role in more instrumental terms as a way of delivering public goods, particularly housing. Indeed, the provision of housing (sometimes defined as 'affordable') was noted a number of times as forming an underlying rationale for planning, particularly by those working in the private sector (and was invoked as a 'human right' by one planner). The delivery of development was thus accorded as a distinct moral purpose for planning, often without attention to the quality or wider implications of what was built (see Slade et al, 2021). This is not to say that planners were unaware of other justifications for planning: there were loosely presented invocations of planning as a connective activity that helps address societal challenges, including climate change and environmental degradation. However, these justifications were not as strongly articulated within the everyday work of planning and tended to be used formulaically as a means of arguing for the merits of a project. While some planners sought to position themselves more centrally in relation to work done to address key challenges (particularly at Simpsons), the reality of much of the work we observed was a long way from the presentation of planning as a crucial solution to these problems.

Planners' lack of much substantive power to fundamentally shape patterns of development and its resulting form led to the celebration of minor changes to developments as significant. For example, developments were praised as 'sustainable' if they included electric-vehicle charging points, and Section 106 monies were viewed more as a means of sustaining services rather than as enabling substantive mitigation or work towards more inclusive or sustainable communities. Our work suggests a rather bleak picture of planning as a relatively narrow, highly pragmatic activity involved in managing and smoothing development and restricted to challenging the worst aspects of proposals, but without the power or position to fundamentally change the nature of development. Limited mitigation is, then, the order of the day, perhaps best exemplified in the production of car-dominant, city-edge housing development in Chapter 2. Here we see a sadly all too typical scenario in which planners are unable to secure renewable-energy schemes yet hope that electric-vehicle charging points and future autonomous vehicles will be enough to achieve sustainability (Transport Planning Society, 2018). Dominant national policy combined with structures of land ownership and a powerful, oligarchic development sector driven by investor demands have led to local planning being restricted in what it can achieve. While this has different implications for public- and private-sector planners, neither group has much power within the creation of our built environment, and this in turn shows how changes to the planning system have restricted the ambition and scope of what planners think planning itself can achieve.

6.6 Conclusion

So, what does following planners in their workplaces tell us about contemporary planning in England? We first should note that planning is a diverse profession, taking place in multiple locations, often working to different agendas and containing a huge variety of work, skills and commitments. Yet, having said this, planners in our study still saw themselves as a particular group of professionals often concerned (albeit in differing ways) with the development of 'better' places (Bickenbach and Hendler 1994; Healey, 2010). The reality of sustaining this group identity within rapidly changing environments and the often very different underlying rationales of professional work has not fully been understood either by academic researchers or policymakers, and we argue that the planning profession's ability to define and value itself is at risk. Much discussion in planning still revolves around policy and procedures rather than the environments in which it is implemented. We believe the ethnographic approach underpinning this book goes some way towards addressing this imbalance. Without knowing how planners work, how they navigate often conflictual circumstances in changing environments and how they understand their practice, we run the risk of developing policies and projects that are unlikely to be sustained and implemented, and we may continue to overlook how planning might be shaped to achieve wider societal goals. In turn, this may hinder the changes we know are needed in our cities and regions.

One of the more concerning elements of our work was the narrowness of much of the planning work we observed. In talking of narrowness, we are referring to professional work focused on procedural box-ticking, delivery and project management, particularly of housing, which is still cast in terms of delivering numbers of units, with insufficient attention paid to quality and affordability (see Layard, 2019). These concerns form the centre of much planning work, whether it is private-sector actors seeking to secure development or public-sector planners dealing with planning applications. It shows the ongoing relevance of Eric Reade's observation that planners and developers 'will come to develop a shared subculture. They will be likely to develop shared attitudes and values, shared perceptions of what is economically possible and socially desirable, and most significantly, shared beliefs as to what kind of development best promotes the "public interest"' (Reade, 1987, p 92).

While many planners we spoke to retained ambitions for a wider scope and the potential for planning to address other concerns, such as climate change, they were often unable to significantly influence outcomes, instead mitigating the worst aspects of development and spending precious time extensively mediating between more powerful players. The narrowness of the work we observed was also often related to the limited scope for planners to substantially develop an agenda for planning squeezed between national government-set targets and developers' and local political interests. Even by a generous reading, the power and distinctiveness of local plans is debatable (certainly beyond housing-land allocation), a point supported by the fact that a key driver for finishing a plan is the avoidance of planning by appeal. With a lack of strategy, it is almost impossible to tell whether an individual proposal is sustainable development, yet this was the task of planners, forcing them to judge proposals as such because they had electric-vehicle charging points or a cycle path. The limited acting space for planners was also partly the product of a continuously highly centralised English polity, which has only gotten worse as local-government resources have diminished. As such, many of the projects in our cases were constrained by the demands of central-government funding schemes such as the Housing Infrastructure Fund, which further diminished planners' ability to act in a cause of 'good' planning, particularly as they imposed time constraints which foreclosed the development and negotiation of 'better' outcomes.

A key focus of our work was to understand planning practice in both public and private sectors. That each sector is highly diverse should be apparent from our work, and we do not wish to state that our work represents all of planning in its many workplace environments. However, we note some trends that were apparent. The first is the ongoing commercialisation of public-sector planning, whether this involves full outsourcing, as seen in Southwell, or organisational change projects such as that seen in Bakerdale. The tendency is towards a more procedural and transactional form of planning, focusing on 'customer service' rather than a broader conception of planning as a public service. There is something to build on. Public-sector planners did retain an ethos of public service and often had deep understandings of, and attachments to, the places they worked. However, continuing organisational change and greater introduction of technology may further erode this more embodied, public-focused way of working. Certainly, austerity has had very significant effects on planning in the UK, and life on the front line of public-sector planning feels stretched, further thinning the potential for it to address the wider agendas mentioned in Section 6.5.

Secondly, for those working in the private sector, the spectre of the early-2010s recession still looms large and illustrates the sector's reliance on a sustained property boom. Planners worked hard to gain and retain clients, sometimes leading to compromises and the setting of boundaries when they felt a client wanted inappropriate development but did not want to explicitly reject the work. As shown in Chapter 3, these ethical compromises, while causing planners to stop and reflect, nonetheless were made. Part of the skill of planners we observed, particularly in the private sector organisations, was the way in which they sought to nudge clients away from very bad proposals, though their power to do so in large projects was often limited (Chan and Protzen, 2018). Many were thoughtful about their work and the compromises it entailed, but the culture of hard work and constant networking had an impact on work-life balance and time for reflection. Sustaining this in a more volatile economic climate, in which business is not guaranteed, could be a major challenge for many planners working in consultancies.

Thirdly, and finally, public- and private-sector planners did work together with a strong relationship in places, particularly as local authorities increasingly relied on consultancy expertise. Yet we also saw planners in each sector stereotyping each other and sharing frustrations, raising the prospect of a rather divided profession, the respective parts of which may view themselves as having increasingly less and less in common with each other.

In conclusion, our concern was to understand how planners are oriented towards public ideals and share a common vision. Values are harder to identify in diverse sectors with different professional identities and drivers of work. Planners still retain some common understanding of the role of planning as seeking to shape places, yet often they approached this question from divergent perspectives. Some saw planning as principally a means to deliver housing; others had rationales for their work embedded in ideas of good design, environmental protection and sustainable development. Many viewed themselves as being in a position to 'balance' these often competing interests, though this might ignore the actual power of planning and planners to effect meaningful change. 'Politics' was often talked of as a dirty word, infecting some notional, 'technical' purity of planning decisions; yet without a clear understanding of the value of democratic politics to planning, planners risk under-appreciating how power might flow in undemocratic ways to shape our built environments (see Grange, 2017).

Looking at the situation in only one country might be seen as rather parochial. However, we would argue that many of the trends we have identified throughout the book are reflected in other locations. The growing dominance of private-sector planning and its business models and ethics has been discussed in many locations, including the USA and Canada (Loh and Arroyo, 2017; Linovski, 2019). The increasingly intertwined nature of public and private planning has been noted in contexts such as Finland and Norway (Mäntysalo and Saglie, 2010), and the commercialisation of public-sector planning has been described in many European locations, from Amsterdam (Koolmees and Majoor, 2019) to Stockholm (Metzger and Zakhour, 2019). These speak to a wider trend towards technocratic planning as the means to sustain a neoliberal approach to land and property markets, one that offers scope for further in-depth ethnographic work in a variety of contexts.

We have observed here the narrowness of much of the planning we saw, and this points to the heart of the profession's situation. While many talked ambitiously about planning's potential to solve issues of climate change, environmental degradation and housing inequality, such talk seemed far removed from the compromises, limited power and conflictual environment which shaped many planners' professional work. The fact that while many planners saw themselves as professionals, they did not talk much about how the profession might be changed to achieve these wider goals, gives an impression of a profession without a clear guiding purpose. We observed good work being done by committed individuals, often working in challenging circumstances. In this sense there is much to build on. But the discretionary nature of English planning creates a multitude of problems, not least in that it undermines the long-term nature of the work required of planners to think about place futures. But this discretionary nature also suggests an opportunity. Not much would need to change for planning to re-emerge as a force to shape places in ways that can help tackle the climate emergency, inequality and a range of societal challenges in the twenty-first century. However, without greater discussion and agreement on what planning is for in this regard, and how planners might serve it, the profession will continue to find itself shaped too much by events rather than in charge of its own destiny.

Notes

Chapter 1
1. A tendency noted historically in organisational studies more generally (Garsten and Nyqvist, 2013).
2. See also this edition of the *50 Shades of Planning* blog: http://samuelstafford.blogspot.com/2021/12/life-on-front-line.html
3. Note that a significant number of planners, approximately 10 per cent, work in the third/voluntary sector, an area worthy of further study but which is outside the scope of our work.
4. Approximately 37 per cent of planning-fee income to consultancies came from the public sector in 2019–20 (Dewar, 2020).

Chapter 2
1. Section 106 (s106) of the Town and Country Planning Act 1990 provides for site specific mitigation of the impact of development, in this case the provision of new transport infrastructure.
2. Southwell was one of the twenty councils worst hit by cuts in the period 2010–11 to 2016–17 (Gray and Barford, 2018).
3. TUPE refers to Transfer of Undertakings (Protection of Employment) Regulations, which protect some of the rights of employees where their employer changes to another business.
4. A common feature in English local government in the 2010s (Slade et al, 2019).
5. Large open-plan offices are not new in local government but there was strong corporate control over the working space at Southwell, and the absence of a library and the lack of things like maps on walls/screens is significant (see Beauregard, 2015).
6. The mascot of Children in Need, an annual UK fundraiser.
7. Routine untidiness and mud on roads caused by developers are persistent problems, generating numerous public complaints. A highways officer told us that he is so frustrated with the issue that he gives the 'Mr Angrys' of this world the mobile number of the developer so they can bear the impact of their actions directly.
8. This extends ideas of public service, showing the importance of kindness, collegiality and compassion in planning (Lyles et al, 2018; Forester, 2021).
9. 'PlanTech' and 'proptech' were significant buzzwords at the time of our fieldwork, not least in central government (Connected Places Catapult, 2020). The rhetoric-reality gap was very sharp, and the IT clutter was not conducive to deep, slow thinking.
10. The 1985 dystopian sci-fi film directed by Terry Gilliam in which bureaucratic excess and machine surveillance feature heavily.
11. Theta's name appears on various background documents and it is unclear whether this work is part of the annually negotiated contract with the local authority or the routine winning of contracts.
12. The council, like many at this time in the UK, declared a climate emergency during the course of our fieldwork, with little discernible consequence.
13. A goalkeeper in football effectively plays a different game to the ten colleagues in their team. They thus find themselves bonded less to their teammates than to other goalkeepers in rival teams through shared experiences, language, practices, humiliations and triumphs. The term was used by a planner in our Chapter 5 case. There are some equivalences with Wenger's (1998) ideas of 'communities of practice'.

14. English legal requirements relating to ecology strengthened significantly during the 2010s and into the 2020s, notably consolidated in the Environment Act 2021 in England, further narrowing the discretionary 'acting space' (Grange, 2013) for planners.
15. How planners and planning committees treat reports from 'domain experts', such as ecology or heritage, is left to their judgement, but it is potentially open to legal challenge.
16. Southwell's ecologist considered the loss of farmland birds the biggest ecological issue facing the district.
17. The village, as noted, has little character, although the only listed building, an industrial premises in continuous use for over a century, was to be demolished to make way for a large roundabout into the development.
18. There is no statutory definition of affordable housing, but typically it is housing available at 80 per cent of the local market value (for rent or purchase).
19. 'The petty thief is hanged, the big thief gets away.'
20. This language is common, and not given enough attention in practice or research (compare Bicquelet-Lock et al, 2020).
21. Such reflections of a patriarchal culture, and the skill required in dealing with it, were common in communicative settings in our research; for a wider illustration see Forester and Kilgore (2020).
22. The officers defend Southwell's 'generous' parking standards on the grounds that, if proper spaces are not provided, people tend to park in a way that obstructs pavements. However, the policy also encourages car ownership, embedding car dependency in housing developments.
23. A heat network is an environmentally friendly system that takes heat from a central source and delivers it to many buildings throughout, for example, a new housing development. Central government advocated for them, but take-up was voluntary, with few financial or other incentives. The UK is highly dependent on gas for heating, and a ban on gas boilers in new-build homes from 2025 was likely. Many of the Everdale Fields houses won't be built by then given the long-term nature of the development, making this particularly disappointing.
24. When the local plan was being developed, Leavesley proposed ambitious carbon targets for heating, which were quickly deleted.

Chapter 3

1. Senior strategic planners were the hardest to recruit at this time (see Blackman, 2021).
2. We recognise that planning officers in local authorities advise elected members, but see the advisory relationship between consultant and client as structured differently, particularly by the paying relationship.
3. See Parker et al (2018). Also see Parker et al (2019), in which advising is seen as one of three main roles of planning consultants.
4. See Loh and Norton (2013). Also see Linovski (2017) for discussion on pro bono practices.
5. See Marcuse (1976) for discussion of autonomy in the provision of planning advice.
6. The packaging up of technical expertise by consultancies might be seen as part of wider trends towards technocracy in management of the built environment (see Raco and Savini, 2019).
7. See Marcuse (1976) for discussion of cases such as these, including the work of consultants advising the mayor of 'Oldport'.
8. See Howe (1994) for typologies including 'traditional technicians' and 'active planners'.
9. See Linovski (2019) for discussion of consultancy as defined by fee-charging. Interestingly, Linovski's US consultant interviewees did not mention the 'fee-for-service' nature of private consultancy.

10. This may be an (outdated) misconception; see Chapter 4 for discussion of counting working time at Bakerdale Council.
11. Autonomy is often seen as a hallmark of knowledge-intensive firms but frequently exists in tension with impulses to control and manage companies (see Alvesson, 2011). Our biographical interviews (Clifford, 2018) also noted a tension inherent in takeovers and mergers in the sector which can disempower middle-ranking and senior planners.
12. There is an extensive literature emerging on planning reform in England and the positioning of planning ideologically – see Inch and Shepherd (2020), Marshall (2021) and Clifford (2020).
13. Mental Health First Aid (mhfaengland.org) is a national guidance and training initiative to support mental health.
14. Deal and Kennedy's (1982) seminal work extols the benefits to employees of a strong culture. However, this claim has also been extensively critiqued by Willmott (1993), Hochschild (1997), Kunda (1992) and others in relation to work-life balance considerations.

Chapter 4

1. Party politics can play a significant role in English local government (Hall and Leach, 2000), but councillors on planning committees tend to prioritise independence, judgement and common sense.
2. There is a significant, emerging body of work on the adoption of market-oriented understandings within planning over the last two decades; see, for example, Harris and Thomas (2011), Clifford (2012) and Raco (2018). For a thorough grounding of Bakerdale's commercialisation agenda within this literature see Slade et al (2021).
3. Bakerdale has thus advanced a process we observed in Chapter 2 at Southwell rather more quickly and efficiently by doing it 'in-house'.
4. For an overview of the roots of this change, see Ferlie et al (1996).
5. See Chapter 2 as well as Colenutt (2020) for a thorough dissection of the UK's 'property lobby' and its disproportionate power.
6. The Housing Infrastructure Fund (HIF) provides central-government money with which to build infrastructure to 'unlock' housing sites.
7. This has rightly proved contentious; see Booth (2020).
8. See Ferm and Raco (2020) for further discussion of the impact of the UK's uneven developmental geographies on market-led planning reform.
9. This was becoming a bugbear for planning at this time. For example, the singer Ed Sheeran built a 'wildlife pond' at his Suffolk mansion complete with handrails, steps and a neighbouring sauna, which attracted the ire of his neighbours and the planning authority.
10. This observation is borne out somewhat by research that suggests slightly more planning students see themselves going into the private than the public sector (Hickman et al, 2021).
11. The bus trip is useful for planners to gauge members' feelings about applications and helps avoid the element of surprise we saw in "Murdered Hedgehogs" in Chapter 2.
12. Some development has always been permitted by the English planning system since the nationalisation of development rights in 1948. However, permitted development rights were significantly extended from 2013 to allow for the conversion of offices, and certain other uses, to housing. See Clifford et al (2020).
13. The Community Infrastructure Levy (CIL) is a planning charge introduced by the Planning Act 2008 as a tool for local authorities in England and Wales to help deliver infrastructure to support the development of their area. It came into force on 6 April 2010 through the Community Infrastructure Levy Regulations 2010.

14 As mentioned in Chapter 2, Section 106 (s106) of the Town and Country Planning Act 1990 provides for site-specific mitigation of the impact of development.

Chapter 5

1. Planning appeals can be dealt with through written representations, informal hearings or full inquiries.
2. See "Murdered Hedgehogs" in Chapter 2.
3. Schwartzmann (1989) exhorts ethnographers to be attentive to spaces around the obvious object of research attention such as meetings!
4. Learning and networking opportunities were less visible in our local-government cases.
5. See Kunda (1992) and Hochschild (1997) for similar findings.
6. Since 2003, although their introduction accelerated somewhat later, local authorities have been able to charge for meeting applicants. See Chapters 2 and 4 and Slade et al (2021).
7. The deficit between the glossy rhetoric of 'PlanTech' and the reality at the coalface was a constant feature of our work; see also Chapter 2.
8. This lack of urgency with regard to decarbonising transport was alarmingly common, alongside a conception of autonomous and/or electric vehicles as a panacea; see Lamb et al (2020), Brand (2021) and Chapter 2.
9. See, Parker, Salter and Wargent (2019) for an outline of the challenges neighbourhood planning poses.
10. It is in the council's interest to suggest more units can go on sites as it contributes to numbers in their five-year housing-land supply.
11. Despite this view, some planning consultancies have undertaken such work using RTPI members to execute it.
12. In contrast with work extension and intensification in our other workplaces, see Chapters 2 and 3, and on employee responses to this, see Nippert-Eng (1996).
13. REG19 forms part of the consultation process on a proposed local plan, outlined in 'The Town and Country Planning (Local Planning) (England) Regulations 2012', whereby prior to submission a full copy of a draft plan must be made available for people to make representations.
14. Leaving work early on Friday to go to the pub was historically associated with British local government.
15. Changes to the NPPF in 2021 made building in flood plains more difficult, but past history, rather as in discussions of sustainable transport, suggests English planning hasn't taken environment and climate-change issues seriously.
16. English Nature was renamed Natural England in 2006, twelve years prior to this encounter.
17. See Chapter 2 and the seabird mitigation payments for a similar example.
18. *The Planners*, and a follow-up, *Permission Impossible*, were fly-on-the-wall documentary series following several teams of local authority planners.
19. See Vigar (2012) on the judgement that comes with experience.
20. This illustrates the yawning gap between planning theory's emphasis on the rich variety of different knowledges that are useful for planning and creeping legalisation which fuels the English system's demand for quantifiable evidence.
21. The UK government's stated intention when introducing the NPPF was to reduce complexity and lawyerly arguments.
22. The government's own research concluded that planning and land supply were not the barriers to delivering more houses, rather it was the 'market absorption rate'; this is to say, housebuilders trickle houses into the market to maintain prices (Letwin, 2018).

[23] Salaries exhibit a fairly flat structure in the branch, although directors earn most of their income through annual bonus payments. In the period following the 2008 recession, no bonuses were paid and directors took home lower wages than most staff to avoid redundancies.

Chapter 6

[1] See Clifford (2018), reporting a survey of local authorities which found that only eight local authorities had a fully outsourced planning department.

References

Abram, S. (2004) 'Personality and professionalism in a Norwegian district council', *Planning Theory*, 3(1): 21–40.

Alvesson, M. (2011) *Management of Knowledge-Intensive Companies*, Berlin: De Gruyter.

Amin-Smith, N., Phillips, D. and Simpson, P. (2016) *Real-Terms Change in Local Government Service Spending by LA Decile of Grant Dependence, 2009–10 to 2016–17, England, Scotland and Wales*, London: Institute for Fiscal Studies.

Anderson-Gough, F., Grey, C. and Robson, K. (2000) 'In the name of the client: the service ethic in two professional services firms', *Human Relations*, 53(9): 1151–74.

Annink, A. and den Dulk, L. (2012) 'Autonomy: the panacea for self-employed women's work-life balance?', *Community, Work & Family*, 15(4): 383–402.

Auty, S. (1996) 'Designing and testing a resource-based method for setting professional fees', *Journal of Professional Services Marketing*, 13(2): 71–92.

Back, L. (2014) 'Journeying through words: Les Back reflects on writing with Thomas Yarrow: Writers on writing', *The Journal of the Royal Anthropological Institute*, 20(4): 766–70.

Barrett, S. and Fudge, C. (1981) *Policy and Action: Essays on the Implementation of Public Policy*, London: Methuen.

Baum, H. (2015) 'Planning with half a mind: why planners resist emotion', *Planning Theory & Practice*, 16(4): 498–516.

Beauregard, R.A. (1998) 'Writing the planner', *Journal of Planning Education and Research*, 18(2): 93–101.

Beauregard, R.A. (2015) *Planning Matter: Acting with Things*, Chicago: University of Chicago Press.

Bickenbach, J. and Hendler, S. (1994) 'The moral mandate of the planning profession', in H. Thomas (ed), *Values and Planning*, Aldershot: Avebury, pp 162–77.

Bicquelet-Lock, A., Divine, J. and Crabb, B. (2020) *Women and Planning: an Analysis of Gender Related Barriers to Professional Advancement*, London: RTPI.

Blackman, D. (2021) 'The most in-demand skills in planning', *Planning*, Autumn: 24–7.

Booth, P. (2003) *Planning By Consent: the Origins and Nature of British Developmental Control*, London: Routledge.

Booth, R. (2020) 'Revealed: London councils take funds from developers to pay for planning guidelines', *The Guardian*, [online] 23 August, Available from: www.theguardian.com/politics/2020/aug/23/revealed-councils-accept-payments-from-developers-to-fund-planning-guidelines [Accessed 26 April 2022].

Boxall, P. and Macky, K. (2014) 'High-involvement work processes, work intensification and employee well-being', *Work, Employment and Society*, 28(6): 963–84.

Brand, C. (2021) 'Obsessing over electric cars is impeding the race to net zero: more active travel is essential', *Our Research: True Planet*, [blog] 14 June, Available from: www.research.ox.ac.uk/article/2021-06-14-obsessing-over-electric-cars-is-impeding-the-race-to-net-zero-more-active-travel-is-essential [Accessed 26 April 2022].

Brewer, J. (2004) 'Ethnography', in C. Cassell and G. Symon (eds) *Essential Guide to Qualitative Methods in Organizational Research*, London: Sage, pp 312–22.

Brindley, T., Rydin, Y. and Stoker, G. (1996) *Remaking Planning: The Politics of Urban Change*, London: Routledge.

Campbell, H. and Marshall, R. (1998) 'Acting on principle: dilemmas in planning practice', *Planning Practice & Research*, 13(2): 117–28.

Campbell, H. and Marshall, R. (2002) 'Utilitarianism's bad breath? A re-evaluation of the public interest justification for planning', *Planning Theory*, 1(2): 163–87.

Carmona, M. and Sieh, L. (2004) *Measuring Quality in Planning: Managing the Performance Process*, London: Spon Press.

Chapman, K., Tait, M. and Inch, A. (2020) 'The dangers of data', *Town and Country Planning*, 89(9/10): 307–11.

Chan, J.K.H. and Protzen, J.P. (2018) 'Between conflict and consensus: searching for an ethical compromise in planning', *Planning Theory*, 17(2): 170–89.

Cherry, G.E. (1974) *The Evolution of British Town Planning: A History of Town Planning in the United Kingdom During the 20th Century and of the Royal Town Planning Institute, 1914–74*, Leighton Buzzard: Leonard Hill Books.

Clarke, J. and Newman, J. (1997) *The Managerial State: Power, Politics and Ideology in the Remaking of Social Welfare*, London: Sage.

Clifford, B. (2012) 'Planning in an age of customers: British local authority practitioners, identity and reactions to public sector reform', *Town Planning Review*, 83(5): 553–74.

Clifford, B. (2018) 'Freedom of information request to support Work Package 2: Charting outsourcing in UK public planning', *Working in the Public Interest*, [online], Available from: sites.google.com/sheffield.ac.uk/witpi/research/foi?authuser=0 [Accessed 8 August 2022].

Clifford, B., Ferm, J., Livingstone, N. and Canelas, P. (2019) *Understanding the Impacts of Deregulation in Planning: Turning Offices into Homes?*, Cham: Palgrave Macmillan.

Clifford, B., Canelas, P., Dunning, R., Ferm, J., Livingstone, N. and Lord, A. (2020) *Research into the Quality Standard of Homes Delivered through Change of Use Permitted Development Rights*, London: MHCLG.

Climate Change Committee (2016) 'Fifth carbon budget infographic', *Climate Change Committee*, [blog] 20 July, Available from: www.theccc.org.uk/2016/07/20/fifth-carbon-budget-infographic/ [Accessed 26 April 2022].

Colenutt, B. (2020) *The Property Lobby: The Hidden Reality Behind the Housing Crisis*, Bristol: Policy Press.

Connected Places Catapult (2020) *Transforming the Digital Architecture of Planning*, London: Connected Places Catapult.

Davoudi, S. and Strange, I. (2009) *Conceptions of Space and Place in Strategic Spatial Planning*, London: Routledge.

Deal, T. and Kennedy, A. (1982) *Corporate Cultures: The Rites and Rituals of Organizational Life*, Reading, MA: Addison-Wesley.

Dewar, D. (2020) 'The planning consultancy market report 2020: overview', *Planning*, Autumn: 17–19.

Duneier, M. (2001) *Sidewalk*, New York: Farrar, Straus and Giroux.

Durning, B., Carpenter, J., Glasson, J. and Watson, G.B. (2010) 'The spiral of knowledge development: professional knowledge development in planning', *Planning Practice & Research*, 25(4): 497–516.

Erickson, K.C. and Stull, D.D. (1998) *Doing Team Ethnography: Warnings and Advice*, Thousand Oaks, CA: Sage.

Etzioni, A. (1969) *The Semi-professions and their Organization: Teachers, Nurses, Social Workers*, New York: Free Press.

Evans, B. (1993) 'Why we no longer need a town planning profession', *Planning Practice & Research*, 8(1): 9–15.

Evetts, J. (2011) 'A new professionalism? Challenges and opportunities', *Current Sociology*, 59(4): 406–22.

Ferlie, E., Ashburner, L., Fitzgerald, L. and Pettigrew, A. (1996) *The New Public Management in Action*, Oxford: Oxford University Press.

Ferm, J. and Raco, M. (2020) 'Viability planning, value capture and the geographies of market-led planning reform in England', *Planning Theory & Practice*, 21(2): 218–35.

Fincham, R., Clark, T., Handley, K. and Sturdy, A. (2008) 'Knowledge narratives and heterogeneity in management consultancy and business services', in D. Muzio, S. Ackroyd and J.-F. Chanlat (eds) *Redirections in the Study of Expert Labour: Established Professions and New Expert Occupations*, Basingstoke: Palgrave Macmillan, pp 183–203.

Fisher, M. (2009) *Capitalist Realism: Is There No Alternative?*, Winchester: Zero Books.

Fleming, P. and Spicer, A. (2003) 'Working at a cynical distance: implications for power, subjectivity and resistance', *Organization*, 10(1): 157–79.

Forester, J. (1999) *The Deliberative Practitioner: Encouraging Participatory Planning Processes*, Cambridge, MA: MIT Press.

Forester, J. (2021) 'Our curious silence about kindness in planning: challenges of addressing vulnerability and suffering', *Planning Theory*, 20(1): 63–83.

Forester, J. and Kilgore, A. (2020) 'Dancing around male violence: the all too ordinary backstory to Barshefsky's extra-ordinary practice', *Negotiation Journal*, 36(2): 189–91.

Frank, A.I. (2007) 'Entrepreneurship and enterprise skills: a missing element of planning education?', *Planning Practice & Research*, 22(4): 635–48.

Friedson, E. (2001) *Professionalism: The Third Logic*, Cambridge: Polity.

Furbey, R., Reid, B. and Cole, I. (2001) 'Housing professionalism in the United Kingdom: the final curtain or a new age?', *Housing, Theory, and Society*, 18(1–2): 36–49.

Gardner, A. (2017) 'Big change, little change? Punctuation, increments and multi-layer institutional change for English local authorities under austerity', *Local Government Studies*, 43(2): 150–69.

Garsten, C. and Nyqvist, A. (2013) *Organisational Anthropology: Doing Ethnography in and Among Complex Organisations*, London: Pluto Press.

Geertz, C. (2000) *The Interpretation of Cultures: Selected Essays*, New York: Basic Books.

Gerard Forsey, M. (2010) 'Ethnography as participant listening', *Ethnography*, 11(4): 558–72.

Glasson, B. and Booth, P. (1992) 'Negotiation and delay in the development control process: case studies in Yorkshire and Humberside', *The Town Planning Review*, 63(1): 63–78.

Goodman, R. (1972) *After the Planners*, Harmondsworth: Penguin Books.

Grange, K. (2013) 'Shaping acting space: in search of a new political awareness among local authority planners', *Planning Theory*, 12(3): 225–43.

Grange, K. (2017) 'Planners – a silenced profession? The politicisation of planning and the need for fearless speech', *Planning Theory*, 16(3): 275–95.

Gray, M. and Barford, A. (2018) 'The depths of the cuts: the uneven geography of local government austerity', *Cambridge Journal of Regions*, 11(3): 541–63.

Green, F. (2004) 'Why has work effort become more intense?', *Industrial Relations*, 43(4): 709–41.

Gunn, S. (2019) 'Planning professionalism in the face of technocracy: ethics, values and practices', in M. Raco and F. Savini (eds) *Planning and Knowledge: How New Forms of Technocracy Are Shaping Contemporary Cities*, Bristol: Policy Press, pp 127–38.

Gunn, S. and Hillier, J. (2014) 'When uncertainty is interpreted as risk: an analysis of tensions relating to spatial planning reform in England', *Planning Practice and Research*, 29(1): 56–74.

Haas, P.M. (1992) 'Introduction: epistemic communities and international policy coordination', *International Organization*, 46(1): 1–35.

Hall, D. and Leach, S. (2000) 'The changing nature of local labour politics', in G. Stoker (ed) *The New Politics of British Local Governance*, Basingstoke: Macmillan, pp 150–65.

Hall, P. (2013) *Good Cities, Better Lives: How Europe Discovered the Lost Art of Urbanism*, London: Taylor & Francis.

Hammersley, M. and Atkinson, P. (2007) *Ethnography: Principles in Practice* (3rd edn), London: Routledge.

Harris, N. and Thomas, H. (2011) 'Clients, customers and consumers: a framework for exploring the user-experience of the planning service', *Planning Theory & Practice*, 12(2): 249–68.

Hatherley, O. (2010) *A Guide to the New Ruins of Great Britain*, London: Verso.

Healey, P. (1992) 'A planner's day: knowledge and action in communicative practice', *Journal of the American Planning Association*, 58(1): 9–20.

Healey, P. (2010) *Making Better Places: The Planning Project in the Twenty-First Century*, London: Bloomsbury.

Healey, P. and Underwood, J. (1978) *Professional Ideals and Planning Practice: A Report on Research into Planners' Ideas in Practice in London Borough Planning Departments*, Oxford: Pergamon.

Hickman, H., McClymont, K. and Sheppard, A. (2021) *Planners of the Future: Expectations, Motivations, and Experiences: A Snapshot from 2019–2020*, London/Bristol: RTPI/UWE.

Historic England (2018) *Tenth Report on Local Authority Staff Resources*, London: Historic England.

Hochschild, A. (1997) *The Time Bind: When Work Becomes Home and Home Becomes Work*, New York: Metropolitan Books.

Hochschild, A. (2008) 'On the edge of the time bind: time and market culture', in C. Warhurst, D.R. Eikhof and A. Haunschild (eds) *Work Less, Live More? Critical Analysis of the Work-Life Boundary*, Basingstoke: Palgrave Macmillan, pp 80–91.

Hoggett, P. (2006) 'Conflict, ambivalence, and the contested purpose of public organizations', *Human Relations*, 59(2): 175–94.

Howe, E. (1994) *Acting on Ethics in City Planning*, New Brunswick, NJ: Center for Urban Policy Research.

Imrie, R. and Thomas, H. (1992) 'The wrong side of the tracks: a case study of local economic regeneration in Britain', *Policy & Politics*, 20(3): 213–26.

Inch, A. (2010) 'Culture change as identity regulation: the micro-politics of producing spatial planners in England', *Planning Theory & Practice*, 11(3): 359–74.

Inch, A. and Shepherd, E. (2020) 'Thinking conjunctively about ideology, housing and English planning', *Planning Theory & Practice*, 19(1): 59–79.

Inch, A., Wargent, M. and Tait, M. (2022) 'Serving the public interest? Towards a history of private sector planning expertise in England', *Planning Perspectives*. DOI: 10.1080/02665433.2022.2063165.

Jackson, J. (2020) 'What do mid-career Melbourne planners profess?', *International Planning Studies*, 25(4): 393–408.

Johnson, T.J. (1972) *Professions and Power*, London: Macmillan

Kenny, T. (2019) *Resourcing Public Planning*, London: RTPI.

Killian, J. and Pretty, D. (2008) *The Killian Pretty Review: Planning applications – a Faster and More Responsive System: Final Report*, London: Department for Communities and Local Government.

Kirk, J. and Vasconcelos, A. (2003) 'Management consultancies and technology consultancies in a converging market: a knowledge management perspective', *Electronic Journal of Knowledge Management*, 1(1): 33–46.

Kitchen, T. (1997) *People, Politics, Policies and Plans: The City Planning Process in Contemporary Britain*, London: Paul Chapman Publishing.

Koolmees, T. and Majoor, S. (2019) 'Local government in the face of crisis: changing public management of urban projects in Amsterdam', in M. Raco and F. Savini (eds) *Planning and Knowledge: How New Forms of Technocracy are Shaping Contemporary Cities*, Bristol: Policy Press, pp 59–75.

Kunda, G. (1992) *Engineering Culture: Control and Commitment in a High-Tech Corporation*, Philadelphia: Temple University Press.

Lamb, W.F., Mattioli, G., Levi, S., Roberts, J.T., Capstick, S., Creutzig, F., et al (2020) 'Discourses of climate delay', *Global Sustainability*, 3: 1–5.

Land, C. and Taylor, S. (2010) 'Surf's up: work, life, balance and brand in a new age capitalist organization', *Sociology*, 44(3): 395–413.

Laurian, L. and Inch, A. (2019) 'On time and planning: opening futures by cultivating a "sense of now"', *Journal of Planning Literature*, 34(3): 267–85.

Layard, A. (2019) 'Planning by numbers: affordable housing and viability in England', in M. Raco and F. Savini (eds) *Planning and Knowledge: How New Forms of Technocracy are Shaping Contemporary Cities*, Bristol: Policy Press, pp 213–24.

Leach, S., Stewart, J. and Jones, G. (2017) *Centralisation, Devolution and the Future of Local Government in England*, Abingdon: Routledge.

Lennon, M. (2017) 'On "the subject" of planning's public interest', *Planning Theory* 16(2): 150–68.

Letwin, O. (2018) *Independent Review of Build Out: Final Report*, London: MHCLG.

Levi-Faur, D. (2005) 'The global diffusion of regulatory capitalism', *The Annals of the American Academy of Political and Social Science*, 598(1): 12–32.

Levi-Faur, D. (2009) 'Regulatory capitalism and the reassertion of the public interest', *Policy & Society*, 27(3): 181–91.

Lindblom, C.E. (1959) 'The science of "muddling through"', *Public Administration Review*, 19(2): 79–88.

Lindgren, M. and Packendorff, J. (2006) 'What's new in new forms of organizing? On the construction of gender in project-based work', *Journal of Management Studies*, 43(4): 841–66.

Linovski, O. (2017) 'Pro bono practices and government agencies', *Journal of the American Planning Association*, 83(2): 180–82.

Linovski, O. (2019) 'Shifting agendas: private consultants and public planning policy', *Urban Affairs Review*, 55(6): 1666–701.

Linovski, O. (2021) 'The value of planning: views from management consultants', *Journal of Planning Education and Research*. https://doi-org.libproxy.ncl.ac.uk/10.1177/0739456X211051420

Loh, C.G. and Arroyo, R.L. (2017) 'Special ethical considerations for planners in private practice', *Journal of the American Planning Association*, 83(2): 168–79.

Loh, C.G. and Norton, R.K. (2013) 'Planning consultants and local planning: roles and values', *Journal of the American Planning Association*, 79(2): 138–47.

Lundin, R.A. and Söderholm, A. (1998) 'Conceptualising a projectified society: discussion of an eco-institutional approach to a theory on temporary organizations', in R.A. Lundin and C. Midler (eds) *Projects as Arenas for Renewal and Learning Processes*, Boston, MA: Kluwer Academic Publishers, pp 13–23.

Lyles, W., White, S.S. and Lavelle, B.D. (2018) 'The prospect of compassionate planning', *Journal of Planning Literature*, 33(3): 247–66.

Mack, J. and Herzfeld, M. (2020) *Life Among Urban Planners: Practice, Professionalism, and Expertise in the Making of the City*, Philadelphia: University of Pennsylvania Press.

Madell, A., McNally, D., McClymont, K., Beebeejaun, Y. and Mathijssen, B. (2021) 'Intersections of (infra)structural violence and cultural inclusion: the geopolitics of minority cemeteries and crematoria provision', *Transactions*, 46(3): 675–88.

Majoor, S. (2018) 'Coping with ambiguity: an urban megaproject ethnography', *Progress in Planning*, 120: 1–28.

Manning, P. and Van Maanen, J. (1978) *Policing: A View from the Street*, Santa Monica, CA: Goodyear Publishing Company.

Mäntysalo, R. and Saglie, I.-L. (2010) 'Private influence preceding public involvement: strategies for legitimizing preliminary partnership arrangements in urban housing planning in Norway and Finland', *Planning Theory & Practice*, 11(3): 317–38.

Marcuse, P. (1976) 'Professional ethics and beyond: values in planning', *Journal of the American Institute of Planners*, 42(3): 264–74.

Marshall, T. (2021) *The Politics and Ideology of Planning*, Bristol: Policy Press.

Mbiba, B. (2003) 'A clash of time cultures and planning: lessons from Zimbabwe', *Planning Theory & Practice*, 4(4): 477–81.

McClymont, K. (2006) 'Ideology, legitimacy and values in practice: reconceptualising professionalism in town planning', PhD thesis, University of Sheffield.

McClymont, K. (2014) 'Stuck in the process, facilitating nothing? Justice, capabilities and planning for value-led outcomes', *Planning Practice & Research*, 29(2): 187–201.

Mescher, B., Benschop, Y. and Doorewaard, J. (2010) 'Representations of work–life balance support', *Human Relations*, 63(1): 21–39.

Metzger, J. and Zakhour, S. (2019) 'The politics of new urban professions: the case of urban development engineers', in M. Raco and F. Savini (eds) *Planning and Knowledge: How New Forms of Technocracy are Shaping Contemporary Cities*, Bristol: Policy Press, pp 181–95.

Muhr, S.L. and Kirkegaard, L. (2013) 'The dream consultant: productive fantasies at work', *Culture and Organization*, 19(2): 105–23.

Nandhakumar, J. and Jones, M. (2001) 'Accounting for time: managing time in project-based teamworking', *Accounting, Organizations and Society*, 26(3): 193–214.

Needham, C.E. (2006) 'Customer care and the public service ethos', *Public Administration*, 84(4): 845–60.

Nelson, S. and Neil, R. (2021) 'Early career planners in a neo-liberal age: experience of working in the south east of England', *Planning Practice & Research*, 36(4): 442–55.

Nippert-Eng., C. (1996) 'Calendars and keys: the classification of "home" and "work"', *Sociological Forum*, 11(3): 563–82.

Othengrafen, F. and Reimer, M. (2013) 'The embeddedness of planning in cultural contexts: theoretical foundations for the analysis of dynamic planning cultures', *Environment and Planning A*, 45(6): 1269–84.

Parker, G. and Street, E. (2021) *Contemporary Planning Practice: Skills, Specialisms and Knowledges*, London: Macmillan Education.

Parker, G., Street, E. and Wargent, M. (2018) 'The rise of the private sector in fragmentary planning in England', *Planning Theory & Practice*, 19(5): 734–50.

Parker, G., Street, E. and Wargent, M. (2019) 'Advocates, advisors and scrutineers: the technocracies of private sector planning in England', in M. Raco and F. Savini (eds) *Planning and Knowledge: How New Forms of Technocracy are Shaping Contemporary Cities*, Bristol: Policy Press, pp 157–67.

Pearson, G. and Rowe, M. (2020) *Police Street Powers and Criminal Justice: Regulation and Discretion in a Time of Change*, Oxford: Bloomsbury.

Pennington, M. (2000) *Planning and the Political Market: Public Choice and the Politics of Government Failure*, London: Athlone.

Perez, F. (2020) 'An anatomy of failure: planning after the fact in contemporary Bogota', in J. Mack and M. Herzfeld (eds) *Life Among Urban Planners: Practice, Professionalism, and Expertise in the Making of the City*, Philadelphia: University of Pennsylvania Press, pp 100–18.

Phelps, N.A. and Wu, F. (2011) *International Perspectives on Suburbanization: a Post-Suburban World?*, Basingstoke: Palgrave Macmillan.

Pink, S. (2021) *Doing Visual Ethnography*, London: Sage.

Pratchett, L. and Wingfield, M. (1996) 'Petty bureaucracy and wooly-minded liberalism? The changing ethos of local government officers', *Public Administration*, 74(4): 639–55.

Prince, R. (2012) 'Policy transfer, consultants and the geographies of governance', *Progress in Human Geography*, 36(2): 188–203.

Raco, M. (2018) 'Private consultants, planning reform and the marketisation of local government finance', in J. Ferm and J. Tomaney (eds) *Planning Practice: Critical Perspectives from the UK*, Abingdon: Routledge, pp 123–37.

Raco, M. and Savini, F. (2019) *Planning and Knowledge: How New Forms of Technocracy Are Shaping Contemporary Cities*, Bristol: Policy Press.

Reade, E. (1987) *British Town and Country Planning*, Milton Keynes: Open University Press.

Rhodes, R.A.W. (2011) *Everyday Life in British Government*, Oxford: Oxford University Press.

Robertson, M. and Swan, J. (2003) '"Control – what control?' Culture and ambiguity within a knowledge intensive firm', *Journal of Management Studies*, 40(4): 831–58.

Robertson, M., Scarbrough, H. and Swan, J. (2003) 'Knowledge creation in professional service firms: institutional effects', *Organization Studies*, 24(6): 831–57.

Rydin, Y. (2007) 'Re-examining the role of knowledge within planning theory', *Planning Theory*, 6(1): 52–68.

Sandercock, L. and Attili, G. (2010) 'Digital ethnography as planning praxis: an experiment with film as social research, community engagement and policy dialogue', *Planning Theory & Practice*, 11(1): 23–45.

Sandler, J. (2017) 'Introduction: exploring the boring', in J. Sandler and R. Thedvall (eds) *Meeting Ethnography: Meetings as Key Technologies of Contemporary Governance, Development, and Resistance*, New York: Routledge, pp 10–23.

Sanyal, B. (2005) *Comparative Planning Cultures*, New York: Routledge.

Sartorio, F.S., Thomas, H. and Harris, N. (2018) 'Interpreting planners' talk about change: an exploratory study', *Planning Theory*, 17(4): 605–27.

Schoneboom, A. and Slade, J. (2020) 'Question your teaspoons: tea-drinking, coping and commercialisation across three planning organisations', *Journal of Organizational Ethnography*, 9(3): 311–26.

Schwartzman, H.B. (1989) *The Meeting: Gatherings in Organizations and Communities*, New York: Plenum Press.

Sehested, K. (2009) 'Urban planners as network managers and metagovernors', *Planning Theory & Practice*, 10(2) 245–63.

Slade, D., Gunn, S. and Schoneboom, A. (2019) *Serving the Public Interest? The Reorganisation of UK Planning Services in an Age of Reluctant Outsourcing*, London: RTPI.

Slade, J., Tait, M. and Inch, A. (2021) '"We need to put what we do in my dad's language, in pounds, shillings and pence": commercialisation and the reshaping of public-sector planning in England', *Urban Studies*, 59(2): 397–413.

Steele, W. (2009) 'Australian urban planners: hybrid roles and professional dilemmas?', *Urban Policy and Research*, 27(2): 189–203.

Suddaby, R., Gendron, Y. and Lam, H. (2009) 'The organizational context of professionalism in accounting', *Accounting, Organizations and Society*, 34(3): 409–27.

Tait, M. (2011) 'Trust and the public interest in the micropolitics of planning practice', *Journal of Planning Education and Research*, 31(2): 157–71.

Tait, M. (2016) 'Planning and the public interest: still a relevant concept for planners?', *Planning Theory*, 15(4): 335–43.

Tait, M., Inch, A., Slade, J., Gunn, Z., Vigar, G., Schoneboom, A. and Clifford, B. (2020) *What Must Planners Do Differently? Critical Thoughts on the State of Planning*, Sheffield: University of Sheffield.

Thomas, H. (2002) 'What future for the RTPI?', *Town and Country Planning*, 71(10): 250–51.

Thomas, J.C. (2013) 'Citizen, customer, partner: rethinking the place of the public in public management', *Public Administration Review*, 73(6): 786–96.

Town and Country Planning Association (2018) *Planning 2020: Raynsford Review of Planning in England*, London: TCPA.

Transport Planning Society (2018) *Transport for New Homes: Project Summary and Recommendations*, London: Transport for New Homes, Available from: www.transportfornewhomes.org.uk/wp-content/uploads/2018/07/transport-for-new-homes-summary-web.pdf [Accessed 8 August 2022].

Twenge, J.M. (2010) 'A review of the empirical evidence on generational differences in work attitudes', *Journal of Business and Psychology*, 25(2): 201–10.

Van Maanen, J. (1988) *Tales of the Field: On Writing Ethnography*, Chicago: University of Chicago Press.

Vickers, S.G. (1968) *Value Systems and Social Process*, New York: Basic Books.

Vigar, G. (2012) 'Planning and professionalism: knowledge, judgement and expertise in English planning', *Planning Theory*, 11(4): 361–78.

Vigar, G., Healey, P., Hull, A. and Davoudi, S. (2000) *Planning, Governance and Spatial Strategy in Britain: an Institutionalist Analysis*, Basingstoke: Macmillan.

Walker, M. (2010) 'The great inertia sector: a whistleblower's account of council work where staff pull six-month sickies', *Daily Mail*, [online] 26 June, Available from: www.dailymail.co.uk/news/article-1289702/Public-sector-inertia-council-office-employees-month-sickies.html [Accessed 7 July 2022].

Watson, T.J. (2000) 'Making sense of managerial work and organizational research processes with Caroline and Terry', *Organization*, 7(3): 489–510.

Wenger, E. (1998) *Communities of Practice: Learning, Meaning, and Identity*, Cambridge: Cambridge University Press.

Willmott, H. (1993) 'Strength is ignorance: slavery is freedom: managing culture in modern organizations', *Journal of Management Studies*, 30(4): 515–52.

Wynn, A.T. and Rao, A.H. (2020) 'Failures of flexibility: how perceived control motivates the individualization of work–life conflict', *Industrial & Labor Relations Review*, 73(1): 61–90.

Yarrow, T. (2019) *Architects: Portraits of a Practice*, Ithaca, NY: Cornell University Press.

Index

References to figures appear in *italic* type.
References to endnotes show the page number,
the note number and the chapter number (202n13(ch5)).

A

Abram, S. 10
action 11
advice 76–84, 123–6, 189
  see also pre-application (pre-app) service
advocacy 78
affordable housing 48, 200n10(ch2)
air quality 152, 166, 167, 170–1, 172
altruism 92
Amin-Smith, N. 10
Anderson-Gough, F. 90
Annink, A. 71
arboricultural officers 113
area of outstanding natural beauty (AONB) 117, 125–6, 130
Arroyo, R.L. 15, 83, 84, 197
Atkinson, P. 14
austerity 5, 21, 69, 71, 183, 185
automation 33–5, 103
autonomy 91, 201n11(ch3)
Auty, S. 74

B

Back, L. 16
bake-off entry *95*
Bakerdale 9, 105–42
  Agile Wall *112*
  Charles Street development 136–41
  collaboration 126–7
  contemporary public practice 110–15
  development-management decision-making *125*
  Go To project 108–10, 111, 114–15, 116, 122–3, 124, 183
  householder application 115–17
  kitchen *124*
  major housebuilders 117–19
  planning committee 134–6
  planning culture 119–23
  planning office *128*
  planning team 106
  reception area *107*
  relations with elected members 129–33
  relations with public 188
  specialist advice 123–6
  workplace culture 128–9, 185

Bakerdale Planning Committee
  committee meeting 134–6
  site vists 129–33
banter 190
  Bakerdale 137, 140, 141
  OIP 145, 146, 164, 165
  Southwell 24, 27–8, 30, 53, 58
Barnes, Y. 24
Barrett, S. 8
Baum, H. 12, 15
Beauregard, R.A. 12
Berkshire County Council 6
Bickenbach, J. 11, 13, 195
biodiversity 37–42, 44, 46, 48, 152
  see also ecological requirements
birds 38, 41, 47, 48, 200n16(ch2)
Blackman, D. 12
Booth, P. 88
Boxall, P. 96
Brewer, J. 14
business development meeting 163–7

C

Campbell, H. 8, 13, 30, 83
capacity-building 70–2
capitalist realism 123
Carmona, M. 88
central government 5, 6, 55
change 119–23
change-management programme *see* Go To project
Charles Street development 136–41
Cherry, G.E. 6
Clarke, J. 4
class 173
Clifford, B. 9, 165
climate change 55, 91–2
collaboration 65–76, 126–7, 154–8, 164
  see also multi-agency projects
commercialisation 2–3, 6, 8–10, 19, 30, 196, 197
  Bakerdale 108, 114–15, 142, 183
  see also Go To project; privatisation
communication 67, 75, 91, 99, 192
communities of practice 3, 11, 13
community engagement 188
  see also public engagement
Community Infrastructure Levy (CIL) 137–8, 201n13(ch4)
compromise 81–2

215

conference calls 161–3
conservation specialists 71, 125
consultancy *see* OIP; Simpsons
councillors 43–6, 129–33, 187–8
   see also politicians
crematoria 165
curiosity 88–9, 90
customer-focused practices 9
cycling 20, 37, 50–1, 52–3, 54

D

Daily Mail 184–5
Davoudi, S. 11
design and build system 138
developers 25, 29, 38
   see also housebuilders
development consortium 49–50
development-management
   decision-making *125*
Dewar, D. 199n4(ch1)
discontinuous outsourcing 8
Downstaple Council 32
Duneier, M. 18
Durning, B. 12

E

ecological requirements 37–43, 125–6,
   200n14(ch2)
   see also biodiversity
Ellis, H. 30
employment land review 154–8
English Nature 166
   see also Natural England
Environment Agency 125
epistemic communities *see* communities
   of practice
equitable wealth 92
Erickson, K.C. 17
ethnographic research 11
   see also planning ethnographies
Evans, B. 5
Everdale Fields housing development
   46–54, 56
Evetts, J. 66

F

Ferlie, E. 9
Fincham, R. 71, 75
Fisher, M. 123
flexitime 35
flooding 125, 166
"Focus Hour" 88–90
Forester, J. 12
Frank, A.I. 91
Friargate County Council 77
Friedson, E. 13
Fudge, C. 8
funding cuts 5, 9, 21
Furbey, R. 12

G

Gardner, A. 15
Geertz, C. 15
Glasson, B. 88
Go To project 9, 108–10, 111, 114–15,
   116, 122–3, 124, 183
goalkeepers' union 40–1
golf courses 126–8, 156
Goodman, B. 30
Grange, K. 6, 59
green belt *39*, 105, 152, 156, 158, 161,
   162–3, 164
Green, F. 94
greenfield housing development 46–54
Gunn, S. 5, 7, 12, 14

H

Haas, P.M. 3, 11
habitats strategies 38
Hall, P. 5, 59
Hammersley, M. 14
Harris, N. 9
Healey, P. 8, 11, 15, 66, 190, 192, 195
heat networks 55–7, 200n23(ch2)
Hendler, S. 11, 13, 195
Hillier, J. 5, 7
Hochschild, A. 99
Hoggett, P. 12
homes in multiple occupations
   (HMOs) 132, 134
hot desking 29, *33*, 72, 110, 145
housebuilders 21, 38, 49, 59, 117–19
householder application 115–17
housing developments 20–1, 22
   Charles Street 136–41
   ecological requirements 37–41
   Everdale Fields 46–54
Housing Infrastructure Fund (HIF) 118,
   201n6(ch4)
housing supply 202n22(ch5)
hybridisation of planners 2, 7

I

identity 13, 192–4, 194–5
Inch, A. 5, 85, 191
independent advice 76–84
infrastructure-led development 88–9
integrity 79–81
interdisciplinary working 161–3

J

Jackson, J. 6
Johnson, T.J. 13
Jones, M. 85

K

Kenny, T. 9
Killian, J. 9

Kirk, J. 71
Kirkegaard, L. 102
knowledge 11, 12–13, 165, 190–2
  see also local knowledge; people knowledge; private-sector knowledge
Koolmees, T. 197

L

Labour governments 5
Land, C. 102
Laurian, L. 85
Leach, S. 21
Lennon, M. 14
Levi-Faur, D. 76, 191
Lindblom, C.E. 60
Lindgren, M. 98
Linovski, O. 76, 197
local governments 5, 6
local knowledge 8, 13, 188, 191–2
  OIP 149, 171, 175, 176, 178
  Southwell 46
Loh, C.G. 15, 78, 83, 84, 197
Lundin, R.A. 75
Lyles, W. 12

M

Macky, K. 96
Majoor, S. 15, 197
managerialism 4–5
Mäntysalo, R. 197
market absorption rate 202n22(ch5)
Marshall, R. 8, 13, 83
Mbiba, B. 85
McClymont, K. 8, 12, 46
mental health 98–9, 185
Merton Wharfside development 83
Mescher, B. 99
Metzger, J. 75, 197
moral-practical knowledge 11
Muhr, S.L. 102
multi-agency projects 75–6, 82–4, 97
  see also collaboration

N

Nandhakumar, J. 85
National Planning Policy Framework (NPPF) 116, 170, 171, 175, 176, 202n21(ch5)
Natural England 38, 39–40
  see also English Nature
negotiation 136–41
network professionalism 12
network professionals 66
networking 67, 145–6, 154, 163, 180, 186, 189–90
neutrality 81
new public management 9
Newman, J. 4

Northby Council 72
Norton, R.K. 78

O

office culture 26–31
  see also organisational culture; workplace culture
OIP 143–81
  business development meeting 163–7
  interdisciplinary working 161–3
  local knowledge 191
  meeting room *144*
  organisational culture 144–9, 160
  planning inquiry 167–80
  planning work and planning culture 158–61
  private-sector knowledge 154–8
  relationships with politicians 187–8
  Undercliffe Planning Committee 149–53
  work context 184
organisational culture 144–9
  see also office culture; workplace culture
organisational ethnography 14–15
Othengrafen, F. 11
othering 31, 166
outsourcing 8, 22, 23, 25, 183, 185, 191
Overcombe 38, 40–1
Overcombe Holdings 49, 50, 51–2

P

Packendorff, J. 98
Parker, G. 5, 11
parking 53, 200n22(ch2)
participant listening 16
pedestrian access *21*
Pennington, M. 13
people knowledge 66
Perez, F. 8
performance indicators 4
performance measurement 9
permitted development (PD) rights 131, 132, 141, 156, 160, 201n12(ch4)
Phelps, N.A. 20
Pink, S. 17
planners
  hybridisation of 2, 7
  knowledge and skills 190–2
  local government 6
  political constraints 5–6
  private sector 6, 7, 10
  professional identity 192–4, 194–5
  professionalism 3–4, 12–14
  third sector 199n3(ch 1)
  work context 182–4
  work done by 3, 10–12
  working practices 184–7
  see also planning teams

planning
   commercialisation 2–3, 6, 8–10, 19, 30, 196, 197
   narrowness of 195–6, 197
   nature and purpose 1–2, 4–6, 197
   privatisation 2, 6–8, 19
planning applications 9, 115–17
planning committees 43–6, 129–36, 134–6, 149
planning culture 3, 119–23, 158–61
planning ethnographies 3, 14–18
planning fees 9, 199n4(ch1)
planning inquiry 167–80
   recommended public inquiry layout 169
Planning Performance Agreements (PPAs) 9, 118–19, 138–40
planning research 15
planning scholarship 11–12
planning surgery 124–6
planning teams 24–6, 63–5, 72, 106
PlanTech 161–3, 187, 192
Polborough Council 72–3
political economy 1–2, 4
politicians 123, 129–33, 164, 180, 187–8, 193
   see also councillors
post-suburbia 20
poverty 22
pre-application (pre-app) service 108, 109, 111–12, 114–15, 116, 117, 126–8, 154
Pretty, D. 9
Prince, R. 15
private sector 4, 6, 183–4, 199n4(ch1)
   ethical compromises 196
   growing dominance of 197
   local knowledge 191–2
   professional identity 193
   see also OIP; Simpsons
private-sector knowledge 154–8
privatisation 2, 6–8, 19, 188
   Theta partnership 23, 32–7, 60
professional development 88
professional identity 192–4, 194–5
professionalism 3–4, 12–14
profit 92–4
project management skills 192
public 83, 131
   see also residents
public complaints 28, 29, 168, 199n7(ch2)
public engagement 48–9, 188
public good 92–4
public inquiry layout 169
public interest 3, 5, 13–14, 78, 92, 180, 193, 195
   see also Working in the Public Interest (WITPI) project
public sector 4, 8, 182–3
   commercialisation 196, 197
   local knowledge 191
   working practices 185
public-sector ethos 11, 193
public-service ethos 25, 29–31, 71

R

Raco, M. 36, 192
Rao, A.H. 96
Reade, E. 5, 195
REG19 162, 202n13(ch5)
regulatory capitalism 76, 191
Reimar, M. 11
relationship-building 87
relationships 43–6, 65–76, 129–33, 187–90, 197
resident engagement 48–9
residents 20, 23, 29, 126, 132, 152, 168, 171
resident's groups 161
retirement homes 165–6
Ridley, N. 4
Robertson, M. 89, 93
Rogers housebuilding firm 117–19
Royal Town Planning Institute (RTPI) 145–6, 165, 192, 193
Rydin, Y. 11

S

Saglie, I.L. 197
Sandercock, L. 13
Sandler, J. 27
Sartorio, F.S. 15
Savini, F. 192
Schoneboom, A. 16, 65, 147, 190
self-reliance 90–1
Sieh, L. 88
Simpsons 61–104
   company culture 88–94, 185–6
   independent advice 76–84
   planning team 63–5
   reception area 62
   relationships 65–76, 188, 189
   time management 84–8
   work context 184
   work environment 61–3
   work-life balance 94–103
site visits 86, 115–16, 122, 126–7, 129–33, 158–61
Slade, D. 8
Slade, J. 5, 16, 65, 147, 185, 190
Söderholm, A. 75
Somfortby Council 73–4, 77, 81–2
Southwell 5, 19–60
   council offices 19–23
   ecological requirements 37–43
   Everdale Fields housing development 46–54, 56
   local knowledge 191
   office culture 26–31
   pedestrian access 21

planning constraints 54–9
planning office 23–4
planning team 24–6
public engagement 188
relations with councillors 43–6
Theta partnership 23, 32–7, 60
work context 182–3
working practices 185
Southwell Planning Committee 43–6
special protection area (SPA) 38, 40
specialist advice 123–6
staff wellbeing 97–9
Steele, W. 2, 7, 189
stereotypes 13, 78, 184, 187, 189–90, 197
Strange, I. 11
strategic assessment (SA) 161–2
Street, E. 5, 11
stress 98–9, 101, 102
student housing 159, 164
subjectivity 17
Suddaby, R. 3
survival crime 22
sustainability 25, 37, 170, 194
Swan, J. 93

T

Tait, M. 5
Taylor, S. 102
team ethnography 17
team spirit 27–9
technical expertise 81
technology 155, 165
  see also PlanTech
Theta partnership 23, 32–7, 60
third sector 199n3(ch 1)
Thomas, H. 9, 12
Thomas, J.C. 9
time management 84–8, 101, 113
Timetracker 33–5
Town and Country Planning Act
  1990 199n1(ch2)
  Section 106 20, 51, 52, 57–9, 152, 166
Town and Country Planning
  Association 5, 30
town planners see planners
town planning see planning
trade unions 35, 186–7
traffic 49, 135, 152, 156, 166
traffic modelling 83
Transfer of Undertakings (Protection
  of Employment) (TUPE) 22, 35,
  199n3(ch2)

translational research 156
Tranton Council 68–70, 80
tree officers 113
tree protection orders (TPOs) 26
TUPE see Transfer of Undertakings
  (Protection of Employment)
Twenge, J.M. 102

U

Undercliffe Planning Committee
  149–53
Underwood, J. 190, 192
unions 35, 185–6

V

values 78, 80, 93
Van Maanen, J. 15, 16
Vasconcelos, A. 71
Vermilion 29, 52
Vickers, S.G. 3
Vigar, G. 6, 12, 13, 193
visitor parking 53, 200n22(ch2)
voice 17

W

walkability 78–9
Walker, M. 185
Watson, T.J. 17
wellbeing 97–9
Wenger, E. 3, 11
West Harbyshire Council 76–7
Women in Property 146
work context 182–4
work extension and intensification 184–5
work-life balance 94–103
working conditions 154
Working in the Public Interest (WITPI)
  project 16, 94, 183, 185
working practices 110–14, 184–7
workload 27, 32–3, 42, 151
workplace culture 119–23, 128–9,
  181, 185
  see also office culture;
    organisational culture
Wynn, A.T. 96

Y

Yarrow, T. 10

Z

Zakhour, S. 75, 197

www.ingramcontent.com/pod-product-compliance
Lightning Source LLC
Chambersburg PA
CBHW071158070526
44584CB00019B/2835